THE RELAXATION & STRESS REDUCTION WORKBOOK

Fifth Edition

Martha Davis, Ph.D.

Elizabeth Robbins Eshelman, M.S.W.

Matthew McKay, Ph.D.

New Harbinger Publications, Inc.

Publisher's Note

This publication is designed to provide accurate and authoritative information in regard to the subject matter covered. It is sold with the understanding that the publisher is not engaged in rendering psychological, financial, legal, or other professional services. If expert assistance or counseling is needed, the services of a competent professional should be sought.

Distributed in Canada by Raincoast Books.

Copyright © 2000 by Martha Davis, Elizabeth Robbins Eshelman, and Matthew McKay
New Harbinger Publications, Inc.
5674 Shattuck Avenue
Oakland, CA 94609

Cover design by SHELBY DESIGNS AND ILLUSTRATES
Edited by Donna Long

Library of Congress Card Catalog Number: 00-134879
ISBN 1-57224-214-0 Paperback

Printed in the United States of America

New Harbinger Publications' Web site address: www.newharbinger.com

FIRST EDITION
Printed from May 1980 to October 1981

SECOND EDITION
Printed from April 1982 to September 1987

THIRD EDITION
Printed from September 1988 to July 1994

FOURTH EDITION
Printed from March 1995 to May 2000

FIFTH EDITION

06   05   04

20   19   18   17   16   15   14   13   12   11   10

All of the authors of this workbook wish to dedicate this book to our families.
Without their continuous support, this book would not be possible.

Thank you, Bill and Amanda, Don, Judy, Rebekah and Jordan.

Contents

Preface to the Fifth Edition

The year 2000 marks the twentieth anniversary of the first edition of *The Stress Management and Relaxation Workbook*. The authors of this book look back over the years, asking what inspired us to write it to begin with and what spurs us to rewrite it today.

In the late seventies and early eighties stress management was not a household word as it is today. But more and more frequently stress was at the root of why people were seeking psychotherapy and medical consultation. There were virtually no classes or groups to teach people how to handle stress. There were no books that provided under one cover sufficient tools for people to manage their own stress. While a few intrepid individuals spent a good deal of time and money on books, workshops, and psychotherapy to piece together their own stress management plan, many people continued to live lives compromised by chronic stress. Observing this problem, the authors of *The Stress Management and Relaxation Workbook* began offering stress management and relaxation workshops. Through trial and error, they compiled their own workbook of techniques that were easy to teach and were most effective in alleviating symptoms of stress. They decided to publish this workbook for the lay public to fill a vacuum in the popular psychology literature.

Stress is defined as any change to which you must adapt. In the past twenty years the rate of change in our society has continued to accelerate, so it is not surprise that the rate of stress related illnesses has also continued to climb at an alarming rate. Fortunately, there has been an increased interest in stress management and relaxation on the part of researchers, the mass media, and the lay public. The authors of this workbook, in reviewing the literature on stress management and relaxation, have found that most of the concepts and techniques presented in our first workbook have stood the test of time and research. Some of the techniques have undergone refinement, while others have multiple variations that give the reader more choices.

As the authors of this workbook continue to work in the field of stress management, we are excited to be able to offer in the fifth edition a number of new techniques for challenging problems. For example, we have added a chapter on "worry control" to help people manage their mental stress. Due to popular demand, we have included in the Coping

Skills chapter a section on how to handle anger-provoking situations. In the Thought Stopping chapter we have added "eye movement therapy" as a means to not only stop distressing thoughts but also to neutralize them. Throughout the book, content, examples, and bibliography have been updated.

One of the major stressors today is information overload. With this thought in mind, the authors have made a number of changes in the fifth edition to simplify your accessing the information you need to address your specific stress management questions. We have added an expanded table of contents and a subject index. We have deleted portions of some chapters that we considered nonessential and shortened others to save you time. We have made the text more readable by breaking it up into more clearly defined learning chunks.

We thank our readers for your continued support and your feedback, which you have generously given us over the years regarding what you find most effective about the book, the situations in which you use it, and what you want to see added or changed in the next edition. As in writing our first edition, today we are motivated to keep improving this workbook on the basis of this feedback.

The authors wish to acknowledge the following contributors to the fifth edition. Their expertise, experience, and collaboration have made this a more valuable edition.

Andrea Epel, M.P.H., R.D. is a Behavioral Health Program Coordinator at Kaiser Permanente's Oakland Medical Center in northern California. She has developed, evaluated, and taught programs in stress and pain management and mind-body approaches to health for over ten years. She has degrees from Stanford University and the University of California at Berkeley. Ms. Epel contributed to the Meditation chapter.

Caryl B. Fairfull, R.D. is a Registered Dietitian and member of the American Dietetic Association. She has provided individual and group nutrition counseling, developed nutrition care guidelines, and managed the Department of Nutrition Services for Kaiser Permanente's Santa Clara Medical Center in northern California. Ms. Fairfull wrote the Nutrition chapter.

Cheryl Pierson-Carey, P.T., M.S. Is currently a Care Management Consultant with the Care Management Institute in the program offices at Kaiser Permanente in Oakland, California. Her clinical specialization is in neurologic physical therapy. She holds degrees from Indiana University, Purdue University, and Samuel Merritt College. Ms. Pierson-Carey wrote the Exercise chapter.

How to Get the Most Out of This Workbook

This workbook is designed to teach you the most popular stress management and relaxation techniques and exercises used today. Consider it your guide to increasing your awareness of your personal reaction to stress and building your sense of control and mastery over the stressors in your life. We hope that this process will give you more pleasure and less frustration in your life.

Read chapters 1 and 2 first. They are the foundation upon which all of the other chapters are built. After you have read the first two chapters, you will know enough about stress and your personal reactions to stress to decide which chapters it will be most helpful for you to read next.

Chapters 3 through 12 teach techniques for relaxation. Chapters 13 through 15 help you with your stressful thoughts. Chapter 16 assists you managing your time more effectively so that you can free up time to relax and do more of what is most important to you. From chapter 17 you can learn to communicate more assertively and chapter 18 gives you many options to deal with environmental and interpersonal stress on the job. Chapters 19 and 20 teach the basics of nutrition and exercise and their relationship to stress management. Chapter 21 gives you some hints to increase motivation, deal with problems that come up along the way, and stick to your plan.

A basic premise of this workbook is that the benefits of relaxation and stress reduction techniques can only be fully realized after they have been practiced regularly over a period of time. Intellectual understanding of most techniques is of little value, unless accompanied by first hand experience. Whether you plan to use these techniques for yourself or in a professional setting to help others who are experiencing stress, your personal experience is key.

The purpose of regular practice is twofold. First, it will ensure that you will be able to consciously carry out the exercise instructions anytime you need to, without having to refer to written materials. Second, regular practice will help you develop the habits at an unconscious level.

The length of time required each day to practice the relaxation techniques in this workbook varies. To start, we suggest that you spend ten to fifteen minutes twice a day doing the exercises of your choice. Make a contract with yourself. Consider the time you spend practicing the exercises you find to be most helpful a reward or a break. You can decide to expand the time you give yourself to relax as you discover which exercises work best for you.

Choose a quiet place where you will not be interrupted to learn the techniques. Since this is new activity for you, it is wise to explain to the people around you what you are doing. Politely ask them to help you by leaving you alone without distractions. You'll find that family members, fellow office workers, and friends tend to be very supportive of these exercises once they understand what you are doing and why.

If you find it difficult to stick to a daily schedule or discover that barriers such as motivation or time get in your way, we have a couple of suggestions.

- Consider doing the exercises with another person. That way you can share your experiences and give and receive encouragement.

- If time is always the excuse, make an appointment with yourself just like you would make an appointment for a haircut or with a friend for lunch. If you have to cancel, immediately set up the next appointment or date.

If you still have trouble accomplishing what you set out to do, turn to chapter 21 for additional suggestions.

If you are over thirty or if your reaction to stress involves physical symptoms such as frequent headaches, stomach problems, or high blood pressure, make an appointment with your doctor for a physical examination before you begin these exercises. Tell your doctor or health-care provider that you intend to practice relaxation and stress management techniques and ask him or her to determine whether your physical symptoms are caused entirely by stress, or if there are physiological causes as well. Your doctor can be a supportive partner in your efforts to live a more healthy life. Once you start your program, consult a physician if you experience any prolonged negative physical effects.

How You React to Stress

Stress is an everyday fact of life. You can't avoid it. Stress is any change that you must adapt to, ranging from the negative extreme of actual physical danger to the exhilaration of falling in love or achieving some long-desired success. In between, day-to-day living confronts even the most well-managed life with a continuous stream of potentially stressful experiences. Not all stress is bad. In fact, stress is not only desirable but also essential to life. Whether the stress you experience is the result of major life changes or the cumulative effect of minor everyday hassles, it is how you respond to these experiences that determines the impact stress will have on your life.

Sources of Stress

You experience stress from four basic sources:

1. Your *environment* bombards you with demands to adjust. You must endure weather, pollens, noise, traffic, and pollution.

2. You also must cope with *social stressors* such as deadlines, financial problems, job interviews, presentations, disagreements, demands for your time and attention, and loss of loved ones.

3. A third source of stress is *physiological*. The rapid growth of adolescence, menopause in women, illness, aging, injuries, lack of exercise, poor nutrition, and inadequate sleep all tax the body. Your physiological reaction to environmental and social threats and changes can also result in stressful symptoms such as muscle tension, headaches, stomach upset, and anxiety.

4. The fourth source of stress is your *thoughts*. Your brain interprets complex changes in your environment and body and determines when to turn on the "emergency response."

How you interpret and label your present experience and what you predict for the future can serve either to relax or to stress you. Interpreting a sour look from your boss to mean that you are doing an inadequate job is likely to be very anxiety provoking. Interpreting the same look as tiredness or preoccupation with personal problems will not be as frightening.

Stress researcher Richard Lazarus has argued that stress begins with your appraisal of a situation. You first ask how dangerous or difficult the situation is and what resources you have to help you cope with it. Anxious, stressed people often decide that (1) an event is dangerous, difficult, or painful and (2) they don't have the resources to cope.

Fight or Flight Response

Walter B. Cannon, a physiologist, laid the groundwork for the modern meaning of "stress" at Harvard around the turn of the century. He was the first to describe the "fight or flight response" as a series of biochemical changes that prepare you to deal with threat or danger. Primitive man needed quick bursts of energy to fight or flee such predators as a saber-toothed tiger. You can thank this response for enabling your ancestors to survive long enough to pass on their genetic heritage to you. Think of occasions in your life when the fight or flight response served you well, such as when you had to respond quickly to a car that cut in front of you on the freeway or you had to weave through an aggressive defense to make a touchdown. These days, however, when social custom prevents you from fighting or running away, this "emergency response" is rarely useful.

Hans Selye, the first major researcher on stress, was able to trace exactly what happens in your body during the fight or flight response. He found that any problem, imagined or real, can cause the cerebral cortex (the thinking part of the brain) to send an alarm to the hypothalamus (the main switch for the stress response, located in the midbrain). The hypothalamus then stimulates the sympathetic nervous system to make a series of changes in your body. Your heart rate, breathing rate, muscle tension, metabolism, and blood pressure all increase. Your hands and feet get cold as blood is directed away from your extremities and digestive system into the larger muscles that can help you fight or run. You experience butterflies in your stomach. Your diaphragm and your anus lock. Your pupils dilate to sharpen your vision and your hearing becomes more acute.

Unfortunately, when the fight or flight response continues unchecked during times of chronic stress, something else happens that can have long-term negative effects. Your adrenal glands start to secret corticoids (adrenaline or epinephrine, and norepinephrine), which inhibit digestion, reproduction, growth, tissue repair, and the responses of your immune and inflammatory systems. In other words, some very important functions that keep your body healthy begin to shut down.

Fortunately, the same mechanism that turns the stress response on can turn it off. This is called the relaxation response. As soon as you decide that a situation is no longer dangerous, your brain stops sending emergency signals to your brain stem, which in turn ceases to send panic messages to your nervous system. Three minutes after you shut off the danger signals, the fight or flight response burns out. Your metabolism, heart rate, breathing rate, muscle tension, and blood pressure all return to their normal levels. Herbert Benson (1975) suggests that you can use your mind to change your physiology for the better, improving your health and perhaps reducing your need for medication. He coined the term "the relaxation response" to refer to this natural restorative process.

Chronic Stress and Disease

Chronic or persistent stress can occur when the stressors of life are unrelenting, as they are during a major reorganization or downsizing at work or while you are undergoing a messy divorce or coping with a chronic or life-threatening illness. Chronic stress also occurs when little stressors accumulate and you are unable to recuperate from any one of them. As long as the mind perceives a threat, the body remains aroused. If the stress response remains turned on, you may be increasing your chances of a stress-related disease.

Researchers have been looking at the relationship between stress and disease for over fifty years. They have observed that people suffering from stress-related disorders tend to show hyperactivity in a particular "preferred system," such as the skeletal-muscular, cardiovascular, or gastrointestinal system. For example, evidence shows that chronic stress can result in muscle tension and fatigue for some people. For others, it can contribute to stress hypertension, migraine headaches, ulcers, or chronic diarrhea.

Almost every system in your body can be damaged by stress. Suppression of the reproduction system can cause amenorrhea (cessation of menstruation) and failure to ovulate in women, impotency in men, and loss of libido in both. Stress-triggered changes in the lungs increase the symptoms of asthma, bronchitis, and other respiratory conditions. Loss of insulin during the stress response may be a factor in the onset of adult diabetes. Stress suspends tissue repair and remodeling, which in turn causes decalcification of the bones, osteoporosis, and susceptibility to fractures. Inhibition of immune and inflammatory systems makes you more susceptible to colds and flu and can exacerbate some diseases such as cancer and AIDS. In addition, a prolonged stress response can worsen conditions such as arthritis, chronic pain, and diabetes. There is also some evidence that the continued release and depletion of norepinephrine during a state of chronic stress can contribute to depression.

The relationship between chronic stress, disease, and aging is another area of research. Experts in aging are looking at the changing patterns of disease and the emergence of degenerative disorders. Over just a few generations, the threat of infectious diseases such as typhoid, pneumonia, and polio have been replaced with such "modern plagues" as cardiovascular disease, cancer, arthritis, respiratory disorders such as asthma and emphysema, and a pervasive incidence of depression. As you age normally, you expect a natural slowing down of your body's functioning. But many of these mid- to late-life disorders are stress-sensitive diseases. Researchers and clinicians are now asking how stress accelerates the aging process and what can be done to counteract this process.

Schedule of Recent Experience

Thomas Holmes, M.D., and his research associates at the University of Washington have found that people are more likely to develop illnesses or clinical symptoms after experiencing a period when they have had to adapt to many life events.

Dr. Holmes and his associates have developed the Schedule of Recent Experience, which allows you to quantify how many changes you have experienced in the past year and consider how these stressful events may increase your vulnerability to illness. The purpose of this scale is to increase your awareness of stressful events and their potential impact on your health so that you can take steps to reduce the stress level in your life.

Instructions: Think about each possible life event listed below and decide how many times, if at all, each has happened to you within the last year. Write that number in the "Number of Times" column. (If an event happened more than four times, give it a four in that column.)

Event	Number of Times	x	Mean Value		Your Score
1. A lot more or a lot less trouble with the boss.		x	23	=	
2. A major change in sleeping habits (sleeping a lot more or a lot less or a change in time of day when you sleep).		x	16	=	
3. A major change in eating habits (eating a lot more or a lot less or very different meal hours or surroundings).		x	15	=	
4. A revision of personal habits (dress, manners, associations, and so on).		x	24	=	
5. A major change in your usual type or amount of recreation.		x	19	=	
6. A major change in your social activities (e.g., clubs, dancing, movies, visiting, and so on).		x	18	=	
7. A major change in church activities (attending a lot more or a lot less than usual).		x	19	=	
8. A major change in the number of family get-togethers (a lot more or a lot fewer than usual).		x	15	=	
9. A major change in your financial state (a lot worse off or a lot better off).		x	38	=	
10. Trouble with in-laws.		x	29	=	
11. A major change in the number of arguments with spouse (a lot more or a lot fewer than usual regarding child rearing, personal habits, and so on).		x	35	=	
12. Sexual difficulties.		x	39	=	
13. Major personal injury or illness.		x	53	=	
14. Death of a close family member (other than spouse).		x	63	=	
15. Death of spouse.		x	100	=	
16. Death of a close friend.		x	37	=	
17. Gaining a new family member (through birth, adoption, oldster moving in, and so on).		x	39	=	
18. Major change in the health or behavior of a family.		x	44	=	
19. Change in residence.		x	20	=	
20. Detention in jail or other institution.		x	63	=	
21. Minor violations of the law (traffic tickets, jaywalking, disturbing the peace, and so on).		x	11	=	

22. Major business readjustment (merger, reorganization, bankruptcy, and so on).	x	39	=
23. Marriage.	x	501	=
24. Divorce.	x	73	=
25. Marital separation from spouse.	x	65	=
26. Outstanding personal achievement.	x	28	=
27. Son or daughter leaving home (marriage, attending college, and so on).	x	29	=
28. Retirement from work.	x	45	=
29. Major change in working hours or conditions.	x	20	=
30. Major change in responsibilities at work (promotion, demotion, lateral transfer).	x	29	=
31. Being fired from work.	x	47	=
32. Major change in living conditions (building a new home or remodeling, deterioration of home or neighborhood).	x	25	=
33. Spouse beginning or ceasing to work outside the home.	x	26	=
34. Taking out a mortgage or loan for a major purchase (purchasing a home or business and so on).	x	31	=
35. Taking out a loan for a lesser purchase (a car, TV, freezer, and so on).	x	17	=
36. Foreclosure on a mortgage or loan.	x	30	=
37. Vacation.	x	13	=
38. Changing to a new school.	x	20	=
39. Changing to a different line of work.	x	36	=
40. Beginning or ceasing formal schooling.	x	26	=
41. Marital reconciliation with mate.	x	45	=
42. Pregnancy.		40	=
Your total score			

Scoring: Multiply the mean value by the number of times an event happened, and enter the result in the "Your Score" column. (Remember, if an event happened more than four times within the past year, give it a four in the "Number of Times" column.) Add up your scores to get your total score and enter it at the bottom of the schedule.

According to Dr. Holmes and his associates, the higher your total score, the greater your risk of developing stress-related symptoms or illnesses. Of those with a score of over 300 for the past year, almost 80 percent get sick in the near future; of those with a score of 200 to 299, about 50 percent get sick in the near future; and of those with a score of 150 to 199, only about 30 percent get sick in the near future. A score of less than 150 indicates that you have a low chance of becoming ill. So, the higher your score, the harder you should work to stay well.

Because individuals vary in their perception of a given life event as well as in their ability to adapt to change, we recommend that you use this standardized test only as a rough predictor of your increased risk.

Stress can be cumulative. Events from two years ago may still be affecting you now. If you think that past events may be a factor for you, repeat this test for the events of the preceding year and compare your scores.

Prevention

Here are some ways that you can use the Schedule of Recent Experience to maintain your health and prevent illness:

1. Remind yourself of the amount of change that has happened to you by posting the Schedule of Recent Experience where you and your family can see it easily.

2. Think about the personal meaning of each change and try to identify some of the feelings you experience.

3. Think about ways that you can best adjust to each change.

4. Take your time in making decisions.

5. Try to anticipate life changes and plan for them well.

6. Pace yourself. Don't rush. It will get done.

7. View accomplishments as part of daily life rather than as a "stopping point" or a "time to let down."

8. Be compassionate and patient with yourself. It is not uncommon for people to become overwhelmed by all the stresses in their lives. It takes a while to put into effect coping strategies to deal with stress.

9. Acknowledge what you can control and what you cannot control and, when possible, choose which changes you take on.

10. Try out the stress management and relaxation techniques presented in this book and incorporate the ones that work best for you into your personalized stress-management program.

Symptoms Checklist

The major objective of this workbook is to help you achieve symptom relief using relaxation and stress-reduction techniques. So that you can determine exactly which symptoms you want to work on, complete the following checklist.

After you have used this workbook to master stress-reduction techniques that work best for your symptoms, you can return to this checklist and use it to measure your symptom relief.

Instructions: Rate your stress-related symptoms below for the degree of discomfort that they cause you, using this ten-point scale:

Slight discomfort				Moderate discomfort			Extreme discomfort		
1	2	3	4	5	6	7	8	9	10

Symptom *(Disregard those that you don't experience)*	Degree of discomfort *(1-10) now*	Degree of discomfort *(1-10) after mastering relaxation and stress reduction techniques*

Anxiety in specific situations
  Tests
  Deadlines
  Interviews
  Other
	_____
	_____
	_____
	_____
		_____
		_____
		_____
		_____

Anxiety in personal relationships
  Spouse
  Parents
  Children
  Other
	_____
	_____
	_____
	_____
		_____
		_____
		_____
		_____

General anxiety (regardless of the situation or the people involved)		
Depression		
Powerlessness		
Poor self-esteem		
Hostility		
Anger		
Irritability		
Resentment		
Phobias		
Fears		
Obsessions, unwanted thoughts		
Muscular tension		

Symptom (Disregard those that you don't experience)	Degree of discomfort (1-10) now	Degree of discomfort (1-10) after mastering relaxation and stress reduction techniques
High blood pressure		
Headaches		
Neckaches		
Backaches		
Indigestion		
Irritable bowel		
Ulcers		
Chronic constipation		
Chronic diarrhea		
Muscle spasms		
Tics		
Tremors		
Fatigue		
Insomnia		
Sleeping difficulties		
Obesity		
Physical weakness		
Job stress		
Other		

Important: Physical symptoms may have purely physiological causes. You should have a medical doctor eliminate the possibility of such physical problems before you proceed on the assumption that your symptoms are completely stress-related.

Tactics for Coping with Stress

As a member of modern society, you have available to you a variety of methods to cope with the negative effects of stress. Doctors can treat your stress-related symptoms and diseases. Over-the-counter remedies can reduce your pain, help you sleep, keep you awake, enable you to relax, and counter your acid indigestion and nervous bowels. You can consume food, alcohol, and recreational drugs to help block feelings of discomfort. You have diversions such as TV, movies, hobbies, and sports. You can withdraw from the world into your home and avoid all but the most necessary contact with the stressful world around you.

Our society rewards people who deal with stress by working harder and faster to produce more in a shorter time. Such people are referred to as "type A" personalities. The type A person has a strong sense of time urgency, is highly competitive, and is easily angered when he doesn't get his way. Although type A personalities may be very successful, they have a significantly higher rate of cardiovascular disease than type B personalities. Unlike their hard-driving, aggressive counterparts, type Bs don't suffer from chronic time urgency. They can play and relax without guilt and are not hostile or excessively competitive. Type Bs can be just as ambitious as type As and often are more successful. Presidents of companies are sometimes clever type Bs who employ type As to do their work for them.

In contrast to anxious, chronically stressed people, certain individuals are less vulnerable to stress, according to University of Chicago research psychologist Suzanne Kobasa. These "stress-hardy" individuals have a lower frequency of illness and work absenteeism. They view stressors as challenges and chances for new opportunities and personal growth rather than as threats. They feel in control of their life circumstances, and they perceive that they have the resources to make choices and influence events around them. They also have a sense of commitment to their homes, families, and work that makes it easier for them to be involved with other people and in other activities. According to Herbert Benson and Eileen Steward, authors of *The Wellness Book,* the incidence of illness is even lower in individuals who have these stress-hardy characteristics and who also have a good social support system, exercise regularly, and maintain a healthy diet.

Tactics for Coping with Stress Inventory

Before you embark on a program of change, it is important to consider how you are currently managing your stress.

Instructions: Listed below are some common ways of coping with stressful events. Mark those that are characteristic of your behavior or that you use frequently.

_____ 1. I ignore my own needs and just work harder and faster.

_____ 2. I seek out friends for conversation and support.

_____ 3. I eat more than usual.

_____ 4. I engage in some type of physical exercise.

_____ 5. I get irritable and take it out on those around me.

_____ 6. I take a little time to relax, breathe, and unwind.

_____ 7. I smoke a cigarette or drink a caffeinated beverage.

_____ 8. I confront my source of stress and work to change it.

_____ 9. I withdraw emotionally and just go through the motions of my day.

_____ 10. I change my outlook on the problem and put it in a better perspective.

_____ 11. I sleep more than I really need to.

_____ 12. I take some time off and get away from my working life.

_____ 13. I go out shopping and buy something to make myself feel good.

_____ 14. I joke with my friends and use humor to take the edge off.

_____ 15. I drink more alcohol than usual.

_____ 16. I get involved in a hobby or interest that helps me unwind and enjoy myself.

_____ 17. I take medicine to help me relax or sleep better.

_____ 18. I maintain a healthy diet.

_____ 19. I just ignore the problem and hope it will go away.

_____ 20. I pray, meditate, or enhance my spiritual life.

_____ 21. I worry about the problem and am afraid to do something about it.

_____ 22. I try to focus on the things I can control and accept the things I can't
.

Evaluate your results: The even-numbered items tend to be more constructive tactics and the odd-numbered items tend to be less constructive tactics for coping with stress. Congratulate yourself for the even-numbered items you checked. Think about whether you need to make some changes in your thinking or behavior if you checked any of the odd-numbered items. Consider experimenting with some even-numbered items you haven't tried before. This workbook will assist you in making these changes.

Adapted from the "Coping Styles Questionnaire." © 1999 by Jim Boyers, Ph.D., Kaiser-Permanente Medical Center and Health Styles, Santa Clara, Calif.

Knowing Your Goal

The goal of stress management is not merely stress reduction. After all, wouldn't life be boring without stress? As mentioned earlier, there is a tendency to think of stressful events or stressors as negative (such as the injury or death of a loved one) but stressors are often positive. For instance, getting a new home or a promotion at work brings with it the stress of change of status and new responsibilities. The physical exertion of a good workout, the excitement of doing something challenging for the first time, or the pleasure of watching a beautiful sunset are all examples of positive stress. Distress or negative stress occurs when you perceive that the challenge facing you is dangerous, difficult, painful, or unfair, and you are concerned that you may lack the resources to cope with it. You can actually increase your ability to deal with distress by integrating into your everyday life positive activities such as solving challenging problems, practicing regular exercise and relaxation, keeping enjoyable social contacts, following sensible dietary practices, and engaging in optimistic and rational thinking, humor, and play.

Research shows that performance and efficiency actually improve with increased stress, until performance peaks as the stress level becomes too great. Stress management involves finding the right types and amounts of stress, given your individual personality, priorities, and life situation, so that you can maximize your performance and satisfaction. By using the tools presented in this workbook, you can learn how to cope more effectively with distress as well as add more positive stress or stimulating challenges, pleasure, and excitement to your life.

Symptom Effectiveness

Now that you have identified the major sources of your stress, your stress-related symptoms, and your current tactics for dealing with stress, it is time to choose one or two symptoms that bother you the most and select the techniques that you will use to relieve them. Defining and achieving a specific goal will give you a sense of accomplishment and motivate you to continue using the tools and ideas that give you the positive change you are seeking. Since everyone reacts differently to stress, we can't tell you which techniques will work best for you. However, the chart on the following pages will give you a general idea of what to try first and where to go from there.

Chapter headings for each stress-reduction method are across the top, and typical stress-related symptoms are listed down the side. As you can see, more than one stress-reduction technique can be effective in treating most symptoms. The most effective techniques for a particular symptom are marked with a boldface X, while other helpful techniques for the same symptom are indicated by a smaller and lighter X.

The techniques fall into roughly two categories: relaxation techniques that focus on relaxing the body, and stress-reduction techniques that condition the mind to handle stress effectively. Your mind, body, and emotions are interrelated. In seeking relief from stress, you will obtain the best results by using at least one technique from each of these two broad categories. For example, if your most painful stress symptom is general anxiety, you might practice progressive relaxation and breathing exercises to calm your body and do exercises from the chapters on refuting irrational ideas and worry control to reduce your mental and emotional stress. If your results on Tactics for Coping with Stress indicate that you do not engage in regular physical exercise and/or your diet is not good, you will also want to refer to the chapters on physical exercise and nutrition to learn how these tactics can reduce your general anxiety.

Symptom Effectiveness Chart

Chapter titles for each stress reduction method are listed across the top, and typical stress-related symptom are listed down the side. The most effective techniques for a particular symptoms are marked with a boldface **X**, while other helpful techniques for that same symptom are indicated by a lighter x.

Techniques

Symptoms	Breathing	Progressive Relaxation	Meditation	Visualization	Applied Relaxation	Self-hypnosis	Auto-genics
Anxiety in specific situations (tests, deadlines, interviews, etc.)	**X**	**X**	x	x		x	
Anxiety in your personal relationships (spouse, parents, children, etc.)	**X**	**X**				x	
Anxiety, general (regardless of the situation or the people involved)	**X**	**X**	**X**	x	**X**		x
Depression, hopelessness, powerlessness, poor self-esteem	x	x	**X**				
Hostility, anger, irritability, resentment	**X**		x				x
Phobias, fears		**X**			**X**		
Obsessions, unwanted thoughts	x		**X**				
Muscular tension	**X**	**X**		x		x	**X**
High blood pressure	x	**X**	x				**X**
Headaches, neckaches, backaches	x	**X**		**X**	**X**	**X**	x
Indigestion, irritable bowel, ulcers, chronic constipation	x	**X**				**X**	**X**
Muscle spasms, tics		**X**		x	**X**	x	
Fatigue, tired all the time	**X**	x				**X**	x
Insomnia, sleeping difficulties	x	**X**			**X**	**X**	x
Obesity	x					x	
Physical weakness	x						
Job stress	x						
Chronic pain	**X**	x	**X**	**X**	x	**X**	**X**
Chronic illness	**X**		**X**	**X**		x	x

Important: Physical symptoms may have purely physiological causes. You should have a medical doctor eliminate the possibility of such physical problems before you proceed on the assumption that your symptoms are completely stress-related.

Brief Combination Techniques	Refuting Irrational Ideas	Thought Stopping	Worry Control	Coping Skills Training	Goal Setting and Time Management	Asser-tiveness Training	Job Stress Manage-ment	Nutrition	Exercise
x	x	X	X	X	X	x			
x	x		X	x		X			
x	X	x	X	x				x	x
	X	X			x	X		x	x
	X				X	X		x	x
	X	X	X	X	x	x			
	X	X	X	x	x				
x					x				X
x					x	x		X	x
						x		x	X
x					x	x		X	x
					x				x
					x			x	x
		X			x			x	x
	x							X	X
	x								X
X	X			x	x	x	X		
x		X		x		x		X	X
x		X				x		X	X

Read chapter 2 before you move on to other chapters. Body awareness is the key to everything else in this workbook, and without it you cannot use any of these techniques effectively.

Further Reading

Amundson, M. E., C. A. Hart, and T. A. Holmes. 1986. *Manual for the Schedule of Recent Experience (SRE)*. Seattle, Wash.: University of Washington Press.

Benson, H. 1994. *Beyond the Relaxation Response*. Berkeley, Calif.: Berkeley Pub. Corp.

Benson, H. 1975. *The Relaxation Response*. New York: Morrow.

Kobasa, S., S. Maddi, M. Puccetti, and M. Zola. 1985. Effectiveness of hardiness, exercise and social support as resources against illness. *Journal of Psychosomatic Research* 29:505–33.

Lazarus, R. S., and S. Folkman. 1984. *Stress Appraisal and Coping*. New York: Springer Publishing.

Lorig, K., H. Holman, D. Sobel, D. Laurent, V. Gonzalez, and M. Menor. 1994. *Living a Healthy Life with Chronic Disease*. Palo Alto, Calif.: Bull Publishing.

Martin, P. R. 1998. *The Healing Mind: The Vital Links between Brain and Behavior, Immunity and Disease*. Dunne Books.

Ornstein, R., and D. Sobel. 1990. *Healthy Pleasures*. Cambridge, Mass.: Perseus Press.

———. 1999. *The Healing Brain*. New York: Major Books.

Rabin, B. 1999. *Stress, Immune Function and Health: The Connection*. New York: Wiley-Liss.

Sapolsky, R. M. 1998. *Why Zebras Don't Get Ulcers: A Guide to Stress, Stress-Related Diseases, and Coping*. New York: W. H. Freeman.

Selye, H. 1978. *The Stress of Life*. New York: McGraw-Hill.

Sobel, D. S., and R. Orstein. 1997. *The Healthy Mind, Healthy Body Handbook*. Los Altos, Calif.: DRx.

Body Awareness 2

In this chapter you will learn:

- [ ] How the mind and body interact

- [ ] How to recognize tension in your body

- [ ] Exercises to recognize and let go of tension in your body

The ability to recognize how your body reacts to the stressors in your life can be a powerful skill. Most people are more aware of the weather, the time of day, or their bank balance than they are of the tension in their own bodies or their personal stress response. Your body registers stress long before the conscious mind does. Muscle tension is your body's way of letting you know that you are under stress, and body awareness is the first step toward acknowledging and reducing stress.

You inevitably tense your body when you experience stress. When the stress is removed, the tension will also go away. Also, chronic muscular tension occurs in people with particular beliefs or attitudes and tends to tighten specific muscle groups. For example, a woman who believes that it is bad to express anger is likely to have chronic neck tension and pain, while a man experiencing a lot of anxiety about the future may develop chronic stomach problems. This chronic muscular tension restricts digestion, limits self-expression, and decreases energy. Every contracted muscle blocks movement.

Differentiating between your external awareness and internal awareness in order to separate the world from your physical reaction to it is important. External awareness includes all stimulation to the five senses from the outside world. Internal awareness refers to any physical sensation, feeling, emotional discomfort, or comfort inside your body. Much of the tension in your body isn't felt because most of your awareness is directed toward the outside world. Below, you will learn about Gestalt exercises designed to locate and explore your body tension.

Background

The importance of body states, their effect on consciousness, and their relationship to stress have been emphasized for many centuries by eastern philosophies such as Zen, yoga, and Sufi. During this century, the work of Wilhelm Reich, originally a student of Freud, kindled Western psychiatry's interest in the body's interaction with emotional conditions. Two modern therapies that concentrate on the body and its relationship to emotional stress are Fritz Perls' Gestalt therapy and Alexander Lowen's bioenergetic therapy. Both of these therapies work closely with the mind-body relationship.

Body Inventory

The following exercises promote body awareness and will help you identify areas of tension.

Internal versus External Awareness

1. First focus your attention on the outside world. Start sentences with, "I am aware of." (For example, "I am aware of the cars going by outside the window, papers moving, the coffee perking, the breeze blowing, and the blue carpet.")

2. After you have become aware of everything that is going on around you, shift to focusing your attention on your body and your physical sensations—your internal world. (For example, "I am aware of feeling warm, my stomach gurgling, tension in my neck, nose tickling, and a cramp in my foot.")

3. Shuttle back and forth between internal and external awareness. (For example, "I am aware of the chair pushing into my buttocks, the circle of yellow light from the lamp, my shoulders hunching up, the smell of bacon.")

4. Used at free moments through the day, this exercise allows you to separate and appreciate the real difference between your inner and outer worlds.

Body Scanning

Close your eyes. Starting with your toes and moving up your body, ask yourself, "Where am I tense?" Whenever you discover a tense area, exaggerate it slightly so you can become aware of it. Be aware of the muscles in your body that are tense. Then, for example, say to yourself, "I am tensing my neck muscles . . . I am hurting myself . . . I am creating tension in my body." Note that all muscular tension is self-produced. At this point, be aware of any life situation that may be causing the tension in your body and what you could do to change it.

Letting Go of Your Body

Lie down on a rug or a firm bed and get comfortable. Pull your feet up until they rest flat on the floor and close your eyes. Check yourself for comfort. (This may require shifting your body around.) Become aware of your breathing. . . . Feel the air move into your nose, mouth, and down your throat into your lungs. Focus on your body and let all of the parts come into your awareness spontaneously. What parts of your body come into awareness first? What parts are you less aware of? Become aware of which parts of your body you can feel easily and which parts of your body have little sensation. Do you notice any difference between the right and left side of your body? Now become aware of any physical discomfort you are feeling. Become aware of this discomfort until you can describe it in detail. Focus and be aware of what happens to this discomfort. It may change. . . . Scan your body for any residual tension or discomfort and let it go with each exhalation. Continue letting go for five to ten minutes, allowing your body to take over.

Stress Awareness Diary

Some parts of the day are more stressful than others, and some stressful events are more likely to produce physical and emotional symptoms than others. Certain types of stressful events often produce characteristic symptoms. For this reason, keeping a record of stressful events, as well as symptoms that may have been a stress reaction, is useful. Make extra copies of the blank form on the next page for your own diary.

Keep a stress-awareness diary for two weeks. Make a note of the time that a stressful event occurs and the time you notice a physical or emotional symptom that could be related to the stress.

The following stress-awareness diary is from the Monday of a department-store clerk:

Time	Stressful event	Symptom
8:00	Alarm doesn't go off, late, rushing	
9:30		Slight headache
11:00	Customer is rude and insulting	
11:15		Anger, tightness in stomach
3:00	Return of three big-ticket items, much paper work	
3:15		Depression, slight headache
5:30	Heavy commute traffic	
6:30	Irritable with son	Anger, pounding headache
6:35	Wife defends son	Tightness in stomach

As you can see, the diary identifies how particular stresses result in predictable symptoms. Interpersonal confrontations may characteristically be followed by stomach tension. Rushing may be causing vasoconstriction (tightening of the blood vessels) for this individual, who as a result experiences irritability and headaches. You can use your stress-awareness diary to discover and chart your stressful events and characteristic reactions.

As you use these body-awareness exercises, you will begin to recognize where your body stores muscular tension. When you allow yourself increased awareness, you can find ways to let go of the tension you discover. Along with the release of tension, you will experience increased energy and a sense of well-being.

To keep a convenient record of how you feel before and after your relaxation exercises, use the following record of general tension.

Stress Awareness Diary

Date _____ Day of the week _____

Time	Stressful event	Symptom
_____	_____	_____
_____	_____	_____
_____	_____	_____
_____	_____	_____
_____	_____	_____
_____	_____	_____
_____	_____	_____
_____	_____	_____
_____	_____	_____
_____	_____	_____
_____	_____	_____
_____	_____	_____
_____	_____	_____
_____	_____	_____
_____	_____	_____
_____	_____	_____
_____	_____	_____
_____	_____	_____

Record of General Tension

Rate yourself on this 10-point scale before and after you do your relaxation exercise.

1	2	3	4	5
totally relaxed no tension	very relaxed	moderately relaxed	fairly relaxed	slightly relaxed

6	7	8	9	10
slightly tense	fairly tense	moderately tense	very tense	extremely tense (the most uncomfortable you could be)

Week of	Before session	After session	Comments
Monday			
Tuesday			
Wednesday			
Thursday			
Friday			
Saturday			
Sunday			

Your personal mind-body connection and the interactions between your thoughts, body, and social environment are an integral part of beginning to manage the stress in your life, as opposed to letting it manage you. This chapter will help you begin that process.

Further Reading

Benson, H., and E. Stuart. 1993. *The Wellness Book.* New York: Birch Lane Press.

Borysenko, J. 1993. *Minding the Body, Mending the Mind.* Reading, Mass.: Bantam Doubleday Dell Publications.

Goleman, D., and J. Gurin. 1995. *Mind Body Medicine: How to Use Your Mind for Better Health*. Yonkers, N.Y.: Consumer Reports Books.

Knaster, M. 1996. *Discovering the Body's Wisdom*. New York: Bantam Books.

Lorig, K., H. Holman, D. Sobel, D. Laurent, V. Gonzalez, and M. Menor. 1994. *Living a Healthy Life with Chronic Conditions*. Palo Alto, Calif.: Bull Publishing.

Lowen, A. 1976. *Bioenergetics*. New York: Viking-Penguin.

Perls, F, and F. S. Perls. 1973. *The Gestalt Approach and Eye Witness to Therapy*. New York: Science and Behavioral Books.

Scheller, M. D. 1993. *Growing Older, Feeling Better*. Palo Alto, Calif.: Bull Publishing.

Breathing

In this chapter you will learn to:

☐   Use breathing to increase your awareness and relaxation

☐   Breathe to release tension

☐   Use breathing for symptom control or release

Background

Breathing is a necessity of life that most people take for granted. With each breath of air, you obtain oxygen and release the waste product carbon dioxide. Poor breathing habits diminish the flow of these gases to and from your body, making it harder for you to cope with stressful situations. Improper breathing contributes to anxiety, panic attacks, depression, muscle tension, headaches, and fatigue. As you learn to be aware of your breathing and practice slowing and normalizing your breaths, your mind will quiet and your body will relax. Breathing awareness and good breathing habits will enhance your psychological and physical well-being, whether you practice them alone or in combination with other relaxation techniques.

Let's examine a breath. When you inhale, air is drawn in through your nose, where it is warmed to body temperature, humidified, and partially cleansed. Your diaphragm, a sheetlike muscle separating the lungs and the abdomen, facilitates your breathing by expanding and contracting as you breathe in and out.

Your lungs are like a tree with many branches (bronchial tubes) that carry air to elastic air sacs (alveoli). The alveoli have the balloonlike ability to expand when air is taken into the lungs and contract when air is let out. Small blood vessels (capillaries) surrounding the alveoli receive oxygen and transport it to your heart.

The blood that your heart pumps carries oxygen to all parts of your body. An exchange occurs in which blood cells receive oxygen and release carbon dioxide, a waste product that is carried back to your heart and lungs and exhaled. This efficient method of transporting and exchanging oxygen is vital to sustain life.

When you breathe, you typically use one of two patterns: (1) chest or thoracic breathing and (2) abdominal or diaphragmatic breathing.

Chest or thoracic breathing is often associated with anxiety or other emotional distress. It is also common in people who wear restricted clothing or lead sedentary or stressful lives. Chest breathing is shallow and often irregular and rapid. When air is inhaled, the chest expands and the shoulders rise to take in the air. Anxious people may experience breath holding, hyperventilation or constricted breathing, shortness of breath, or fear of passing out. If an insufficient amount of air reaches your lungs, your blood is not properly oxygenated, your heart rate and muscle tension increase, and your stress response is turned on.

Abdominal or diaphragmatic breathing is the natural breathing of newborn babies and sleeping adults. Inhaled air is drawn deep into the lungs and exhaled as the diaphragm contracts and expands. Breathing is even and nonconstricting. The respiratory system is able to do its job of producing energy from oxygen and removing waste products.

By increasing your awareness of your breathing patterns and shifting to more abdominal breathing, you can reduce the muscle tension and anxiety present with stress-related symptoms or thoughts. Diaphragmatic breathing is the easiest way of eliciting the relaxation response.

Symptom Effectiveness

Breathing exercises have been found to be effective in reducing generalized anxiety disorders, panic attacks and agoraphobia, depression, irritability, muscle tension, headaches, and fatigue. They are used in the treatment and prevention of breath holding, hyperventilation, shallow breathing, and cold hands and feet.

Time to Master

While a breathing exercise can be learned in a matter of minutes and some benefits experienced immediately, the profound effects of the exercise may not be fully appreciated until after months of persistent practice. After you have tried the exercises presented in this chapter, develop a breathing program incorporating those exercises you find most beneficial and follow your program with patience and persistence.

Instructions

This chapter is divided into three sections: breathing for awareness and relaxation, breathing to release tension, and breathing for symptom control.

Breathing for Awareness and Relaxation

Your first step is to increase your awareness of your breathing habits and to learn how to use breathing as a relaxation skill.

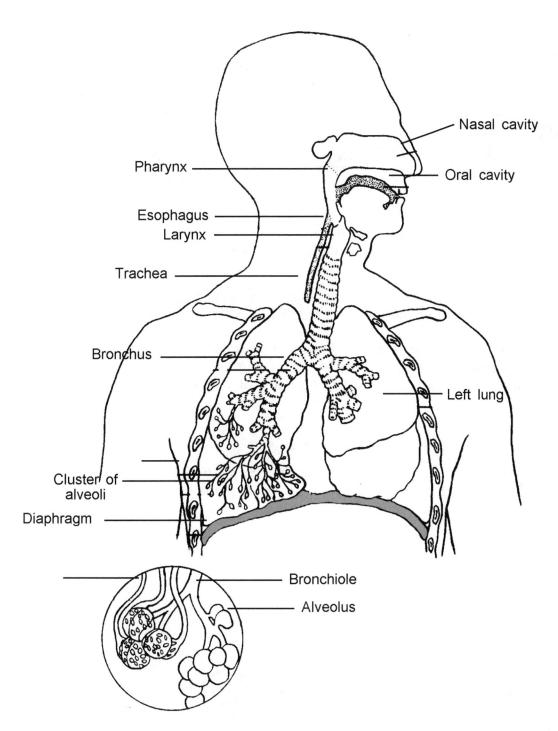

Nasal cavity

Pharynx

Oral cavity

Esophagus

Larynx

Trachea

Bronchus

Left lung

Cluster of
alveoli

Diaphragm

Bronchiole

Alveolus

Adapted from *The Anatomy Coloring Book* by Wynn Kapit and Lawrence M. Elson, Harper & Row, New York, 1977.

Breathing Awareness

1. Close your eyes. Put your right hand on your abdomen, right at the waistline, and put your left hand on your chest, right in the center.

2. Without trying to change your breathing, simply notice how you are breathing. Which hand rises the most as you inhale—the hand on your chest or the hand on your belly?

If your abdomen expands, you are breathing from your abdomen or diaphragm. If your belly doesn't move or moves less than your chest, you are breathing from your chest.

The trick to shifting from chest to abdominal breathing is to make one or two full exhalations that push out the air from the bottom of your lungs. This will create a vacuum that will pull in a deep, diaphragmatic breath on your next inhalation.

Diaphragmatic or Abdominal Breathing

1. Lie down on a rug or blanket on the floor in a "dead body" pose—your legs straight and slightly apart, your toes pointed comfortably outward, your arms at your sides and not touching your body, your palms up, and your eyes closed.

2. Bring your attention to your breathing and place your hand on the spot that seems to rise and fall the most as you inhale and exhale.

3. Gently place both of your hands or a book on your abdomen and follow your breathing. Notice how your abdomen rises with each inhalation and falls with each exhalation.

4. Breathe through your nose. (If possible, always clear your nasal passages before doing breathing exercises.)

5. If you experience difficulty breathing into your abdomen, press your hand down on your abdomen as you exhale and let your abdomen push your hand back up as you inhale deeply.

6. Is your chest moving in harmony with your abdomen or is it rigid? Spend a minute or two letting your chest follow the movement of your abdomen.

7. If you continue to experience difficulty breathing into your abdomen, an alternative is to lie on your stomach, with your head rested on your folded hands. Take deep abdominal breaths so you can feel your abdomen pushing against the floor.

Deep Breathing

1. Although this exercise can be practiced in a variety of poses, the following is recommended: Lie down on a blanket or rug on the floor. Bend your knees and move your feet about eight inches apart, with your toes turned slightly outward. Make sure that your spine is straight.

2. Scan your body for tension.

3. Place one hand on your abdomen and one hand on your chest.

4. Inhale slowly and deeply through your nose into your abdomen to push up your hand as much as feels comfortable. Your chest should move only a little and only with your abdomen.

5. When you feel at ease with step 4, smile slightly and inhale through your nose and exhale through your mouth, making a quiet, relaxing, whooshing sound like the wind as you blow gently out. Your mouth, tongue, and jaw will be relaxed. Take long, slow, deep breaths that raise and lower your abdomen. Focus on the sound and feeling of breathing as you become more and more relaxed.

6. Continue deep breathing for about five or ten minutes at a time, once or twice a day. Then, if you like, gradually extend this period to twenty minutes.

7. At the end of each deep-breathing session, take a little time to once more scan your body for tension. Compare the tension you feel at the conclusion of the exercise with that which you experienced when you began. Use the Record of General Tension in chapter 2 to monitor your progress.

8. When you become at ease with breathing into your abdomen, practice it any time during the day when you feel like it and you are sitting down or standing still. Concentrate on your abdomen moving up and down, the air moving in and out of your lungs, and the feeling of relaxation that deep breathing gives you.

9. When you have learned to relax yourself using deep breathing, practice it whenever you feel yourself getting tense.

Breathing to Release Tension

Use the following exercises to enhance relaxation and release tension.

Breath Counting

1. Sit or lie in a comfortable position with your arms and legs uncrossed and your spine straight.

2. Breathe in deeply into your abdomen. Let yourself pause before you exhale.

3. As you exhale, count "one" to yourself. As you continue to inhale and exhale, count each exhalation: "Two ... three ... four."

4. Continue counting your exhalations in sets of four for five to ten minutes.

5. Notice your breathing gradually slowing, your body relaxing, and your mind calming as you practice this breathing meditation.

The Relaxing Sigh

During the day, you probably catch yourself sighing or yawning. This is generally a sign that you are not getting enough oxygen. Sighing and yawning are your body's way of remedying the situation. A sigh is often accompanied by a sense that things are not quite as they should be, and a feeling of tension. Since a sigh actually does release a bit of this tension, you can practice sighing at will as a means of relaxing.

1. Sit or stand up straight.

2. Sigh deeply, letting out a sound of deep relief as the air rushes out of your lungs.

3. Don't think about inhaling—just let the air come in naturally.

4. Take eight to twelve of these relaxing sighs and let yourself experience the feeling of relaxation. Repeat whenever you feel the need for it.

Letting Go of Tension

1. Sit comfortably in a chair with your feet on the floor.

2. Breathe in deeply into your abdomen and say to yourself, "Breathe in relaxation." Let yourself pause before you exhale.

3. Breathe out from your abdomen and say to yourself, "Breathe out tension." Pause before you inhale.

4. Use each inhalation as a moment to become aware of any tension in your body.

5. Use each exhalation as an opportunity to let go of tension.

6. You may find it helpful to use your imagination to picture or feel the relaxation entering and the tension leaving your body.

Breathing for Symptom Control or Release

Abdominal Breathing and Imagination

This exercise combines the relaxing benefits of complete natural breathing with the curative value of positive autosuggestion.

1. Lie down on a rug or blanket on the floor in a "dead body" pose.

2. Place your hands gently on your solar plexus (the point where your ribs start to separate above your abdomen) and practice complete natural breathing for a few minutes.

3. Imagine that energy is rushing into your lungs with each incoming breath of air and being immediately stored in your solar plexus. Imagine that this energy is flowing out to all parts of your body with each exhalation. Form a mental picture of this energizing process.

4. Continue on a daily basis for at least five to ten minutes a day.

Alternatives to step 3:

Keep one hand on your solar plexus and move the other hand to a point on your body that hurts. As you inhale, imagine energy coming in and being stored. As you exhale, imagine the energy flowing to the spot that hurts and stimulating it. As you continue to inhale more energy, imagine this energy driving out the pain with each exhalation. Keep a clear picture of this process in your mind as you alternately stimulate the spot that hurts and then drive out the pain.

Keep one hand on your solar plexus and move the other hand to a point on your body that has been injured or is infected. Imagine the energy coming in and being stored as you inhale. As you exhale, imagine that you are directing energy to the affected point and stimulating it, driving out the infection or healing it. Picture this process in your mind's eye.

Alternative Breathing

Most people will find this relaxation exercise useful, but those suffering from tension or sinus headaches often find it particularly beneficial. Begin by doing five cycles, then slowly raise the number to between ten and twenty-five cycles.

1. Sit in a comfortable position with good posture.

2. Rest the index and second finger of your right hand on your forehead.

3. Close your right nostril with your thumb.

4. Inhale slowly and soundlessly through your left nostril.

5. Close your left nostril with your ring finger and simultaneously open your right nostril by removing your thumb.

6. Exhale slowly and soundlessly and as thoroughly as possible through your right nostril.

7. Inhale through your right nostril.

8. Close your right nostril with your thumb and open your left nostril.

Alternative breathing

9. Exhale through your left nostril.

10. Inhale through your left nostril, beginning the next cycle.

Breath Training

This exercise, adapted from Masi (1993), has also been called "breathing retraining" and "controlled breathing." Individuals with panic disorder or agoraphobia have found it particularly helpful. When most people feel panic, they have a tendency to gasp, take in a breath, and hold onto it. The resulting sensation of fullness and inability to get enough air in turn produces quick, shallow breathing or hyperventilation. The hyperventilation triggers the panic attack. Breath training provides a crucial counting or pacing procedure that helps counteract this process. Here are the steps to follow.

1. Exhale first. At the first sign of nervousness or panic, at the first "what if" thought that you might pass out, have a heart attack, or be unable to breathe, always exhale. It is important to exhale first so that your lungs open up and you'll feel as though there's plenty of room to take a good deep breath.

2. Inhale and exhale through your nose. Exhaling through your nose will slow down your breathing and prevent hyperventilation. As an alternative to breathing

through your nose, inhale through your mouth and make a purifying exhalation through your mouth by pretending that you are blowing out through a straw.

3. Lie on your back with your hand over your abdomen, and the other hand on your chest. Exhale first, and then breathe in through your nose, counting, "One . . . two . . . three." Pause a second, and then breathe out through your mouth, counting, "One . . . two . . . three . . . four." Make sure that your exhalation is always longer than your inhalation. This will protect you from taking short, gasping panic breaths.

4. After you feel comfortable with step 3, you can slow your breathing even further. Breathe in and count, "One . . . two . . . three . . . four"; pause and breathe out, counting, "One . . . two . . . three . . . four . . . five." Keep practicing these slow deep breaths, pushing the hand on your abdomen up but allowing very little movement for the hand on your chest. When your minds drifts, refocus on your breathing.

Alternative positions:

Lie on your stomach with your hands folded under your head. Continue to count, "One . . . two . . . three" as you breathe in and, "One . . . two . . . three . . . four" as you breathe out. As in step 4 above, breathe even more slowly by counting to four as you inhale and to five as you exhale.

Step 4 can also be done while you are standing, walking, and sitting. Pace your steps to match the same slow rate of your breathing.

When paced breathing feels comfortable and natural, you can replace counting with the words "in" as you inhale and "calm" as you exhale. Maintain the same pace, making each exhalation last slightly longer than each inhalation. Breathe in through your nose and breathe out through your mouth. Always exhale first.

Controlled Breathing

If you find that it is difficult to use the counting techniques described above, you can make a pacing tape that will teach you controlled breathing. First you need to decide how to set the breathing rate that is best for you. Depending on how slowly you breathe when you are at rest, your rate can be set at either eight or twelve breaths a minute. To determine which interval will be better for you, relax and count how many breaths you take over a period of three minutes. If you counted more than thirty breaths, follow the instructions for the twelve-breaths-per-minute tape. If you counted thirty or fewer, follow the instructions for the eight-breaths-per-minute tape.

To make a twelve-breaths-per-minute pacing tape:

1. Say the word "in" for two seconds.

2. Say the word "out" for two seconds.

3. Pause for one second.

4. Continue to repeat "in" for two seconds and "out" for two seconds, followed by a one-second pause.

5. Keep the tape going for about five minutes.

To make an eight-breaths-per-minute pacing tape:

1. Say the word "in" for three seconds.

2. Say the word "out" for three seconds.

3. Pause for one second.

4. Continue to repeat that sequence for about five minutes.

After you have made your pacing tape, practice breathing with the tape four times per day. When you feel comfortable, practice controlled breathing with the tape off for thirty seconds and then turn the tape back on for one minute to see if your pace still matches the tape. If your breath rate remains the same, try turning the tape off for two minutes at a time, and then for five minutes. Each time you finish breathing on your own, turn the tape back on again to see if your pace still matches.

Further Reading

Benson, H., and E. Stuart. 1992. *The Wellness Book: The Comprehensive Guide to Maintaining Health and Treating Stress-Related Illness.* Secaucus, N.J.: Birch Lane Press.

Borysensko, J. 1993. *Minding the Body, Mending the Mind.* New York: Bantam Doubleday Dell Publications.

Farhi, D. 1996. *The Breathing Book.* New York: Henry Holt.

Hendricks, G. *Conscious Breathing: Breathwork for Health, Stress Release and Personal Mastery.* 1995. New York: Bantam Books.

Audiotapes

Hendricks, G. 1989. *The Art of Breathing and Centering.* Audio Renaissance.

Masi, N. 1993. *Breath of Life.* Plantation, Fla.: Resource Warehouse.

Progressive Relaxation and Breathing. 1987. Oakland, Calif.: New Harbinger Publications.

Ten Minutes to Relax. 1990. Manhasset, N.Y.: Vital Body Marketing Company.

Progressive Relaxation

In this chapter you will learn to:

☐ Distinguish between tense and relaxed muscles

☐ Progressively relax all of the muscles of your body

☐ Relax quickly in stressful situations

Background

You cannot have the feeling of warm well-being in your body and at the same time experience psychological stress. Progressive relaxation of your muscles reduces pulse rate and blood pressure as well as decreases perspiration and respiration rates. Deep muscle relaxation, when successfully mastered, can be used as an antianxiety pill.

Edmund Jacobson, a Chicago physician, published the book *Progressive Relaxation* in 1929. In this book he described his deep muscle relaxation technique, which he asserted required no imagination, willpower, or suggestion. His technique is based on the premise that the body responds to anxiety-provoking thoughts and events with muscle tension. This physiological tension, in turn, increases the subjective experience of anxiety. Deep muscle relaxation reduces physiological tension and is incompatible with anxiety: the habit of responding with one blocks the habit of responding with the other.

Symptom Effectiveness

Excellent results have been found in the treatment of muscular tension, anxiety, insomnia, depression, fatigue, irritable bowel, muscle spasms, neck and back pain, high blood pressure, mild phobias, and stuttering.

Time to Master

One to two weeks, employing two fifteen-minute sessions per day.

Instructions

Most people do not realize which of their muscles are chronically tense. Progressive relaxation provides a way of identifying particular muscles and muscle groups and distinguishing between sensations of tension and deep relaxation.

Progressive relaxation can be practiced lying down or in a chair. Each muscle or muscle group is tensed from five to seven seconds and then relaxed for twenty to thirty seconds. This procedure is repeated at least once. If a particular muscle is difficult to relax, you can practice tensing and releasing it up to five times. You may also find it helpful to say to yourself as you are doing progressive relaxation one or more of the following expressions:

Let go of the tension.
Calm and rested.
Relax and smooth out the muscles.
Let the tension dissolve away.
Let go more and more.
Deeper and deeper.

Once the procedure is familiar enough to be remembered, keep your eyes closed and focus attention on just one muscle group at a time. The instructions for progressive relaxation are divided into two sections. The first part is the basic procedure, which you may wish to tape and replay while practicing. This will familiarize you with the muscles in your body that are most commonly tense. If you do tape it, be sure to pause long enough for tensing and relaxing. The second section shortens the procedure by simultaneously tensing and relaxing many muscles at one time, so that deep muscle relaxation can be achieved in a very brief period.

Basic Procedure

Get into a comfortable position in a quiet room where you won't be disturbed. You may want to loosen your clothing and remove your shoes. Begin to relax as you take a few slow, deep breaths. . . . Now as you let the rest of your body relax, clench your fists and bend them back at the wrist . . . tighter and tighter . . . feel the tension in your fists and forearms. . . . Now relax. . . . Feel the looseness in your hands and forearms. . . . Notice the contrast with the tension. . . . (If you have time, repeat this, and all succeeding procedures, at least one more time.) Now bend your elbows and tense your biceps. . . . Tense them as hard as you can and observe the feeling of tautness. . . . Let your hands drop down and relax. . . . Feel that difference. . . . Turn your attention to your head and wrinkle your forehead as tight as you can. . . . Feel the tension in your forehead and scalp. Now relax and smooth it out. Imagine your entire forehead and scalp becoming smooth and at rest. . . . Now frown and notice the strain spreading throughout your forehead. . . . Let go. Allow your brow to become smooth again. . . . Squeeze your eyes closed . . . tighter. . . . Relax your eyes. Let them remain closed gently and comfortably. . . . Now open your mouth wide and feel the tension in your jaw. . . . Relax your jaw. . . . When the jaw is relaxed, your lips will be slightly parted. Notice the contrast between tension and relaxation.... Now press your tongue against the roof of your mouth. Experience the ache in the back of your mouth.... Relax.... Press your lips now, purse them into an "O."... Relax your lips.... Feel the relaxation in your forehead, scalp, eyes, jaw, tongue, and lips.... Let go more and more....

Roll your head slowly around on your neck, feeling the point of tension shifting as your head moves ... and then slowly roll your head the other way. Relax, allowing your head to return to a comfortable upright position.... Now shrug your shoulders; bring your shoulders up toward your ears ... hold it.... Drop your shoulders back down and feel the relaxation spreading through your neck, throat, and shoulders ... pure relaxation, deeper and deeper....

Now breathe in and fill your lungs completely. Hold your breath. Experience the tension.... Now exhale and let your chest become loose.... Continue relaxing, letting your breath come freely and gently.... Notice the tension draining out of your muscles with each exhalation.... Next, tighten your stomach and hold. Feel the tension.... Relax.... Now place your hand on your stomach. Breathe deeply into your stomach, pushing your hand up. Hold ... and relax. Feel the contrast of relaxation as the air rushes out.... Now arch your back, without straining. Keep the rest of your body as relaxed as possible. Focus on the tension in your lower back.... Now relax.... Let the tension dissolve away.

Tighten your buttocks and thighs.... Relax and feel the difference.... Now straighten and tense your legs and curl your toes downward. Experience the tension.... Relax.... Straighten and tense your legs and bend your toes toward your face.... Relax.

Feel the comfortable warmth and heaviness of deep relaxation throughout your entire body as you continue to breathe slowly and deeply.... You can relax even more as you move up through your body, letting go of the last bit of tension in your body. Relax your feet ... relax your ankles ... relax your calves ... relax your shins ... relax your knees ... relax your thighs ... relax your buttocks.... Let the relaxation spread to your stomach ... to your lower back ... to your chest.... Let go more and more. Feel the relaxation deepening in your shoulders ... in your arms ... and in your hands.... Deeper and deeper. Notice the feeling of looseness and relaxation in your neck ... your jaw ... your face ... and your scalp.... Continue to breathe slowly and deeply. Your entire body is comfortably loose and relaxed, calm and rested.

Shorthand Procedure

Once you have mastered the basic procedure, use the following procedure to relax your muscles quickly. Whole muscle groups are simultaneously tensed and then relaxed. As before, repeat each procedure at least once, tensing each muscle group from five to seven seconds and then relaxing from fifteen to thirty seconds. Remember to notice the contrast between the sensations of tension and relaxation.

1. Curl both fists, tightening biceps and forearms (Charles Atlas pose). Relax.

2. Roll your head around on your neck clockwise in a complete circle, then reverse. Relax.

3. Wrinkle up the muscles of your face like a walnut: wrinkle forehead, eyes squinted, mouth open, and shoulders hunched. Relax.

4. Arch your shoulders back as you take a deep breath into your chest. Hold. Relax. Take a deep breath, pressing out the stomach. Hold. Relax.

5. Straighten your legs and point your toes back toward your face, tightening your shins. Hold. Relax. Straighten your legs and curl your toes, simultaneously tightening calves, thighs, and buttocks. Relax.

Special Considerations

1. If you make a tape of the basic procedure to facilitate your relaxation program, remember to space each procedure so that time is allowed to experience the tension and relaxation before going on to the next muscle or muscle group.

2. As with all relaxation techniques, regular practice of progressive relaxation will enhance the speed and depth of your relaxation.

3. Caution should be taken in tensing the neck and back, because excessive tightening can result in muscle or spinal damage. Also, overtightening the toes or feet can result in muscle cramping.

4. People new to this technique sometimes make the error of relaxing tension gradually. This slow-motion release of tension may look relaxed, but it actually requires sustained tension. When you release the tension in a particular muscle, let it go instantly; let your muscles become suddenly limp.

5. This chapter has described active tensing of muscles. People with injuries or very painful muscles may prefer passive tensing of muscles. You can use the same basic procedure and substitute the words, "Notice the tension in your _____" whenever the instructions call for tensing a muscle. If you feel no tension in a particular muscle, tense it just enough to notice the slightest amount of tension. This kind of minimal tensing is usually not visibly noticeable.

6. While initially you will learn progressive relaxation in a quiet place, eventually you will be able to use at least a shortened version of it any time during the day when you notice you are tense.

Further Reading

Bernstein, D. A., T. D. Borkovec, and H. Hazlett-Stevens. 2000. *New Directions in Progressive Relaxation Training: A Guidebook for Helping Professionals.* New York: Praeger Publishing.

Jacobson, E. 1974. *Progressive Relaxation.* Chicago: The University of Chicago Press, Midway Reprint. Out of print.

Wolpe, J. 1992. *The Practice of Behavior Therapy.* New York: Pergamon Press.

Meditation

In this chapter you will learn to:

☐ Use basic meditation techniques

Background

Meditation is the practice of uncritically attempting to focus your attention on one thing at a time. Exactly what that thing is is relatively unimportant and varies from one tradition to the next. Often the meditator repeats, either aloud or silently, a syllable, word, or group of words. This is known as mantra meditation. Focusing on a fixed object such as a flame or flower can also anchor the attention. Many meditators find that a convenient and relaxing point of focus is the rising and falling of their own breath. But you can use anything as an object of meditation ... the calendar on your desk, the tip of your nose, or even Aunt Mary's maiden name.

It is important to understand that the heart of meditation lies not simply in focusing on one object to the exclusion of all other thought, but rather in the attempt to achieve this type of focus. The nature of the mind is such that it does not want to stay concentrated. A myriad of thoughts will appear and seemingly interfere with the meditation. A typical meditation might go something like this (the meditator in this case has chosen the task of counting to three repeatedly):

> One ... two ... this isn't so hard ... one ... two ... three ... one ... I'm not having many thoughts at all ... oh, oh, I just had a thought ... that was another one ... two ... my nose itches ... one ... I wonder if it's okay to scratch it ... darn, there was another thought. I've got to try harder ... one ... two ... three ... one ... two ... I was judging myself pretty harshly. I'm not supposed to do that ... one ... two ... three ... one ... I'm hungry ... wonder what I'll cook tonight ... one ... two ... three ... I'm having way too many thoughts ... I'll

never get this right . . . one . . . two . . . now don't judge . . . one . . . two . . . three . . . one. . . .

Each time this meditator realizes that his mind has drifted to other thoughts, he chooses instead to dwell on the original object of his attention. By repeating this one moment of awareness, a moment that consists of noticing the thought and then refocusing the attention, over time a number of surprising realizations will become apparent:

- It is impossible to worry, fear, or hate when your mind is thinking about something other than the object of these emotions.

- It isn't necessary to think about everything that pops into your head. You have the ability to choose which thoughts you will think about.

- The seemingly diverse contents of your mind can really fit into a few simple categories: grudging thoughts, fearful thoughts, angry thoughts, wanting thoughts, planning thoughts, memories, and so on.

- You act in certain ways because you have certain thoughts that over your lifetime have become habitual. Habitual patterns of thought and perception will begin to lose their influence over your life once you become aware of them.

- Emotion, aside from the thoughts and pictures in your mind, consists entirely of physical sensations in your body.

- Even the strongest emotion will become manageable if you concentrate on the sensations in your body and not the content of the thought that produced the emotion.

- Thought and emotion are not permanent. They pass into and out of your body and mind. They need not leave a trace.

- When you are awake to what is happening right now and open to "what is," the extreme highs and extreme lows of your emotional response to life will disappear. You will live life with equanimity.

In 1968, Dr. Herbert Benson and his colleagues at Harvard Medical School decided to put meditation to the test. Volunteer practitioners of transcendental meditation were tested to see if meditation really could counter the physiological effects of stress. Benson scientifically proved that:

1. Heartbeat and breathing rates slow down.

2. Oxygen consumption falls by 20 percent.

3. Blood lactate levels drop. (This level rises with stress and fatigue.)

4. Skin resistance to electrical current, a sign of relaxation, increases fourfold.

5. EEG ratings of brain wave patterns indicate increased alpha activity, another sign of relaxation.

Benson went on to prove that any meditation practice could duplicate these physiological changes as long as four factors were present:

1. a relatively quiet environment,

2. a mental device that provides a constant stimulus,

3. a comfortable position, and

4. a passive attitude.

Today, meditation is practiced by athletes, performers, business people, and anyone who wants to feel more focused and calm in his or her life. Meditation can assist with making new choices in the moment, reducing struggle, and limiting responses that are reactive.

Symptom Effectiveness

Meditation has been used successfully in the treatment and prevention of high blood pressure, heart disease, migraine headaches, and autoimmune diseases such as diabetes and arthritis. It has proved helpful in curtailing obsessive thinking, anxiety, depression, and hostility.

Time to Master

The benefits of meditation increase with practice: Levels of relaxation deepen. Attention becomes steadier. You become more adept at living in the present moment. Therefore, it is important to meditate regularly.

Instructions

Establishing Your Posture

A. From the following, select a position that is comfortable for you:

- In a chair with your knees comfortably apart, your legs uncrossed, and your hands resting in your lap.

- Tailor-fashion (cross-legged) on the floor. This position is most comfortable and stable when a cushion is placed under your buttocks so that both knees touch the floor.

- On your knees with your big toes touching and your heels pointed outward so that your buttocks rest on the soles of your feet. Again, if you place a cushion between your feet for your buttocks to rest on, you will be able to hold the position for a much longer period of time.

- The yoga "full lotus" position. This position requires so much physical conditioning that it is not recommended for beginners.

B. Sit with your back straight (but not ramrod rigid) and let the weight of your head fall directly down upon your spinal column. This can be accomplished by pulling your chin in slightly. Allow the small of your back to arch.

Establishing Your Posture

Yoga lotus position

Japanese-fashion

Tailor-fashoin

C. Rock briefly from side to side, then from front to back, and establish the point at which your upper torso feels balanced on your hips.

D. Close your mouth and breathe through your nose. Place your tongue on the roof of your mouth.

Centering Yourself

A. Grounding

Close your eyes and focus on the place where your body touches the cushion or chair. What are the sensations there? Next, notice the places where your body touches itself. Are your hands crossed? Are your legs crossed? Pay attention to the sensation at these places of contact. Finally, focus on the way your body takes up space. Does it take up a lot of space? A small amount? Can you feel the boundary between your body and space? Notice the feelings there.

B. Breathing

With your eyes closed, take several deep breaths and notice the quality of your breathing. Is it fast or slow? Deep or shallow? Notice where your breath rests in your body. Is it up high in your chest? Is it in the midsection around your stomach? Down low in your belly? Try moving your breath from one area to the other. Breathe into your upper chest, then into your stomach, then drop your breath into your lower belly. Feel your abdomen expand and contract as the air goes in and out. Notice how the upper chest and stomach areas seem almost still. This "dropped breath" is the most relaxing stance to meditate from. However, if you have difficulty taking deep belly breaths, don't worry. Your breath will drop of its own accord as you become more practiced in meditation.

C. Attitude

Maintaining a passive attitude during meditation is perhaps the most important element in eliciting relaxation. It is important to realize that, especially as a beginner, you will have many thoughts and relatively few moments of clear concentration. This is natural and to be expected. Realize that your thoughts are not really interruptions but are an integral part of meditation. Without thoughts, you would not be able to develop the ability to let them go.

A passive attitude includes a lack of concern about whether you are doing things correctly, whether you are accomplishing any goals, or whether this meditation is right for you. Sit with the attitude of, "I'm going to put in my time here, just sitting, and whatever happens is exactly what should happen."

A Word about Time

In general, any amount of time spent in meditation is more relaxing than not meditating at all. When you first begin to practice, maintain the meditation for only as long as is comfortable, even if this is only for five minutes a day. If you feel that you are forcing yourself to sit, you may develop an aversion to practicing meditation at all. As you progress in your practice and meditation becomes easier, you will find yourself wanting to extend your time. In terms of relaxation, twenty to thirty minutes once or twice a day is sufficient.

Exercises

The following exercises are divided into five groups.

- Group 1 explains the mechanics of three basic meditations. Try each one a few times, then settle on the one you like best. Practice it regularly, at least once a day.

- Group 2 consists of meditation exercises that will help you develop the skill of relaxing muscle groups at will.

- Group 3 introduces you to mindfulness exercises. You don't need to go off by yourself and sit in silence in order to concentrate and build mindfulness. These exercises can be practiced anywhere and can be helpful in calming your body as it responds to stress throughout the day.

- Group 4 builds on the mindfulness techniques in group 3. In real life you may often find yourself in the presence of minor pain, annoyances, or disappointments, all of which cause you to tense up. By practicing feeling relaxed around small irritations while you meditate, you will become more adept at handling life's larger irritations when they occur.

- Group 5 teaches you how to let go of obsessive thoughts and feelings that make it difficult to relax because your mind wants to hold on to an idea or emotion that you experienced at an earlier time.

Group 1: Three Basic Meditations

Mantra Meditation

This is the most common form of meditation throughout the world. Before you begin, select a word or syllable that you like. Perhaps there's a word that has special meaning for you. Or you may use nonsense syllables, the sound of which you find pleasant. Benson recommended using the word "one." Many meditators prefer the universal mantra, "OM."

A. Find your posture and center yourself. Take several deep breaths.

B. Chant your mantra silently to yourself. Say the word or syllables over and over within your mind. When your thought strays, note that, then bring your attention back to your mantra. If you notice any sensations in your body, note the feeling, then return to the repetition of your own special word. You needn't force it. Let your mantra find its own rhythm as you repeat it over and over again.

C. If you have the opportunity, you may want to try chanting your mantra aloud. Let the sound of your voice fill you as you relax. Notice whether the sensations in your body are different from those you felt when you chanted silently. Which is more relaxing?

D. Remember that meditation is to be practiced with awareness. You may find that the repetition of a mantra, especially when repeated silently, can easily become mechanical. When this happens, you may have the sense that an inner voice is repeating your mantra while you are actually lost in thought or rapidly approaching sleep. Try to stay aware of each repetition of each syllable.

Sitting Meditation

The simplest way to begin meditation is by focusing on your breath.

A. Choose a comfortable sitting posture.

B. Bring your attention to the gentle rise and fall of your breath. Like ocean waves coming in and out, your breath is always there. You can focus on your inhale and exhale, the sensations of your breath entering your nose or mouth, or the sensations of your breath filling your lungs and diaphragm.

C. Whenever your mind wanders, gently bring your attention back to rest upon your breath. Let your breath be your anchor to this present moment.

D. When you find yourself becoming distracted by thoughts, simply notice them and acknowledge them.

E. One way to work with thoughts is to "name" them as you notice them. If you notice you are worrying, silently say to yourself, "Worry, worry, there is worry." You can name *planning, reminiscing, longing, thinking,* or whatever it is in just the same way: label it and move on. This will help you disidentify with your thinking and let go to create more spaciousness and peace.

This can take between twenty and thirty minutes. With practice, you will be able to rest your attention on your breath more effortlessly and let go of your thoughts more easily.

Breath-Counting Meditation

An alternative form of sitting meditation is the use of counting with the rhythm of the breath. Following the gentle ins and outs of the breath creates a sense of peace and restfulness.

A. Find your posture and center yourself. Take several deep breaths. Either close your eyes or fix them on a spot on the floor about four feet in front of you. Your eyes may or may not be focused.

B. Take deep but not forced belly breaths. As you do, focus your attention on each part of the breath: the inhale, the turn (the point at which you stop inhaling and start exhaling), the exhale, the pause (between the exhale and inhale), the turn (the point at which you start to inhale), the inhale, and so on. Pay careful attention to the pause. What are the sensations in your body as you pause between breaths?

C. As you exhale, say "one." Continue counting each exhale: "two ... three ... four." Then begin again with "one." If you lose count, simply start over.

D. When you discover that your mind has slipped into thought, note this, then gently return to the counting of your breath.

E. If a particular sensation in your body catches your attention, focus on the sensation until it recedes. Then return your attention to the inhale and the exhale and the counting of your breath.

Special Considerations

1. It is not necessary to feel as though you are relaxing while you meditate in order for you to actually become relaxed. You may feel as though you are thinking thousands of thoughts and are very restless. However, when you open your eyes at the end of your meditation, you will realize you feel much more relaxed than you did before meditating.

2. As your mind quiets with meditation, old or hidden pain can arise from your subconscious. If you find that when you meditate you suddenly feel angry, depressed, or frightened, try to gently allow yourself to experience the feeling without resistance and let go of the temptation to make sense out of your feelings. If you feel the need, talk to a friend, counselor, or meditation teacher.

3. You may hear or read about ideal conditions for meditation: that you should meditate only in a quiet place, only two hours after you've eaten, or only in a position that you can hold comfortably for twenty minutes, and so on. Yes, these are ideal conditions, but life is seldom ideal. If the place isn't absolutely quiet or the only time you have to meditate is right after lunch, don't let these small obstacles keep you from meditating. If you find yourself being particularly bothered by noises or the rumblings of a full stomach, simply incorporate the annoying sensation in with the object of your meditation.

4. If you adopt a daily sitting practice, you may find that there are stretches of time during which you will not want to meditate. Do not expect that your desire to meditate will grow constantly with your practice. If you feel discouraged, be gentle with yourself and try to work creatively on ways to make your practice more comfortable. Know that these periods of discouragement will go away by themselves in time. Here are two things you can do to help maintain a schedule: Pick a regular time of the day to meditate and honor it as you would any other appointment. Find a group to meditate with—the value of finding such a group cannot be overstated.

Group 2: Releasing Muscular Tension

The Inner Exploration or Body Scan

The goal of this exercise is for you to open to each part of your body, notice any sensation that is present, and let go of tension in your body.

A. Begin by becoming aware of the rising and falling of your breath in your chest and belly. You can ride the waves of your breath and let it begin to anchor you to the present moment.

B. Bring your attention to the soles of your feet. Notice any sensation that is present there. Without judging or trying to make it different, simply be present with the sensation. After a few moments imagine that your breath is flowing into the soles of your feet. As you breathe in and out you might experience an opening or softening and a release of tension. Just simply observe with no expectations.

C. Now bring your attention to the rest of your feet, up to your ankles. Become aware of any sensation in this part of your body. After a few moments imagine that your breath, instead of stopping at the diaphragm, flows all the way down to your feet. Breathe into and out of your feet, simply noticing the sensations.

D. Proceed up your body in this manner with all the parts of your body—lower legs, knees, upper legs, pelvis, hips and buttocks, lower back, upper back, chest and belly, upper shoulders, neck, head, and face. Take your time as you really feel each body part and notice whatever sensations are present, without forcing them or trying to make them be different, then breathe into the body part and let go of it as you move on to the next body part.

E. Go back to your neck and shoulders or any place that has pain, tension, or discomfort. Simply be with the sensations in a nonjudging way. As you breathe, imagine the breath opening up any tight muscles or painful areas and creating more spaciousness. As you breathe out imagine the tension or pain flowing out.

F. When you reach the top of your body, scan your body one last time for any areas of tension or discomfort. Then imagine that you have a breath hole at the top of your head, much like that of a whale or dolphin. Breathe in from the top of your head, bringing the breath all the way down to the soles of your feet and up again. Allow your breath to wash away tension or uncomfortable sensations.

The entire body scan can take anywhere from a few minutes to thirty minutes. Ideally, try to allow for twenty to thirty minutes to complete a body scan each day.

Moving Band Meditation

A. Find your posture, center yourself, and take several deep breaths.

B. Imagine that a three-inch-wide band encircles the top of your head. Focus your attention on the part of your head surrounded by the imaginary band. Notice the sensations. Is there any tension in your forehead? If so, try to relax it. Are there any other sensations in this area? Focus on them for a moment.

C. Lower the imaginary band three inches—the width of the band. Again, focus your attention on the area encompassed by the band. Really try to feel around in there. What does the back of your eyeball feel like? The right wall of your nose? How are the muscles of your upper lip set? Any tension? Try to completely relax this area of your head. Breathe deeply and whisper to yourself, "Let it go, let it all go."

D. Continue to move the band down your body. Focus intently on any sensations. Wherever you notice tension, try to release it. As you do, take several deep belly breaths and relax. See if you can be aware of how the muscles feel as they relax.

E. When the band gets down to your torso, imagine that it goes around one arm, then across your upper body, around the other arm, then across your back. Scan a section of each arm and your torso at the same time as though they were one part. Notice the sensations where the arms are separate from the body. What do these boundaries feel like? Can you make the sensation of the boundaries less distinct so that your arms feel as though they are merging with your torso? Is there any tension? In the shoulders? The back? If so, relax these areas.

F. Move the band down your torso and arms to your legs, noting tension and releasing it. Focus on the sensation where your legs touch each other (if they do), and where they touch the floor. Again, feel the sensations at the points of contact, then try to experience the sensation of your legs merging together.

This exercise can be practiced in two different ways. Try both ways and see which is more relaxing:

1. Move the band slowly down your body, carefully experiencing each sensation, noting all the points of tension, and letting them go.

2. Quickly lower the band down your body. Move it as soon as your attention has given the encompassed area a brief scan. If practiced this way, repeat the entire exercise several times in a row.

Group 3: Mindfulness and Present-Moment Awareness

Much of our stress comes from thinking about the past or worrying about the future. When you live in the present moment and your attention is focused on what you are doing right now, there is no room for anything else to enter—including fears, desires, or anything that could be stressful.

In the meditative state, your attention is focused on the object of meditation, whether that's the inhale, the exhale, or the mantra that quiets the mind and allows you to be more in the present moment. When thoughts of past or future, desires or aversions, or anything else arise, note this and then turn your awareness gently back to the present. This concentration on the now allows your body and mind to enter a state of relaxation.

Mindfulness meditation is a form of meditation that offers both deep relaxation and insight. It cultivates a way of being in a harmonious relationship with what is, whether that's nagging or obsessive thoughts, uncomfortable feelings, external stressors, or physical discomfort. Through fully opening to what is present in your internal experience and not resisting or pushing it away, a deep acceptance and ability to rest more fully in the present moment can be cultivated. In the beginning stages of mindfulness practice, present-moment awareness is usually cultivated by focusing on the breath. Beginning practices can also include focusing on sounds, feelings, or body sensations. The body scan or mindful movement such as yoga, tai chi, or *chi kong* can also help cultivate mindfulness.

Whatever your focus of attention, a gentle, nonjudgmental, and embracing attitude should be used to encounter what arises during the course of meditation. The stories you tell yourself about what you notice and the reactivity to *what is* creates your suffering or pain. Use a bare-bones attention to simply notice wherever your attention goes during meditation, let go of it without judgment, and return back to the object of focus that you have chosen. If you find yourself creating a story about it, such as, *Oh my left knee is really hurting, it will never stop, it's going to get worse* . . . simply notice the thought or story and return back to the breath without getting caught up in the content. Continue this process throughout the sitting period. Meditating in this way actually trains you to encounter stressors in your life, whether internal or external, in a similar fashion. When you encounter stressors, catch yourself before you go into a habitual reaction that leads to suffering—rather than getting stuck in reactivity, breathe, pause, and make new choices about how to respond. Make choices that bring you healthier thinking, relaxation, insight, health, connection with others, and more love.

Eating Meditation

You eat every day, but how often do you really pay attention to what you are eating while you are eating it? Do you usually eat with other people? In front of the TV? While reading a book? Can you usually finish a three-course meal in ten minutes or less?

The following is a conscious-eating meditation. Try it someplace where it is unlikely anyone will want to come over and eat with you. For the sake of this example, the food in question is a cheese sandwich.

A. Sit down in front of your food and take several deep breaths. Note the color, shape, and texture. Does it seem appealing to you? Can you barely restrain yourself from gobbling it up? Whatever you're feeling, notice it.

B. Be aware of your intention to begin eating. Move your hand slowly toward the sandwich. As you do this, make a quiet mental note of the action. You may say to yourself, "Reaching . . . reaching . . . reaching." By labeling your actions you are more likely to keep in mind your purpose—to stay aware. As you pick up the sandwich, notice that you are "lifting . . . lifting . . . lifting."

C. Watch your hand move the sandwich closer to your mouth. When it nears your mouth, take a moment to smell the food. What smells do you recognize? Can you smell the mayonnaise? How is your body reacting to the smell? Is your mouth watering? Notice the sensation of your body desiring food.

D. As you take your first bite, feel your teeth penetrate the bread. When the bite is complete, how is the food positioned in your mouth? How does your tongue position the food so that it's between your teeth? Begin chewing slowly. What are the sensations in your teeth? Your tongue? How does your tongue move when you chew? What tastes are you experiencing? The tomato? The cheese? What part of your tongue experiences the taste? Where is your arm? Did you put it back on the table? If so, did you notice the motion?

E. When you swallow, try to be aware of how the muscles in your esophagus contract and relax as they push the food to your stomach. Where is the food when you have finished swallowing? Can you feel the sensations in your stomach? Where is your stomach? What size is it? Is it empty, full, or somewhere in between?

F. As you continue to eat your sandwich, try to stay aware of as many sensations as you can. Silently label each movement if this helps. Try eating with the hand you don't normally use, because the awkwardness may serve as a reminder to pay attention. As with your basic meditation, when thoughts arise, notice them and then return your attention to your food.

Walking Meditation

Most people cover miles in the course of their daily routines. This makes walking a good opportunity to practice mindfulness. Focus on the act of walking much the same way as you focus on your breath in sitting meditation.

A. Stand up and relax your abdominal muscles. Take several deep belly breaths. Feel your abdomen expand and contract with each breath. As you practice this exercise, try to continue breathing from this relaxed stance. Mentally repeat the word "in" with each inhalation and "out" with each exhalation.

B. Without controlling your breathing too much, try to arrange it so that one of your feet touches the ground at the beginning of each *in* breath and each *out* breath. Now, see how many steps seem natural to take during each inhalation and each exhalation.

C. As with all meditations, when thoughts or images interrupt your focus, make a mental note of this and then return to your walking and breathing.

D. Pay attention to the sensations of walking. Concentrate on your feet and lower legs. Notice which muscles contract and which relax as you lift your legs up and down. Which part of your foot touches the ground first? Pay attention to how your weight shifts from one foot to the other. What are the feelings in your knees as they bend and straighten? And, while you're at it, pay attention to the ground. What is its texture? Is it hard or soft? Notice any cracks or stones. How does the sensation of walking on grass differ from that of walking on a sidewalk? Catch the thoughts, let them go, and notice everything.

An alternative way of practicing walking meditation is to count your steps in time with your breathing as you walk. If you are taking three steps during each inhalation and exhalation, mentally say to yourself, "In . . . two . . . three. Out . . . two . . . three. In . . . two . . . three . . . " and so on. Your *in* breaths may be longer or shorter than your *out* breaths and therefore may accommodate either more or fewer steps. Or your step count may vary from breath to breath. Just pay attention and readjust your walking to the ins and outs of your breathing as needed.

Seeing Meditation

You can gaze at something during a meeting, on a bus, or in a waiting room. This is wonderfully inconspicuous meditation practice.

A. Find an object within your line of vision that you might want to fix your eyes on. Take several belly breaths as you glue your eyes to the object. Let it capture your interest, as though it were the only object around you. Try not to judge what you are seeing, or have any thoughts about it at all. See if you can have the experience of "just seeing." When thoughts arise, note them and then return your focus to the object.

B. Try practicing this exercise with different types of objects. Here are a few suggestions:

- Concrete objects—objects with a definite size and shape that are usually stationary.

- Natural objects—such as clouds, sand, a pile of dry leaves, the ocean, and so on.

- Vastness—any large, uniform surface such as a wall or a finely patterned rug.

- Moving objects—a crowd of people, cars on a busy street, and so on. With objects of this nature, don't follow individual shapes with your eyes. Instead, fix your eyes on a point in space and let the movement pass in front of you.

Any simple activity can become a meditation when you try to continuously focus your attention on it. A good mindfulness exercise is to choose an activity you do every day, preferably a short one. Concentrate on every action and every sensation involved in the activity. Use the type of mental notation discussed earlier, under Eating Meditation, if that helps. You could practice concentrating when you shave, brush your teeth, wash dishes, fold clothes, or pull weeds. As thoughts occur, note them and then go back to the task with renewed concentration. It is often helpful to switch to your nondominant hand (though you might not want to do this while shaving). The resulting awkwardness will serve as a constant reminder that you want to concentrate on what you are doing.

Group 4: Mindfulness of Pain or Discomfort

People usually respond to pain, irritation, or any discomfort by trying to build a solid wall of tightness around it, attempting to block off the feeling or avoid it. However, the more you resist pain, the more it hurts. And the more it hurts, the more you will try to resist it. This vicious circle produces one big knot of pain and resistance that is extremely difficult to untie.

An alternative way to deal with pain is to learn to soften around it. This means you first acknowledge the pain's presence, and then simply allow yourself to experience, physically and mentally, whatever it is that hurts. Be your own good nurse, hold your own hand, tell yourself it's all right, and then sit with yourself compassionately as you experience sensations of discomfort.

When you open to an irritation, you consciously relax your tense, clenched muscles around the spot that hurts. You focus on the hurting itself, without all the tightness you tend to add to it.

Softening also means that you notice but disregard your thoughts about how awful the discomfort is, how you have to move, how you have to scratch, how you can't stand it, and so on.

Softening is like working the hard lumps out of a mound of clay so that you can feel a tiny pearl in the center. It's like removing screens placed around a candle flame so that you can see it clearly. It's like thawing out the frozen core of a large piece of meat so that you can remove the bone. It's like cleaning layers of grime off the outside of a window so that you can see what's inside more clearly.

The following exercises introduce minor irritations into your basic meditation. By practicing with small irritations in a safe setting, you can begin to understand the process of softening.

Don't Move

A. Find your posture and center yourself. Take several deep breaths.

B. Make an agreement with yourself that for a preset period of time you will not move. Then begin your basic meditation.

C. As time passes, you may find yourself moving your head or shifting in your seat without realizing it. This is fine. Note the movement and return to your meditation. After a while you will be able to notice your intention to move a part of your body before you actually move it.

D. Once you are able to identify your intention to move, try to focus on what exactly your desire is. Do you want to squirm around in your chair? Stretch your back muscles? Maybe you have an itch, or an ant is crawling across your foot. Try to precisely identify the uncomfortable sensation. Remember, don't move.

E. As you focus on the discomfort, try to soften around it. If muscle groups are tightening, try to relax them. Check these muscle groups often, because they will not want to stay relaxed. Where is your breath? Is it high in your chest? If so, try to drop it into your belly. Focus on the sensation of discomfort. What is the feeling here? Stay with it for a while.

F. When time is up, move your body slowly to the position you've been wanting to sit in. Focus on the sensations. Is the relief immediate? Is the relief gradual? In what way does your body feel better? Is there any tension? If so, release it.

Any irritating sound or sensation can be used as a focal point for meditation. Focusing on your body's minor aches or the sound of a lawn mower or a dog barking can teach you how your body responds to life's irritations. Once you realize this, you can begin to learn how to soften around such irritations.

Group 5: Letting Go of Thoughts

This highly structured exercise is found in many cultures in one form or another. In it, you passively observe the flow of your thoughts, feelings, and perceptions, one after another, without being concerned with their meaning or their relationship to one another. This will allow you to see what's on your mind and then let it go.

A. Find your posture and center yourself. Take several deep breaths.

B. Close your eyes and imagine yourself sitting at the bottom of a deep pool of water. When you have a thought, feeling, or perception, see it as a bubble and let it rise away from you and disappear. When it's gone, wait for the next one to appear and repeat the process. Don't think about the contents of the bubble. Just observe it. Sometimes the same bubble may come up many times, or several bubbles will seem related to each other, or the bubbles may be empty. That's okay. Don't allow yourself to be concerned with these thoughts. Just watch them pass in front of your mind's eye.

C. If you feel uncomfortable imagining being underwater, imagine that you are sitting on the bank of a river, watching a leaf drift slowly downstream. Observe one thought, feeling, or perception as the leaf, and then let it drift out of sight. Return to gazing at the river, waiting for the next leaf to float by with a new thought. Or, if you prefer, you can imagine your thoughts rising in puffs of smoke from a campfire.

Further Reading

Benson, H. 1996. *Timeless Healing: The Power of Biology and Belief.* Accord, Mass: Wheeler Publishing.

Goldstein, J. 1987. *The Experience of Insight.* Boston: Shambala Publications.

Goldstein, J., and J. Kornfield. 1987. *Seeking the Heart of Wisdom.* Boston: Shambala Publications.

———. 1995. *The Path of Insight Meditation.* Boston: Shambala Publications.

Harp, D., and N. Feldman. 1996. *The Three-Minute Meditator.* Oakland, Calif.: New Harbinger Publications. (This book is particularly recommended as an excellent introduction to meditation practice.)

Hewitt, J. 1990. *The Complete Yoga Book.* New York: Shocken Books.

Kabat-Zinn, J. 1990. *Full Catastrophe Living: Using the Wisdom of Your Body and Mind to Face Stress, Pain, and Illness.* New York: Delacorte.

———. 1995. *Wherever You Go, There You Are: Mindfulness Meditation in Everyday Life.* New York: Hyperion.

Kornfield, J. 1993. *A Path with Heart: A Guide Through the Perils and Promises of Spiritual Life.* New York: Bantam Doubleday Dell.

LeShan, L. 1984. *How to Meditate.* New York: Bantam Books.

Thich, N. H. 1987. *Being Peace.* Berkeley, Calif: Parallax Press.

———. *Touching Peace.* 1992. Berkeley, Calif.: Parallax Press.

Visualization

In this chapter you will learn to:

☐   Use your imagination to relax

☐   Manage stress-related conditions

☐   Create a safe and relaxing place in your mind

Background

You can significantly reduce stress with something enormously powerful: your imagination. The practice of positive thinking in the treatment of physical symptoms was popularized by Emil Coué, a French pharmacist, around the turn of this century. He believed that the power of the imagination far exceeds that of the will. It is hard to will yourself into a relaxed state, but you can imagine relaxation spreading through your body, and you can visualize yourself in a safe and beautiful retreat.

Coué asserted that all of your thoughts become reality—you are what you think you are. For example, if you think sad thoughts, you feel unhappy. If you think anxious thoughts, you become tense. In order to overcome the feeling of unhappiness or tension, you can refocus your mind on positive, healing images. When you predict that you are going to be lonely and miserable, your prediction will probably come true, because your negative thoughts will be reflected in asocial behavior. A woman who predicts that she will get a stomachache when her boss yells her at is likely to have her thoughts take a somatic form. Coué found that organic diseases such as fibrous tumors, tuberculosis, hemorrhages, and constipation are often worsened when you focus on them. He recommended to his patients that they repeat to themselves on waking, twenty times, the now-famous phrase, "Every day in every way I am getting better and better."

Coué also encouraged his patients to get into a comfortable, relaxed position upon retiring, close their eyes, and practice general relaxation of all their muscles. As they started to doze off in the "stage of semi-consciousness," he suggested that they introduce into their minds any desired idea, for example, "I am going to be relaxed tomorrow." This is a way of bridging your conscious and unconscious minds and allowing your unconscious to make a wish come true.

Carl Jung, in his work in the early part of this century, used a technique for healing he referred to as "active imagination." He instructed his patients to meditate without having any goal or program in mind. Images would come to consciousness that the patient was to observe and experience without interference. Later, if he or she wanted, the patient could actually communicate with the images by asking them questions or talking to them. Jung used active imagination to help the individual appreciate his or her rich inner life and learn to draw on its healing power in times of stress. Jungian and Gestalt therapists have since devised several stress-reduction techniques using the intuitive, imaginative part of the mind.

Visualization is practiced and studied in cancer and pain centers throughout the country. Stephanie Matthews and O. Carl Simonton, who pioneered the use of visualization with cancer patients, wrote *Getting Well Again* in 1980. Two other visualization scientists, therapists, and writers are Jeanne Achterberg, who wrote *Imagery in Healing* in 1985, and Connecticut surgeon and Yale professor Bernie S. Siegel, who wrote *Love, Medicine, and Miracles* in 1986.

Shakti Gawain, author of *Creative Visualization* and *Living in the Light*, states that visualization is a form of energy creating life and life's happenings. Everything is energy and our mind creates our world, much as a movie projector projects a world upon a blank screen.

Symptom Effectiveness

Visualization is effective in treating many stress-related and physical illnesses, including headaches, muscle spasms, chronic pain, and general or situation-specific anxiety.

Time to Master

Symptom relief can be immediate or take several weeks of practice.

Instructions

Kinds of Visualization

Everybody visualizes. Daydreams, memories, and inner talk are all types of visualization. You can harness your visualizations and consciously employ them for bettering yourself and your life. Visualizations or mental sense impressions that you create consciously can train your body to relax and ignore stress.

There are three types of visualization for change:

1. **Receptive visualization.** Here you relax, empty your mind, sketch a vague scene, ask a question, and wait for a response. You might imagine you are on the beach and the breeze is caressing your skin. You can hear and smell the sea. You might ask, "Why can't I relax?" The response might surface into your consciousness,

"Because you can't say no to people," or "Because you can't detach yourself from your husband's depression."

2. **Programmed visualization.** Create an image, replete with sight, taste, sound, and smell. Imagine a goal that you want to attain or a healing that you want to accelerate. Harriet used programmed visualization when she started to run. For her first race, she daily visualized her race on that course. She would feel the pressure to run up a hill, the exhaustion after several miles, and the sprint to the finish line. When she finally ran that race she set a state record for her age group.

3. **Guided visualization.** Again, visualize your scene in detail, but omit crucial elements. Then wait for your subconscious, or your inner guide, to supply the missing pieces in your puzzle. Jane imagines visiting a special place where she likes to relax. She constructs the smells, tastes, sounds, touch, and sights associated with the place, a forest clearing that she used to visit with the Girl Scouts. She sees herself roasting marshmallows over a campfire at twilight. (There are no mosquitoes.) She imagines her Girl Scout leader, someone she loves, and asks the leader how she can relax. Sometimes her leader reminds her of songs Jane loves and tells Jane to sing them whenever she feels tense. Sometimes she reminds Jane of old jokes and old times that made Jane laugh, and tells Jane that she needs to laugh more. Often the leader gives Jane a hug, to remind her that she is loved and that she needs to search for affirmations of that love.

Rules for Effective Visualization

1. Loosen your clothing, lie down in a quiet place, and close your eyes softly.

2. Scan your body, seeking tension in specific muscles. Relax those muscles as much as you can.

3. Form mental sense impressions. Involve all your senses: sight, hearing, smell, touch, and taste. For instance, imagine the sights of a green forest with the trees, blue sky, white clouds, and pine needles underfoot. Then add the sounds: wind in the trees, water running, birdcalls, and so on. Include the feel of the ground under your shoes, the smell of pine, and the taste of a grass stem or mountain spring water.

4. Use affirmations. Repeat short, positive statements that affirm your ability to relax now. Use the present tense and avoid negatives such as, "I am not tense," in favor of positive versions such as, "I am letting go of tension." Here are some other examples of affirmations:

Tension flows from my body.

I can relax at will.

I am in harmony with life.

Peace is within me.

5. Visualize three times a day. Visualization practice is easiest in the morning and night while you lie in bed. After some practice, you will be able to visualize while waiting in the doctor's office, at the service station, before going into a parent-teacher conference, or during an IRS audit.

Basic Tension and Relaxation Exercises

1. *Eye Relaxation (Palming)*

Put your palms directly over your closed eyes. Block out all light without putting too much pressure on your eyelids. Try to see the color black. You may see other colors or images, but focus on the color black. Use a mental image to remember the color black (black fur, black object in the room).

Continue this way for two to three minutes, thinking and focusing on black. Lower your hands and slowly open your eyes, gradually getting accustomed to the light. Experience the sense of relaxation in the muscles that control the opening and closing of your eyes.

2. *Metaphorical Images*

Lie down, close your eyes, and relax. Visualize an image for tension and then supplant it with an image for relaxation. The best images are those you make up yourself. But to get you started, images for tension might include:

- the color red
- the screech of chalk on a blackboard
- the tension of a cable
- the scream of a siren in the night
- the glare of a searchlight
- the smell of ammonia
- the confinement of a dark tunnel
- the pounding of a jackhammer

These tension images during visualization can soften, expand, and fade, creating relaxation and harmony:

- The color red can fade to pale blue.
- The chalk can crumble into powder.
- The cable can slacken.
- The siren might soften to a whisper of a flute.
- The searchlight might fade into a soft rosy glow.
- The smell of ammonia might soften into the smell of lemon.
- The dark tunnel might open into a light, airy beach.
- The jackhammer can become the hands of a masseuse kneading your muscles.

As you scan your body, apply a tension image to a tense muscle. Allow it to develop into your relaxation image. For example, if your neck is tense, you may visualize a tightened vise. Imagine the vise opening as you say an affirmation such as, "Relax" or, "I can relax at will."

End by reciting your affirmation. Speak to the specific tenseness as you apply your relaxation image. Notice what happens to your tension.

3. *Creating Your Special Place*

In creating your special place you will be making a retreat for relaxation and guidance. This place may be indoors or out. In structuring your place, follow a few guidelines:

- Allow a private entry into your place.

- Make it peaceful, comfortable, and safe.

- Fill your place with sensuous detail. Create a midground, a foreground, and a background.

- Allow room for an inner guide or other person to comfortably be with you.

A special place might be at the end of a path that leads to a pond. Grass is under your feet, the pond is about thirty yards away, and mountains are in the distance. You can feel the coolness of the air in this shady spot. The mockingbird is singing. The sun is bright on the pond. The honeysuckle's pungent odor attracts the bee buzzing over the flower with its sweet nectar.

Or your special place might be a sparkling-clean kitchen, with cinnamon buns baking in the oven. Through the kitchen window you can see fields of yellow wheat. A window chime flutters in the breeze. At the table is a cup of tea for your guest.

Try taping this exercise and playing it, or have a friend read it to you slowly:

To go to your safe place, lie down and be totally comfortable. Close your eyes. . . . . Walk slowly to a quiet place in your mind. . . . Your place can be inside or outside. . . . It needs to be peaceful and safe. . . . Picture yourself unloading your anxieties, your worries. . . . Notice the view in the distance. . . . What do you smell?. . . What do you hear?. . . Notice what is before you. . . . Reach out and touch it. . . . How does it feel?. . . . Smell it. . . . Hear it. . . . Make the temperature omfortable. . . . Be safe here. . . . Look around for a special spot, a private spot. . . . Find the path to this place. . . . Feel the ground with your feet. . . . Look above you. . . . What do you see? . . . Hear? . . . Smell? . . . Walk down this path until you can enter your own quiet, comfortable, safe place.

You have arrived at your special place. . . . What is under your feet? . . . How does it feel?. . . Take several steps. . . . What do you see above you? What do you hear? Do you hear something else? Reach and touch something. . . . What is its texture? Are there pens, paper, paints nearby, or is there sand to draw in, clay to work? Go to them, handle them, smell them. These are your special tools, or tools for your inner guide to reveal ideas or feelings to you. . . . Look as far as you can see. . . . What do you see? What do you hear? What aromas do you notice?

Sit or lie in your special place. . . . Notice its smells, sounds, sights. . . . This is your place and nothing can harm you here. . . . If danger is here, expel it. . . . Spend three to five minutes realizing you are relaxed, safe, and comfortable.

Memorize this place's smells, tastes, sights, sounds. . . . You can come back and relax here whenever you want. . . . Leave by the same path or entrance. . . . Notice the ground, touch things near you. . . . Look far away and appreciate the view. . . . Remind yourself this special place you created can be entered whenever you wish. Say an affirmation such as, "I can relax here" or, "This is my special place. I can come here whenever I wish."

Now open your eyes and spend a few seconds appreciating your relaxation.

4. *Finding Your Inner Guide*

Your inner guide is an imaginary person or animal that clarifies and instructs. This being is your link to your inner wisdom and subconscious. Your inner guide can tell you how to relax and can clarify what is causing your stress. With practice, you can meet your inner guide in your special place whenever you want.

Perhaps you already have an inner guide, a deceased parent or other spiritual presence. If so, invite this person into your special place and ask him or her to show you how to relax.

Try this exercise using your tape recorder or a friend.

Relax and follow the path to your special place, as you have been doing. Invite an inner guide to your place. Wait. Watch your guide's path. Notice a speck in the distance. Wait. Watch your guide's approach. Listen to the footfalls. Can you smell the guide's fragrance? As your guide gains shape and clarity, if you feel unsafe, send it away. Wait for other guides until you find one you like, even though its appearance may surprise you or seem odd.

When your guide is comfortable, ask him or her questions. Wait for the answers. An answer may be a laugh, a saying, a feeling, a dream, a frown, or a purr. Ask your guide, "How can I relax? What is causing my tension?" When your guide answers, you will probably be surprised at the simplicity and clarity of its answers.

Before your guide leaves you, or immediately after, say your affirmation to yourself. Affirm your ability to relax with a simple, "I can relax here" or, "I can relax at will."

Do this exercise several times a day for at least seven days. By the seventh day, you will probably have found a guide and some answers.

One student who has lost his mother and his house and has a father unable to care for him uses his mother as his inner guide. He goes to her to relax, to seek guidance when pressure from life and his peers is overwhelming. She doesn't say much, but her presence and her look of approval or disapproval is often enough.

Another person's guide can create relaxation simply because of the emptying of the mind that occurs in her presence. Rarely are words spoken, but her guide's actions in small stories guide her.

Each person's inner guide is different and instructs them in a unique manner.

5. *Listening to Music*

Listening to music is one of the most common forms of relaxation. Each person gives his or her own meaning to music. It is important, therefore, that you select music you find peaceful and soothing when you want to listen to music for the purpose of relaxation. If possible, make a half hour tape of uninterrupted relaxing music that you can play daily or whenever you decide to use music to relax. Repetition of the same music that helped you relax in the past carries with it a positive association that is likely to be beneficial in the future.

To get the most out of your music session, find a half hour of uninterrupted time alone. Put on the music you have chosen, settle back in a comfortable position, and close your eyes. Mentally scan your body, noting areas of tension, pain, and relaxation. Be aware of your mood as you focus your attention on the music. Each time an unrelated thought enters your head, note it and then discard it, remembering your goal of focusing on the music and relaxing. Say an affirmation such as, "Relax" or, "Music relaxes me." When the music ends, allow your mind to again scan your body and become aware of how it feels. Does your body feel different than before you started? Is there any difference in your mood?

Special Considerations

A. If you have trouble getting impressions from all senses, work on your strongest sense first. The rest will improve in time.

B. Practice often—three times a day. And be patient, it takes time.

C. If recording your own tapes doesn't work, you might want to buy a prerecorded tape. A few are listed at the end of this chapter.

D. Remember to laugh. Laughter reduces emotional and physical tension by producing an internal message. Laughing stimulates your circulatory, respiratory, vascular, and nervous systems. When the internal spasms subside, the release of pressure reduces muscle tension and creates a feeling of well-being.

In his book *Anatomy of an Illness,* Norman Cousins describes how he used laughter to overcome a rare and painful illness. His laughter therapy included watching old Marx Brothers movies and *Candid Camera* shows. He says that laughter has astounding rejuvenating effects on mind and body and "serves as a bulletproof vest that protects you against the ravages of negative thinking."

It is difficult to remain anxious, angry, or depressed when you are laughing. Laughter gets your attention off yourself and your situation. It gives you the distance necessary to gain perspective on a situation you are probably taking too seriously. And laughter is just plain fun to do. Give yourself more opportunities to laugh as a break from your stressful life. Here's a humor exercise.

Close your eyes . . . experience yourself becoming more and more relaxed as the tension gradually leaves your body . . . once you are relaxed, begin imagining yourself using humor in a difficult situation . . . it might be telling your boss you made a mistake . . . or presenting a paper you have written. Choose something that is happening in your life right now and create a humorous alternative to your usual stress response.

E. Use creativity. Accessing the imaginative, creative aspect of the brain can be a powerful stress-management tool and a relief from anxiety, worrying, and negative thinking. Scientific research done since the 1950s supports the value and validity of creative thought and has demonstrated that there are two distinct hemispheres in the human brain that mediate and process different kinds of tasks and problems.

The left brain or hemisphere, named the major or dominant brain by scientists, controls verbal and numerical information processed sequentially in a linear fashion. The left brain is the active, verbal, logical, rational, and analytic part of our brain. In contrast, the right brain or hemisphere manages the intuitive, experimental, nonverbal part of our brain and deals in images and holistic patterns and structures. It deals in dreams, metaphors, analogies, and new combinations of ideas. The key concept is that there are two ways of perceiving the world, and the right-brain mode is more conducive to the relaxation response.

In her book *Drawing on the Right Side of the Brain*, Betty Edwards, an art teacher and researcher on the relationship of drawing and brain-hemisphere process, states that anyone can draw. Edwards writes, "It is not a matter of 'talent,' but a process of developing and turning on the perceptual skills available in the right hemisphere." In her work with beginning art students, Edwards uses upside down or inverted drawing to force a cognitive shift from the dominant left brain to the subdominant right brain. This shift takes the student out of the labeling, rational, abstract mode, and puts them in the nonverbal, visual, concrete, intuitive mode, which allows them to learn the artist's way of perceiving and attending to visual information that the left brain cannot or will not process. After experiencing this shift, the students reported less time urgency, less attachment to meaning, and a heightened sense of alertness, while feeling relaxed, calm, confident, and exhilarated. This pleasurable experience is derived from resting the left hemisphere, stopping its chatter, and keeping it quiet for a change. Visualization and guided imagery are methods of accessing the right brain and using its relaxing power.

Here is an exercise taken in part from *Drawing on the Right Side of the Brain*.

Find a quiet place to draw where no one will disturb you . . . play music if you like. From an art book choose a drawing that interests you. Turn the drawing you are going to copy upside down. Do not turn the drawing right side up until you have finished. Plan to finish the drawing in one sitting . . . allow thirty to forty minutes to complete it . . . you might want to set a timer so you can forget about keeping time.

Look at the upside-down drawing for a minute. Regard the angles and shapes and lines. . . . You can see the lines all fit together . . . where one line ends another starts. . . . When you begin to draw, start at the top and copy each line, moving from line to adjacent line, putting it all together just like a jigsaw puzzle. Stay away from naming parts.

Begin to draw . . . work your way through the drawing by moving from line to line, part to adjacent part. Take your time . . . don't make the exercise too complicated . . . allow your movements to be slow and easy.

After you have finished, notice your state of mind. Do you feel calm and relaxed? Did you lose track of time and meaning? Did you turn off the chatter? Were you able to get away from labeling and focus on the whole rather than the parts of the drawing? Turn your drawing right side up. You will probably be quite surprised by how well your drawing came out . . . give yourself a pat on the back.

Further Reading

Achterberg, J., B. Dossey, L. Kolkmeier. 1994. *Rituals of Healing: Using Imagery for Health and Wellness.* New York: Bantam.

Cousins, N. 1990. *Head First: The Biology of Hope and the Healing Power of the Human Spirit.* New York: Penguin Books.

———. 1991. *Anatomy of an Illness.* New York: Bantam Doubleday Dell.

Epstein, G. 1989. *Healing Visualization: Creating Health Through Imagery.* New York: Bantam.

Fanning, P. 1994. *Visualization for Change.* Oakland, Calif.: New Harbinger Publications.

Gawain, S. 1995. *Creative Visualization.* Mill Valley, Calif.: Whatever Publishing.

Klein, A. 1989. *The Healing Power of Humor.* Los Angeles: J. P. Tarcher.

Ornstein, R. 1996. *The Psychology of Consciousness.* San Francisco: W. H. Freeman.

Russman, M. 1987. *Healing Yourself.* New York: Pocket Books.

Samuels, M., and N. Samuels. 1975. *Seeing with the Mind's Eye.* New York: Random House.

Siegel, B. 1988. *Love, Medicine, and Miracles.* New York: Harper & Row.

Simonton, O. C., S. Matthews-Simonton, and J. L. Creighton. 1980. *Getting Well Again.* New York: Bantam Books.

Wells, V. 1990. *The Joy of Visualization: 75 Creative Ways to Enhance Your Life.* Vancouver: Raincoast Books.

Tape Publishers

New Harbinger Publications
5674 Shattuck Ave.
Oakland, CA 94609
800-748-6273

Health Journeys, Image Paths, Inc.
P. O. Box 5714
Cleveland, OH 44101
800-800-8661

Sources Cassette Tapes
P. O. Box W
Stanford, CA 94305
800-52-TAPES

7

Applied Relaxation Training

In this chapter you will learn to:

☐ Relax quickly in stressful situations

Background

Applied relaxation training brings together a number of proven relaxation techniques, including some already covered in this book. The combined effect is both rapid and powerful, helping you reverse the effects of high stress in under a minute. Since the program is progressive, you will be adding new features to the exercise over the course of several weeks, while taking away other features once they have become habitual. Eventually you will be able to achieve deep relaxation in twenty to thirty seconds, quickly calming both your body and your mind when you encounter a stressful situation.

The Swedish physician L. G. Öst developed applied relaxation in the late 1980s. Öst worked with phobic patients, who needed rapid and reliable methods to cut through the anxiety that struck when they encountered phobic situations. Finding that the technique could achieve high rates of success even with severely phobic patients, Öst realized that applied relaxation could be helpful in a variety of life situations, from daily fights and frustrations to difficulty falling asleep at night.

In general, the program first teaches you to relax by using a physical-relaxation process. You then progress to a conditioned relaxation response and finally learn to relax on command. You will also progress from practicing in a relaxed exercise setting to using the technique in real-life situations.

Applied relaxation training progresses through five stages:

1. Progressive relaxation

2. Release-only relaxation

3. Cue-controlled relaxation

4. Rapid relaxation

5. Applied relaxation

In his original version of applied relaxation, Öst included another stage after cue-controlled relaxation called differential relaxation, in which one part of the body at a time is tensed while the rest of the body remains relaxed. This is a variant of progressive relaxation and is not essential to learning to do applied relaxation.

Symptom Effectiveness

Although applied relaxation was developed to treat patients with phobias, it has a wide range of applications in other areas, including panic disorder, generalized anxiety disorder, headache (tension, migraine, and mixed), back and joint pain, epilepsy in both children and adults, and tinnitus. In clinical practice, applied relaxation training has also proven useful for sleep-onset insomnia, for cardiac neurosis, and for cancer patients with chemotherapy-induced nausea (Öst 1987). Öst found that almost everyone can learn applied relaxation and that 90 to 95 percent of the patients in his studies experienced benefits from the training.

Time to Master

You will notice some relaxation after just one or two sessions of applied relaxation training. Remember that this is a progressive program. Each new stage will help you relax more quickly and more deeply, until you can relax at will in less than a minute. Don't rush yourself. You'll want to master each step of the program before you move on to the next step. Allow yourself one to two weeks, with two practice sessions a day, to feel comfortable with each step. If this sounds like a lot of time, keep in mind that your practice sessions can become the most refreshing part of your day.

Clinical applications of applied relaxation have ranged from an unusually quick two-week course for in-patients suffering from tinnitus to a fourteen-week program for in-patients with panic disorders (Öst 1987). A middle range is more usual; you can expect to spend from five to eight weeks progressing through the program.

Instructions

Applied relaxation training involves learning five separate stages. Each stage builds on the one before it, so be sure to follow all five stages in their listed order.

You may find it useful to record a tape to guide yourself through the exercises that follow. A tape will help you focus on relaxing your body and free you to close your eyes. To make a tape, use the instructions for each step as your script. Speak in a slow, even voice and be sure not to rush through the process. (Chapter 11 offers some additional tips on recording relaxation exercises.) If you'd prefer to order a prerecorded tape, a few are listed at the end of this chapter.

1. *Progressive Muscle Relaxation*

Progressive muscle relaxation will help you recognize the difference between tension and relaxation in each of the major muscle groups. Surprising as it may sound, these distinctions are easy to overlook. Once you can really feel the difference between a tense muscle and a deeply relaxed one, you will be able to identify your chronic trouble spots and consciously rid them of their locked-in tension. You will also be able to bring your muscles to a deeper state of relaxation after you relax them than you could have if you hadn't tensed them first. Follow the instructions under Basic Procedure described in chapter 4. Give yourself one to two weeks to master the technique, with two fifteen-minute practice sessions per day. Your goal should be to relax your entire body in one fifteen-to-twenty-minute session.

2. *Release-Only Relaxation*

Now that you've felt the difference between tensing and relaxing each muscle group, you're ready to move on to the next stage of applied relaxation training. As you might guess from its name, release-only relaxation cuts out the first step in progressive muscle relaxation: the tensing step. This means that you can cut the time down by half (or more) that you need to achieve deep relaxation in each muscle group.

With practice, you'll find that mental focus alone is enough to drain your muscles of their tension, with no need for you to tense them first. Developing this skill depends on your ability to recognize the difference between clenched muscles and deeply relaxed ones. Be sure that you're comfortable with progressive muscle relaxation before you begin the following release-only instructions.

A. Sit in a comfortable chair with your arms at your side and move around a bit until you're comfortable.

B. Begin to focus on your breathing. Breathe in deeply and feel the pure air fill your stomach, your lower chest, and your upper chest. Hold your breath for a moment as you sit up straighter . . . and then breathe out slowly through your mouth, feeling all tension and worry blow out in a stream. After you've exhaled completely, relax your stomach and your chest. Continue to take full, calm, even breaths, noticing that you become more relaxed with each breath.

C. Now relax your forehead, smoothing out all the lines. Keep breathing deeply . . . and now relax your eyebrows. Just let all the tension melt away, all the way down to your jaw. Let it all go. Now let your lips separate and relax your tongue. Breathe in and breathe out and relax your throat. Notice how peaceful and loose your entire face feels now.

D. Roll your head gently and feel your neck relax. Release your shoulders. Just let them drop all the way down. Your neck is loose, and your shoulders are heavy and low. Now let the relaxation travel down through your arms to your fingertips. Your arms are heavy and loose. Your lips are still separated because your jaw is relaxed too.

E. Breathe in deeply and feel your stomach expand and then your chest. Hold your breath for a moment and then breathe out slowly in a smooth stream through your mouth.

F. Let the feeling of relaxation spread to your stomach. Feel all the muscles in your abdomen release their tension as it assumes its natural shape. Relax your waist and relax your back. Continue to breathe deeply. Notice how loose and heavy the upper half of your body feels.

G. Now relax the lower half of your body. Feel your buttocks sink into the chair. Relax your thighs. Relax your knees. Feel the relaxation travel through your calves to your ankles, to the bottoms of your feet, all the way down to the tips of your toes. Your feet feel warm and heavy on the floor in front of you. With each breath, feel the relaxation deepen.

H. Now scan your body for tension as you continue to breathe. Your legs are relaxed. Your back is relaxed. Your shoulders and arms are relaxed. Your face is relaxed. There's only a feeling of peace and warmth and relaxation.

I. If any muscle felt hard to relax, turn your attention to it now. Is it your back? Your shoulders? Your thighs? Your jaw? Tune in to the muscle and now tense it. Hold it tighter and release. Feel it join the rest of your body in a deep, deep relaxation.

The directions for release-only relaxation may seem simpler than those for progressive muscle relaxation, but the tasks involved are actually a bit more complex. Be certain that you are draining all of the tension out of each muscle you focus on. Don't let the tension creep back in as you turn your attention to different muscles. When you stand up after a session of release-only, you should feel as relaxed (or more so) as you did after a session of progressive muscle relaxation.

Of course, you don't want to stress yourself out by pushing yourself through a set of strict directions. Try to allow your body to relax, rather than forcing it. If you have trouble with a particular step, take a deep breath and try it again—or skip it. Let negative, critical thoughts blow away with each breath and hold on to the feeling of success and deepening peace.

Allow yourself one to two weeks with two practice sessions a day to master release-only relaxation. When you can relax your entire body in one five-to-seven-minute session, you're ready to move on to step three.

3. Cue-Controlled Relaxation

Cue-controlled relaxation reduces the time you need to relax even further—down to two or three minutes in most cases. In this stage, you will focus on your breathing and condition yourself to relax exactly when you tell yourself to. The instructions will help you build an association between a cue—for example, the command "relax"—and true muscle relaxation. Be sure that you are comfortable with release-only relaxation before you begin.

A. Make yourself comfortable in your chair, with your arms at your sides and your feet flat on the ground. Take a deep breath and hold it for a moment. Concentrate on blowing the worries of the day far, far away as you release the air in a smooth stream from your mouth. Empty your lungs entirely and then feel your stomach and your chest relax.

B. Now begin to relax yourself, from your forehead all the way down to your toes, using the release-only technique. See if you can relax yourself completely in thirty seconds. If you need more time, that's fine. (If you're making a tape, pause here for half a minute to allow time to relax.)

C. You feel peaceful and at ease now. Your stomach and chest are moving in and out with slow, even breaths. With each breath, the feeling of relaxation deepens.

D. Continue to breathe deeply and regularly, saying "breathe in" to yourself as you inhale and "relax" as you exhale. (If you're making a tape, record these words on the tape, allowing about eight seconds for each repetition.)

Breathe in . . . relax . . .

Breathe in . . . relax . . .

Breathe in . . . relax . . .

Breathe in . . . relax . . .

Breathe in . . . relax . . .

Feel each breath bring peace and calm in and float worry and tension out.

E. Continue to breathe this way for several minutes now, saying the words "breathe in" and "relax" as you breathe. (Do not record the words again on your tape; this section is most effective when you say the words to yourself in silence.) Focus all your attention on the words in your head and on the process of breathing. Feel your muscles relax more and more deeply with each breath. Let the word "relax" crowd every other thought from your mind. Close your eyes, if you can, to deepen your focus. (If you're making a tape, allow one to two minutes of silence before continuing to record the instructions.)

F. Now listen to the words again as you continue to breathe in . . . and relax.

Breathe in . . . relax . . .

Breathe in . . . relax . . .

Breathe in . . . relax . . .

Breathe in . . . relax . . .

Breathe in . . . relax . . .

G. Continue to breathe, saying these words in your head, for a few minutes now. Feel each breath bring peace and calm in and float worry and tension out. (Stop recording the tape here.)

H. If you have time, repeat the entire process of cue-controlled relaxation after a recovery period of between ten and fifteen minutes.

Practice cue-controlled relaxation twice a day, as you did with the earlier stages. After each session, you may want to make a note of the amount of time you needed to relax and how deeply relaxed you became. Most people find that the actual time required to relax at this stage is shorter than they imagine. Aim to relax completely using cue-controlled relaxation within two to three minutes before moving on to rapid relaxation.

4. *Rapid Relaxation*

Rapid relaxation can bring the time you need to relax down to thirty seconds. Being able to relax that quickly can mean real relief during stressful situations. It's a good idea to practice rapid relaxation many times a day as you move through different activities and states of mind.

In rapid relaxation, you will pick a special relaxation cue. Choose something that you see regularly throughout the day, such as your watch or a certain clock or the picture you pass as you walk down the hall to the bathroom. If you can, mark that special cue with a piece of colored tape while you're practicing this technique.

When you're ready to begin, look at your special cue. Breathe in and relax. Breathe in and relax. Continue to look at your cue and think "relax." Breathe in and relax. You are breathing deeply and evenly, and you continue to think "relax" each time you exhale. Let the relaxation spread throughout your body. Scan your body for tension and relax as much as possible in every muscle that is not needed for whatever activity you are currently doing.

Every time you look at your cue throughout the day, go through these simple steps:

1. Take two or three deep, even breaths, exhaling slowly through your mouth.

2. Think "relax" each time you exhale, as you continue to breathe deeply.

3. Scan your body for any tension. Focus on muscles that need to relax and empty them of tension.

Try to use your relaxation cue fifteen to twenty times a day to relax quickly in natural, nonstressful situations. This will instill the habit of checking yourself for tension and moving back to a state of deep relaxation throughout the day. After your first few days of practice, you may want to change the color of the tape on your relaxation cue—or even change the cue altogether. This will keep the idea of relaxation fresh in your mind. Finally, see if you can use rapid relaxation to calm yourself during one or two particularly stressful moments of the day. (The next stage, applied relaxation, will help you refine this ability, but it's a good idea to open yourself up early to the idea of relaxation during crisis.)

When you feel comfortable with rapid relaxation and are able to achieve a state of deep relaxation in twenty to thirty seconds many times during the day, you are ready to move on to the final stage of applied relaxation training.

5. *Applied Relaxation*

The final stage of applied relaxation training involves relaxing quickly in the face of anxiety-provoking situations. You will use the same techniques that you practiced in rapid relaxation, beginning your deep breathing the moment you notice a stress reaction setting in.

If you're unsure of your body's particular stress warning signs—such as rapid breathing, sweating, or an increased heart rate—turn to the exercises for body awareness in chapter 2. The earlier you can identify the physiological signs that accompany stress, the more effectively you can cut in on a stress reaction before it builds.

As soon as you note a sign of stress—if you catch your breath, feel your heart leap, or feel a flush of heat—begin your three steps:

1. Take two to three deep, even breaths.

2. Think these calming words to yourself as you continue to breathe deeply:

Breathe in . . . relax . . .

Breathe in . . . relax . . .

Breathe in . . . relax . . .

If you prefer, you need only hear yourself think "relax" each time you exhale.

3. Scan your body for tension and concentrate on relaxing the muscles that you don't need to continue your activity.

To begin coming close to the feeling of your stress reaction, start by practicing these instructions after you have run up a flight of stairs or completed some jumping jacks. When you feel confident, visualize a stressful situation such as a fight with your spouse or an unpleasant encounter with your boss. (Chapter 6 offers ideas and exercises to help you build your visualization skills.) Finally, practice using these three steps when you encounter a stressful situation in real life. Take a brief moment to collect yourself and remember the three steps and then put them into effect immediately. No one but you needs to know what you're doing, and you and those around you will all benefit from the calmness with which you approach the crisis at hand.

Be patient with yourself. Applied relaxation is a skill, and as with other skills you will refine your ability with practice. Chances are you won't feel complete relief the first time you try to cut through a deeply stressful situation with applied relaxation. Notice the improvements that you do make. Most people are able to stop anxiety from increasing with relatively little practice. From that point, it's just a few short steps to actually decreasing the anxiety and replacing panic with a feeling of calm and control.

Special Considerations

If you have progressed methodically from one step of applied relaxation to the next, you have the control you need to bring your body to a state of deep and full relaxation. You can control your breathing and your thoughts and let go of tension you don't need.

As with any other skill, you'll want to practice applied relaxation regularly to keep yourself in top form. Make it a habit to scan your body for tension at least once a day. Focus on ridding your body of that tension using the rapid-relaxation technique. Whatever activity you may be doing, bring yourself to a calm and deep relaxation.

If there are times when your anxiety doesn't seem to respond or you worry that you've forgotten the skill you once had, remember that setbacks do happen. No treatment can guarantee permanent freedom from anxiety attacks or stress. View setbacks as an opportunity to practice applied relaxation. At other times, enjoy the feeling of deep relaxation that you have achieved. Remind yourself that you can bring yourself there whenever you need to.

Further Reading

Öst, L.-G. 1987. Applied relaxation: Description of a coping technique and review of controlled studies. *Behavior Research Therapy* 25:397–409.

———. 1988. Applied relaxation vs. progressive relaxation in the treatment of panic disorder. *Behavior Research Therapy* 26:13–22.

Audiotape

Fanning, P., M. McKay, and N. Sonenberg. 1991. *Applied Relaxation Training*. Oakland, Calif.: New Harbinger Publications.

Self-Hypnosis

In this chapter you will learn to:

☐ Use self-suggestions for deep relaxation and positive change

☐ Fight stress and stress-related illnesses

☐ Alleviate specific problems such as insomnia

Background

"Hypnosis" is a term derived from the Greek word for sleep. In some ways, hypnosis is similar to sleep: there is a narrowing of consciousness accompanied by inertia and passivity. Hypnosis is very relaxing. But unlike sleep you never completely lose awareness during hypnosis. While hypnotized, you are able to respond to things going on around you. While hypnosis is usually done with eyes closed to facilitate concentration and imagination, it can be done with eyes opened.

Hypnosis allows you to experience your thoughts and images as real. During hypnosis you willingly suspend disbelief for the moment, just as you do when you become absorbed in a compelling fantasy or play. For instance, when you are watching a violent chase scene in a movie, your mind and body respond in many ways as though you are actually participating in the chase: your muscles tense, your stomach knots, your heart rate increases, and you feel excited or scared. The brain-wave patterns traced on an electroencephalogram (EEG) during hypnosis resemble the patterns that typically occur during the actual activities that the hypnotized person is imagining (participating in a chase, relaxing at the beach, playing a musical instrument, and so on).

You are no stranger to hypnosis. Frequently, when you are concentrating on something of great interest to you, you enter hypnosis without any formal induction.

Daydreaming, for example, is a hypnotic state. Long-distance driving is highly conducive to hypnosis (and commonly results in amnesia for various parts of the trip). You may have entered hypnosis many times while attempting to remember a shopping list or a past sequence of events or while watching TV or feeling a strong emotion such as fear.

Every hypnotic trance includes the following elements:

1. Economy of action and relaxation. The hypnotized person experiences a reduction of muscular activity and energy output.

2. Limb catalepsy: a sort of rigidity in the muscles of the limbs, with a tendency for the arms and legs to stay in any position in which they are placed. This is sometimes described as the "lead pipe effect."

3. Understanding words at a literal level. If you ask a hypnotized person, "Can you tell me your birthday?" he or she is likely to reply, "Yes."

4. Narrowing of attention. Background noises may be heard but are not important and are therefore ignored.

5. Increased suggestibility. A hypnotized person who is told, "Your arms are feeling very heavy" will actually feel a sensation of heaviness.

In this chapter you will learn to use self-hypnosis to experience positive thoughts and images of your own choosing for the purpose of relaxation and stress reduction. You can learn self-hypnosis quickly and safely. There are no reported cases of harm resulting from self-hypnosis. Since hypnosis is your experience of your own thoughts and images, it can only take place when your participation is active and voluntary. (This is true even when you are undergoing hypnotic induction by someone else.) You can extend, modify, or shorten any of the hypnosis exercises in this chapter to meet your specific needs.

Symptom Effectiveness

Self-hypnosis has been clinically effective with symptoms of insomnia, minor chronic pain, headache, nervous tics and tremors, chronic muscular tension, and minor anxiety. It is a well-established treatment for chronic fatigue. You may also consider using self-hypnosis for any subjective experience that could be improved with positive words and images (for example, the rapid heartbeat, cold sweaty palms, and knotted stomach associated with anticipatory anxiety).

Counterindications

Poor hypnotic candidates include people who are disoriented due to organic brain syndrome or psychosis, people who are severely mentally retarded, and people who are paranoid or hypervigilant.

Time to Master

Significant relaxation effects can be achieved within two days. To become proficient in the skill of self-hypnosis, practice the basic hypnotic induction once a day for a week. Then adapt the basic induction to your personal goals by adding specific hypnotic suggestions. Plan on practicing this modified induction until you no longer need it.

Instructions

The Power of Suggestion

The first step in self-hypnosis is to learn the power of suggestion. Here are two simple exercises that can demonstrate the power of suggestion:

Postural Sway

1. Stand up with your eyes closed and imagine holding a suitcase in your right hand.

2. Imagine bigger and bigger suitcases weighing down your right side, pulling you over.

3. After two or three minutes, open your eyes and notice any changes in your posture.

4. Close your eyes again and imagine that the north wind is blowing you, pushing you back on your heels. Feel the gusts. Notice if your weight is shifting in response to your imagination.

Postural Suggestion

1. Stretch both arms in front of you at shoulder level. With eyes closed, imagine a weight being tied onto your right arm as it strains to stay up.

2. Imagine a second weight, and then a third. Feel the strain in your arm as it gets heavier and heavier, heavier and heavier.

3. Now imagine that a huge balloon filled with helium has been tied to your left arm and is tugging it up into the air . . . higher and higher . . . higher and higher.

4. Open your eyes and notice where your arms are relative to each other.

Most people who try these two exercises notice that their bodies move at least a little in response to these self-suggestions. If you do not notice any movement, practice the exercises a couple more times. If you still do not notice even the slightest amount of movement, hypnosis may not be for you.

Personalized Self-Induction

The second step of self-hypnosis is to learn how to write a self-induction script. The following suggestions will provide you with a basic outline for self-induction that you can adapt and change to suit your particular style and purposes.

Position. If possible, sit in a reclining chair or comfortable high-backed chair with support for your arms, hands, neck, and head. Choose a comfortable position with your feet flat on the floor and your legs and arms uncrossed. Loosen your clothing. You may prefer to remove contact lenses or glasses. Set aside enough time to do this exercise without being interrupted.

Key word or phrase. Choose something that is the opposite of your problem and hence the essence of the goal you are using hypnosis for. For instance, if your problem is anxiety prior to giving a presentation, your goal and key phrase might be, "Calm and clear" or, "Relax now." You can repeat this statement slowly at the moment your eyes close and in your special place so that it becomes associated with deep relaxation. You could also use your favorite color, sound, or location. A meaningful key phrase may occur to you spontaneously when you experience being in your special place during hypnosis. With enough practice, this key word or phrase will be sufficient to quickly induce hypnosis.

Breathing. After your eyes close, take several deep breaths. Breathe deeply all the way down into your abdomen and feel the spreading sense of relaxation as you exhale.

Muscle relaxation. You will be relaxing your legs, arms, face, neck, shoulders, chest, and abdomen in that order. As you relax your legs and arms, the key phrase is, "heavier and heavier, more and more deeply relaxed." As you relax your forehead and cheeks, the key phrase is, "smooth and relaxed, letting go of tension." As you relax your jaw, the key phrase is, "loose and relaxed." Your neck, too, becomes "loose and relaxed." Your shoulders are "relaxed and drooping." You relax your chest, abdomen, and back by first taking a deep breath. As you exhale, use the key phrase, "calm and relaxed."

Staircase or path to a special place. You will count each step going down to that peaceful place, and with each step you will become more and more relaxed. Count backward slowly from ten to zero. Each number you count is a step going down. Imagine that saying each number and taking each step helps you feel more deeply relaxed. You can count backward from ten to zero once, twice, or even three times. Each complete count will deepen your relaxation.

Your special place. In this special place you feel total peace and complete safety. Your special place could be a meadow or a beach or the bedroom you grew up in. You will look around and notice the shapes and colors. You will listen to the sounds and smell the fragrances of your special place. You will also notice the temperature and how your body feels there.

Practice imagining your special place before attempting your first self-induction. Make sure that the image is detailed and evocative. If you are at the beach, make sure you can hear the waves crashing and hear the hiss of foam as the waves recede. See and hear the seagulls overhead. Notice the salty sea breeze, the warmth of the sun on your body, and the feel of the sand beneath you. Try to involve all your senses in building the scene: sight, sound, taste, smell, and touch.

Deepening hypnosis. Use the following four key suggestions over and over, in various combinations, until you feel a deep sense of calm and letting go.

- *Drifting deeper and deeper, deeper and deeper*
- *Feeling more and more drowsy, peaceful, and calm*
- *Drifting and drowsy, drowsy and drifting*
- *Drifting down, down, down into total relaxation*

Posthypnotic suggestion. Once you've spent time relaxing in your special place, you may wish to give yourself posthypnotic suggestions. Read the sections Hypnotic Suggestions and Practice Writing Hypnotic Suggestions, later in this chapter, for rules and techniques that will help you craft your posthypnotic suggestions.

Coming out of hypnosis. When it is time to end your trance, you can count back up from one to ten. In between numbers, tell yourself that you are becoming "more and more alert, refreshed, and wide awake." As you reach number nine, tell yourself that your eyes are opening. As you say the number ten, tell yourself that you are totally alert and wide awake.

Here is a summary of the key rules for a successful self-induction.

1. Allow at least twenty minutes to enter and deepen the hypnotic state.

2. Don't worry about success or how you are doing. Hypnosis will get easier with practice.

3. Always allow time to relax your muscles and take deep breaths.

4. Use compelling instructions ("I am feeling more and more heaviness in my arms").

5. Use adjectives such as "drowsy, peaceful, comfortable" during self-induction.

6. Repeat everything until the suggestion begins to take hold.

7. Use creative imagery. For example, to induce heaviness, imagine your legs as lead pipes. For lightness, imagine helium-filled balloons pulling up your arm or floating on a cloud.

Basic Self-Induction Script

The third step to self-hypnosis is to tape-record the basic script below and play it back for your initial inductions. When you read the induction aloud, speak in a monotone. Keep the tempo slow and monotonous. Pronounce one word after another with an even beat. Pause between each sentence. Speaking slowly, with little inflection, will help your mind drift and increase your relaxation and suggestibility. After some experience with this induction, you will be ready to write your own personalized self-induction.

Sit in a comfortable position with your arms and legs uncrossed. Let your eyes focus gently on a point in front of you . . . and take a deep relaxing breath all the way down into your abdomen. . . . Take another slow, deep, relaxing breath . . . and another. . . . Even though your eyes are getting tired, keep them open a little longer and take another deep breath . . . and another. . . . Your eyes become heavier and heavier . . . let them close, as you say to yourself, [Insert your key word or phrase here].

Now you can begin to relax the muscles in your body. Let your legs begin to relax . . . let your legs begin to feel heavy . . . heavier and heavier as they relax. Your legs are heavier and heavier as they let go of the last bit of muscular tension. . . . Your legs are becoming more and more heavy and relaxed, heavy and relaxed. . . . Your arms, too, are becoming more and more heavy . . . heavier and heavier as they let go of the last bit of muscular tension. You can feel gravity pulling them down. . . . You feel your arms growing heavier and heavier, more and more deeply relaxed. Your arms are letting go . . . letting go . . . letting go of tension as they become heavier and heavier . . . more and more deeply relaxed. Your arms and legs feel heavy, heavy, and relaxed. . . . Your arms and legs feel totally relaxed as they let go of the last bit of muscular tension . . . more and more heavy and relaxed. . . .

And your face, too, begins to relax. Your forehead is becoming smooth and relaxed. Your forehead is letting go of tension as it becomes more and more smooth and relaxed.... And your cheeks too are becoming relaxed, smooth and relaxed. Your cheeks are relaxed and letting go of tension ... your forehead and cheeks are totally relaxed ... smooth and relaxed. And your jaw can now begin to relax ... feeling more and more loose and relaxed. As your jaw becomes more and more deeply relaxed, feel the muscles letting go ... and your lips beginning to part ... and your jaw becoming more and more loose and relaxed.

Now your neck and shoulders can begin to relax. Your neck is loose and relaxed ... your shoulders are relaxed and drooping.... Feel your neck and shoulders becoming more and more deeply relaxed ... so loose and relaxed....

Now, take another deep breath, and as you exhale let the relaxation spread into your chest and stomach and back.... Take another deep breath and, as you exhale, feel yourself becoming calm and relaxed ... calm and relaxed. Take another deep breath ... and as you exhale, feel your chest and stomach and back become calm and relaxed ... calm and relaxed.

Feel yourself drifting deeper and deeper ... deeper and deeper ... becoming more and more drowsy, peaceful, and calm. Drifting and drowsy ... drowsy and drifting ... drifting down, down, down into total relaxation ... drifting deeper and deeper ... deeper and deeper.

Now it's time to go to your special place ... a place of safety and peace. You can go down the stairway to your special place or down a path, and with each step you can count backward from ten to zero ... and with each step become more and more deeply relaxed. In ten steps you will be there ... feeling peaceful and safe as you move toward your special place. Now you grow more and more relaxed with each step. Ten ... nine ... eight ... seven ... six ... five ... four ... three ... two ... one ... zero.

[If you want to repeat this countdown two or even three times to deepen hypnosis, that's perfectly fine.]

Now see the shapes and colors of your special place ... hear the sounds ... feel the sensations of your special place ... smell the smells of your special place. See it ... feel it ... hear it ... smell it.... You can feel safe and calm in your special place, safe and calm.

Feel yourself drifting deeper and deeper, deeper and deeper ... more and more drowsy, peaceful, and calm. You feel drowsy and drifting, drifting and drowsy ... drifting down, down, down into total relaxation. You are so relaxed, peaceful and calm.

[Pause and spend time relaxing in your special place.]

Now you know that you can ...

[Leave a blank space on the tape here for any posthypnotic suggestion that you wish to use. Give yourself time to repeat the suggestion at least three times.]

Now, when you are ready, it is time to come back up ... to come all the way back, feeling alert, refreshed, and wide awake. Starting to come up now: one ... two ... three ... four ... more and more alert and aware ... five ... six ... seven ... more and more alert and awake ... eight ... nine ... beginning to open your eyes ... and ten ... completely alert, refreshed, and wide awake. Alert, refreshed, and wide awake.

Abbreviated Inductions

An optional fourth step to self-hypnosis is to learn abbreviated inductions. These are shorthand techniques that can produce hypnosis in thirty seconds to two minutes. Here are some examples.

Pendulum drop. To make a pendulum, tie an object such as a paper clip, pen, or ring to the end of a heavy thread ten inches long. Hold the thread in your dominant hand and let the pendulum dangle above the floor. Ask your subconscious for permission to go into hypnosis for two minutes. If the answer is yes, your eyes will want to close. As your eyes close, picture a candle flame. Take several deep breaths and allow yourself to slip deeper and deeper. Tell yourself that when you have entered hypnosis, your hand will relax and drop the pendulum. Count down slowly from ten to zero.

Pencil drop. This technique is the same as the pendulum drop, except that you hold a pencil poised above a table. Pinch the point between your thumb and index finger.

Yes repetition. Think the thought "yes" over and over, as you focus on an imagined candle flame. Go down the stairs or down a path while you continue to think "yes."

Coin flip. Place a penny in your palm. Suggest to yourself that your hand will gradually begin to turn over. Just allow your hand to turn slowly, until the coin drops out. As the coin drops, permit your eyes to close and enter hypnosis.

Eye fixation. Fix your eyes on a point slightly above your normal line of vision. Let your peripheral vision narrow and your eyes lose focus. Allow your eyes to close, accompanied by a feeling of drowsiness. To increase the drowsiness, roll your eyes up to the top of your head two or three times.

Key word or phrase. Breathe deeply and slowly, and repeat the key word or phrase that you used on your self-induction talk. As you say the word or phrase, close your eyes and enter hypnosis.

These abbreviated methods are useful after you have become relatively proficient at self-hypnosis. Always remember to end an induction by suggesting that you will awaken refreshed and feeling good.

Five-finger exercise. The following exercise has been used very effectively for relaxation. Memorize the following steps. After you have gone through them, you can use the feeling of calm that follows to enter hypnosis.

1. Touch your thumb to your index finger. As you do so, go back to a time when your body felt healthy fatigue, such as just after swimming, playing tennis, jogging, or some other exhilarating physical activity.

2. Touch your thumb to your middle finger. As you do so, go back to a time when you had a loving experience. You may choose to remember a moment of sexual fulfillment, a warm embrace, or an intimate conversation.

3. Touch your thumb to your ring finger. As you do so, recall the nicest compliment you have ever received. Try to really accept it now. By accepting it, you are showing your high regard for the person who said it. You are really paying him or her a compliment in return.

4. Touch your thumb to your little finger. As you do so, go back to the most beautiful place you have ever been. Dwell there for a while.

The five-finger exercise takes less than ten minutes, but it pays off with increased vitality, inner peace, and self-esteem. It can be done any time you feel tension.

Hypnotic Suggestions

A very useful fifth step to self-hypnosis is to learn to give yourself positive suggestions for change. For best results, say these suggestions to yourself when you are in a relaxed and receptive frame of mind, such as when you are in your special place during the basic self-induction. Or you may find that you prefer to intersperse suggestions throughout an induction.

Remember that autosuggestions are thoughts and images that influence your subjective experience. Here is a list of rules to keep in mind when you are creating suggestions for yourself.

Autosuggestions are most effective when they are:

1. . . . direct. Tell yourself, "I will be calm, confident, and in control."

2. . . . positive. Avoid wording suggestions in a negative way, such as, "I won't feel tired tonight."

3. . . . permissive. Try saying, "I *can* feel relaxed and refreshed tonight" instead of, "I *will* feel relaxed and refreshed." But some people do respond better to commands. You can experiment with both to find out which approach works best for you.

4. . . . about the immediate future, not the present: "Soon the drowsiness is going to come."

5. . . . repeated at least three times.

6. . . . represented with a visual image. If you are trying to overcome a feeling of exhaustion, imagine yourself bouncing along with springs on your feet and see yourself looking athletic and happy.

7. . . . reinforced with an emotion or sensation. If you are attempting to give up cigarettes, imagine how bad the first one tasted or think of the unpleasant burning in your lungs. If you are attempting to improve your confidence for a first date, imagine the feeling of closeness and belonging that you are looking for.

8. . . . not associated with the word "try," since "try" implies doubt and the possibility of failure.

9. . . . exaggerated at first when working toward the control of unpleasant emotions or painful physical symptoms. Start out by suggesting that the negative emotion or symptom is growing more intense. You might say, "My anger is getting bigger, I can feel the blood pushing at my veins, I'm getting hot, my muscles are tensing." Bring the feeling up to a peak and then tell yourself that the emotion or symptom is diminishing: "My anger is subsiding, my heart is slowing and beating normally, my flush is receding, my muscles are unknotting and beginning to relax." When an unpleasant emotion or symptom reaches its peak, it can only get better. Suggestion can rush that process of recovery. When you can turn your emotions and symptoms on and off during hypnosis, you will have gained enormous control over your life.

10. ... written out in advance and then distilled into a catchword or phrase that you can easily remember when you are in the hypnotic state.

Practice writing hypnotic suggestions. Once hypnotized and relaxed, your subconscious mind is ready to believe what you tell it. Many of the symptoms that bother you, as well as your habitual tension responses to stress, were learned through suggestion. They can be unlearned through suggestion. For example, if you watched your father get angry every time he was forced to wait, and if on the first occasion when you delayed him he became angry at you, you may have learned by suggestion to respond exactly the same way. You can use hypnosis to learn new methods of coping with delay. Suggestions such as, "Waiting is a chance to relax" and, "I can let go of rushing" may undo the old habit.

In order to get the flavor of how suggestions can be written, write down hypnotic suggestions that you could use for the following problems:

1. fear of coming into a dark house at night

2. chronic fatigue

3. obsessive and fearful thoughts about death

4. fear of illness

5. minor chronic head or back pain

6. chronic anger and guilt

7. self-criticism and worry about making mistakes

8. low self-esteem

9. lack of motivation

10. feelings of insecurity and self-consciousness in the presence of other people

11. anxiety about an upcoming evaluation or test

12. improving performance

13. pain or muscle tension

14. disease and injury

Now that you have written your own suggestions, examine these possible scripts for each of the fourteen problems.

1. Fear of coming into the house at night

I can come in tonight feeling relaxed and glad to be home, safe, and secure.

2. Chronic fatigue

I can waken refreshed and rested. I can enjoy the evening ahead. I can pace myself today so that I will accomplish my priorities. Whenever I feel my energy flagging, I can do [the five-finger exercise or other relaxation technique] *and then return to my daily activities relaxed and revitalized.*

3. Obsessive and fearful thoughts about death

I am full of life now. I will enjoy today. Very soon I can let go of these thoughts. [Visualize a blackboard and see the date written there.]

4. Fear of illness

My body is feeling more and more healthy and strong. Each time I relax, my body becomes stronger. [Visualize yourself as healthy, strong, and relaxed while doing a favorite activity.]

5. Minor chronic head or back pain

Soon my head will be cool and relaxed. [Imagine cool images.] *Gradually I will feel the muscles in my neck and back loosen.* [Imagine smooth, flowing, loosening images.] *In an hour, they will be completely relaxed. Whenever these symptoms come back, I will simply turn my ring a quarter turn to the right and the pain will relax away.*

6. Chronic anger and guilt

I can turn off anger and guilt because I am the one who turns it on. [Practice turning up and turning down the unwanted emotion.] *I will relax my body and breathe deeply.*

7. Self-criticism and worry about making mistakes

When I catch myself being self-critical or worried, I can take a deep breath and let go. I can breathe out negative tension and breathe in positive energy. [Practice five-finger exercise.]

8. Low self-esteem

Each day I will feel more capable and self-assured. I can do it. I am doing the best I can with my prevailing level of awareness. I can feel myself becoming more and more happy and successful every day. I can be kind to myself. I am liking myself more and more. I am an intelligent, creative, and talented person.

9. Lack of motivation

I can feel confident that I will achieve my goals. I have the power within myself to change. I can see myself solving my problems and getting beyond them. The decisions I make are the right ones for now. I can put aside distractions and focus my attention on one goal. As I get into my project, I will get more and more interested in it. As I work toward my goal, step by step, new energy and enthusiasm will emerge. When I finish this, I will feel great! When I achieve my goal, I will reward myself. I deserve success.

10. Feelings of insecurity and self-consciousness in the presence of other people

The next time I see Ben, I can feel secure in myself. I can respond to Ben in a firm and assertive manner. I can feel relaxed and at ease because I am perfectly all right. I can relax and enjoy the thought that there are people in my life who see me as a good friend, valuable co-worker, and loving family member. Whenever I lace my fingers together, I will feel confidence flowing throughout my entire body.

11. Anxiety about an upcoming evaluation or test

I can concentrate on my studies, remembering everything I need to know for the test. When I feel nervous, I will take a deep breath and relax. My mind is becoming more and more calm and sharp. When I successfully complete this test, I will reward myself with _____. I can imagine myself getting an "A."

12. Improving performance

I can be calm and in control in response to stressful situations. [Imagine yourself maintaining your cool and concentration in the face of specific pressures and fears.] *I can imagine myself playing a perfect game from start to finish. I can recall a time when I played a perfect game.* [Reflect on every perfect move and strategy.] *I will achieve my goal.* [Be specific about your objectives and visualize them in detail.]

13. Pain or muscle tension

   I can see my back pain as a saber of dry ice burning and stabbing me. Now I see the sun shining, warming my back. The ice saber is gradually melting away into a puddle in the warmth of the sun and my pain is beginning to subside. My tension is starting to flow; as it flows, it turns color into a warm, orange fluid moving slowly through my body toward my right shoulder, down my right arm, and into my clenched fist. When I am ready, I can let go of it. I can just scoop my pain up and throw it away. [Imagine a symbol that best represents your pain or tension. Have it interact with another symbol that eliminates the first symbol or transforms it into something more tolerable or makes it disappear.]

14. Disease and injury

   I can imagine a healing white light at the top of my head. I can see and feel it surrounding my entire body. I can feel it begin to move within my body, cleansing and healing as it slowly spreads throughout my entire body. I can imagine myself healthy, strong, and energetic while doing what I want to do.

Self-Hypnotic Induction for a Specific Problem

An optional sixth step is to consider how self-hypnosis might fit into an overall plan to solve a specific problem in your life. The specific problem addressed here is sleep disturbance. This section is adapted from Josie Hadley's and Carol Staudacher's *Hypnosis for Change*.

Before you are ready to begin hypnosis for a specific problem, there are a few issues you need to address:

Define your problem and your goal. Do you have difficulty falling asleep or staying asleep, or do you wake up too early? Is your sleep restless? Do you have great difficulty waking up in the morning? Once you have clearly labeled your problem, you can easily define your goal in the form of a positive autosuggestion. For example, "I can fall asleep quickly and easily," "I will wake up refreshed and alert at the appropriate time," or "Soon I will be able to sleep deeply and continuously throughout the night."

Identify and eliminate any possible external factors that may be contributing to your problem. Ask yourself what might be interfering with getting a good night's sleep. Is your bedroom a comfortable place that invites sleep, or is it filled with clutter, noise, and light? Do you spend half the night coping with a restless bed partner and staring at a glowing clock face that keeps reminding you of how much sleep you are losing? Are you consuming too many stimulants during the day? You need to address these problems before you use self-hypnosis for sleep, since you cannot expect self-hypnosis to solve these problems for you.

Notice what you are telling yourself that may be contributing to your problem. For example, people who have difficulty with sleep often focus on time. They say things to themselves such as, "If I don't get to sleep by midnight, I know I won't be able to sleep at all." If you tend to worry, your mind can go wild when you turn off the light. "I really blew it today. Wait until my boss finds out!" "I know I didn't study enough for the test tomorrow." Do you use the quiet hours of the night to solve problems? "Until this question is answered, we can't go on!" "I'll tell her I didn't mean what I said, and then she'll say . . . "

If part of your problem has to do with what you are telling yourself, you can use the chapters on Thought Stopping, Refuting Irrational Ideas, Worry Control, and Coping Skills to help you identify and change the way you think. If you are being kept awake by your thoughts, here are some suggestions to calm your mind before you fall asleep.

- If you are a clock watcher, turn the clock to the wall, direct your thoughts away from time, and tell yourself, "As I rest, my mind will become calm and my body will relax."

- If you tend to dwell on the negative or on things that you cannot control, think about the positive things you did during the day.

- If you are a nighttime problem solver, write your "to do" list *before* you go to bed and then make an agreement with yourself to put aside your problems until tomorrow when you are at your sharpest and to save the night for restorative sleep.

When you create your own sleep induction, write in positive suggestions that incorporate these ideas so as to reinforce your new desired behavior.

Record an induction tailored to your particular problem. Begin by taping the basic induction up through the section about your special place, and then add your special suggestions. For sleep disturbance, you might add the following script to the basic induction:

Now just linger in your special place. There's no place to go, nothing to do. Just rest, just let yourself drift and float, drift and float into a sound and restful sleep. And as you drift deeper and deeper, imagine the positive things that you can think and do to allow yourself a sound and restful sleep. Your new positive thoughts are true. You have released negative thoughts and feelings. You have released stress and tension from your mind, body, and thoughts. Each new positive statement becomes stronger and stronger as you continue to drift deeper and deeper into relaxation. Just let yourself drift deeper and deeper into sleep. Just let those positive statements float in your mind as you drift into a sound and restful sleep.

Now become aware of how comfortable you feel, so relaxed, your head and shoulders are in just the right position, your back is supported, and you are becoming less aware of all the normal sounds of your surroundings. As you drift deeper and deeper you may experience a negative thought or worry that is trying to surface in your mind and disrupt your slumber and your rest. Simply take that thought and sweep it up as you would sweep up the crumbs from the floor and place that thought or worry into the box. The box has a nice tight lid. Put the lid on the box and place the box on the top shelf of your closet. You can go back to that box at another time, a time that is more appropriate, a time that will not interfere with your sleep. As other unwanted thoughts appear, sweep them up and place them in the box, put the lid on the box, and place it on the top shelf of your closet to let them go. Let them go and continue to drift deeper and deeper into sleep.

Shift your thoughts back to your positive thoughts and positive statements. Just let these thoughts flow though your mind, thoughts such as, "I am a worthwhile person." [Pause.] "I have accomplished many good things." [Pause.] "I have reached positive goals." [Pause.] Just let your positive ideas flow though your mind. Let them flow and drift, becoming stronger and stronger as you drift deeper and deeper into sleep.

You may begin to see them slowly fade, slowly fade, as you become even more relaxed, sleepier, more drowsy, more relaxed. Just imagine yourself in your peaceful and special place, smiling, feeling so good, so comfortable, so relaxed. [Pause.] From your special place you can easily drift into a sound and restful sleep, a sound and restful sleep, undisturbed in a sound and restful sleep. You sleep through the night in a sound and restful sleep. If you should awaken you simply imagine your special place once again and drift easily back into a sound and restful sleep, a sound and restful sleep. Your breathing becomes so relaxed, your thoughts wind down, wind down, wind down, and relax. You drift and float into a sound and restful sleep, undisturbed through out the night. You will awaken at your designated time feeling rested and refreshed.

Now there's nothing to do, nothing to think about, nothing to do but enjoy your special place, your special place that is so peaceful for you, so relaxing. Just imagine how it feels to relax in your special place. You may become aware of how clean and fresh your special place smells, or you may become aware of the different sounds of your special place, of the birds singing in the background or the water cascading over river rocks in a stream. Or you may become aware of how warm the sun feels as you lounge in a hammock or how cool the breeze feels from the ocean air. Or you may experience something else that is unique and wonderful in your special place. Just experience it, drift and float, all thought just fading, drifting into a sound and restful sleep. Just drift into a comfortable, cozy, restful sleep, your body feeling heavy and relaxed as you sink into your bed, so relaxed, just drifting into sleep . . . sleep . . . sleep . . . sleep . . . sleep . . . sleep . . .

Special Considerations

Do not practice a hypnotic induction in a car or in any other situation where your safety requires you to be fully alert and able to respond quickly. After an induction, always make sure that you are completely awake and alert before reentering such situations.

Some people, especially those who are sleep deprived, fall asleep during self-hypnosis. If sleep is not your goal and you have this problem, you may want to shorten the induction so that you are awake to hear the suggestions specifically geared to your goals. Keep in mind that many people who think they are asleep during hypnosis are still able to hear and benefit from positive suggestions. If you are prone to falling asleep, use a timer to wake yourself up rather than worry about being late for your next activity.

You may find that as the symptom you are concerned about fades, you lose your motivation to continue practicing self-hypnosis. This is a typical experience and nothing to worry about. If your symptom returns at a later time, you can use self-hypnosis again.

You can use your key phrase when you experience your symptom or any time you feel tense or uncomfortable in a stressful situation. Although you are unlikely to feel as relaxed as you do after a full self-hypnotic induction, you will still experience some measure of relief. In this way, your key phrase can also serve as a reminder that you do have a choice about how you respond to stress.

Further Reading

Alman, B. M., and P. Lambrou. 1991. *Self-Hypnosis: The Complete Manual for Health and Self-Change*. New York: Brunner-Mazel.

Hadley, J., and C. Staudacher. 1989. *Hypnosis for Change: A Manual of Proven Techniques*. Second Edition. Oakland, Calif.: New Harbinger Publications.

Haley, J. 1993. *Uncommon Therapy: The Psychiatric Techniques of Milton Erickson*. New York: Norton.

Hunter, C. R. 1998. *Master the Power of Self-Hypnosis*. New York: Sterling Publications.

Rosen, S. 1998. *My Voice Will Go with You*. New York: W. W. Norton.

Soskis, D. A. 1986. *Self-Hypnosis: An Introductory Guide for Clinicians*. New York: W. W. Norton.

Audiotapes

McKay, M., and P. Fanning. 1987. *Self-Hypnosis*. Oakland, Calif.: New Harbinger Publications.

Miller, E. 1980. *Letting Go of Stress*. Stanford, Calif.: Source.

Autogenics

In this chapter you will learn to:

☐ Respond quickly to verbal commands to relax

☐ Return your body to a balanced, normal state

☐ Calm your mind

☐ Resolve specific physical problems

Background

Autogenic training (AT) has its origins in research on hypnosis conducted by the famous brain physiologist Oskar Vogt at the Berlin Institute during the last decade of the nineteenth century. Vogt taught some of his experienced hypnotic subjects to put themselves in a trance that had the effect of reducing their fatigue, tension, and painful symptoms such as headaches. It also appeared to help the subjects deal more effectively with their everyday lives. They usually reported that when their fatigue and tension lifted, they felt warm and heavy.

Johannes H. Schultz, a Berlin psychiatrist, became interested in Vogt's work. He found that his subjects could create a state very much like a hypnotic trance just by thinking of heaviness and warmth in their extremities. Essentially, all they had to do was relax, undisturbed, in a comfortable position and concentrate passively on verbal formulas that suggested warmth and heaviness in their limbs. Schultz combined some of the autosuggestions of Vogt with some yoga techniques and in 1932 published his new system in the book *Autogenic Training*.

In its present form, AT not only provides you with the recuperative effects of traditional hypnosis, it also frees you from dependence on a hypnotist. You can learn to induce the feeling of warmth and heaviness associated with relaxation whenever you choose.

Schultz's verbal formulas fall into four main kinds of exercises: verbal formulas to normalize the body, verbal formulas to calm the mind, autogenic modification exercises designed to address specific problems, and meditative exercises that develop mental concentration and creativity. This introductory chapter will teach you to use verbal suggestions to relax your body, calm your mind, and resolve specific problems.

The verbal formulas to normalize the body fall under six standard themes. They are aimed at reversing the fight or flight state, or alarm state, that occurs when you experience physical or emotional stress. The first standard theme is heaviness, which promotes relaxation of the striped muscles in your body, the voluntary muscles used to move your arms and legs. There are six verbal formulas that suggest the theme of heaviness (see Set 1 under Autogenic Verbal Formulas). The second standard theme is warmth, which brings about peripheral vasodilatation—as you say the verbal formula, "My right hand is warm," the smooth muscles that control the diameter of the blood vessels in your hand relax so that more warming blood flows into your hand. This helps reverse the pooling of blood in the trunk and head that is a characteristic of the fight or flight reaction to stress.

The third standard theme focuses on normalizing cardiac activity. The verbal formula is simply, "My heartbeat is calm." The fourth standard theme regulates the respiratory system. The verbal formula is, "It breathes me." The fifth standard theme relaxes and warms the abdominal region. "My solar plexus is warm." The last standard theme reduces the flow of blood to the head as you say, "My forehead is cool." The verbal formulas to calm the mind are used in conjunction with these six themes and serve to intensify the effect of the themes.

Symptom Effectiveness

AT has been found to be effective in the treatment of muscle tension and various disorders of the respiratory tract (hyperventilation and bronchial asthma), the gastrointestinal tract (constipation, diarrhea, gastritis, ulcers, and spasms), the circulatory system (racing heart, irregular heartbeat, high blood pressure, cold extremities, and headaches), and the endocrine system (thyroid problems). AT is also useful in reducing general anxiety, irritability, and fatigue. It can be employed to modify your reaction to pain, increase your resistance to stress, and reduce or eliminate sleeping disorders.

Contraindications

AT is not recommended for children under five years old, persons who lack motivation, or individuals with severe mental or emotional disorders. Prior to beginning AT, you should have a physical exam and discuss with your medical doctor what physiological effects AT will be likely to have on you. Persons with serious diseases such as diabetes, hypoglycemic conditions, or heart conditions should be under the supervision of a medical doctor while in AT. Some people experience an increase in blood pressure and a few have a sharp drop in blood pressure when they do these exercises. If you have high or low blood pressure, you should check with your medical doctor to be sure that AT is regularizing it. If you feel very anxious or restless during or after AT exercises or experience recurring disquieting side effects, you should continue AT only under the supervision of a professional AT instructor.

Time to Master

In the past, AT specialists recommended moving at a slow but sure pace, taking many months to master all six themes. We have found this timetable unrealistic for people who want and typically get some positive results in the very first session of AT. Others require a week or two of regular practice to experience relaxation. Plan on practicing your autogenic formulas at least twice a day for twenty minutes. If you find this too long for you, shorten the length of the session and add more sessions each day.

By the end of one month of regular practice, you should be able to relax quickly using all six themes. At that time you may choose to use all six themes in a twenty-minute relaxation exercise, or perhaps only a few themes that rapidly bring about deep relaxation for you. For instance, the formulas "My arms and legs are warm and heavy," "My heartbeat is calm and regular," and "It breathes me" may be sufficient to induce immediate relaxation. You can experiment to find what works best for you.

Instructions

How to Facilitate Your Relaxation When Doing AT

- Keep external stimuli to a minimum.

- Choose a quiet room where you won't be disturbed.

- Keep the room temperature at a moderately warm, comfortable level.

- Turn the lights down low.

- Wear loose clothing.

- Choose one of the three basic AT postures:

1. Sit in an armchair in which your head, back, and extremities are supported and you are as comfortable as possible.

2. Sit on a stool, slightly stooped over, with your arms resting on your thighs and your hands draped between your knees.

3. Lie down with your head supported and your legs about eight inches apart, your toes pointed slightly outward, and your arms resting comfortably at your sides but not touching your body.

- Scan your body to be sure that the position you choose is tension free. In particular, look for overextension of limbs such as unsupported arms, head, or legs, tightening of the limbs at the joints, or a crooked spine.

- Close your eyes or pick a point in front of you to softly focus on.

- Take a few slow, deep, and relaxing breaths before you begin to repeat your autogenic formulas.

How to Practice the Six Basic Autogenic Themes to Normalize Your Body

There are two ways to learn the six basic autogenic themes. The first option is to make an audiotape of the verbal formulas listed on the next page and listen to it twice a day. Or, you can memorize and practice one set of verbal formulas at a time until you include all of the themes in your practice. Slowly repeat each formula over and over to yourself, keeping up a steady silent verbal stream.

As a general rule of thumb, repeat each formula four times, saying it slowly (taking about five seconds) and then pausing for about three seconds. Using the first three verbal formulas of the first set as an example, you would say to yourself, "My right arm is heavy.... My right arm is heavy.... My right arm is heavy.... My right arm is heavy." This should take you about half a minute. Then you would say to yourself, "My left arm is heavy.... My left arm is heavy.... My left arm is heavy.... My left arm is heavy...." Then, "Both of my arms are heavy.... Both of my arms are heavy.... Both of my arms are heavy.... Both of my arms are heavy...." The entire set should take you less than four minutes. If you are focusing on memorizing one set at a time, you can repeat the set up to twenty minutes in one practice session or create many minipractice sessions of one or a few sets throughout the day. If you are taping the verbal formulas, be sure to leave about half a minute between each formula for silent repetition.

As you silently repeat a verbal formula, "passively concentrate" on the part of the body it refers to. In other words, just notice what happens without harboring any expectations or judgments. Passive concentration does not mean spacing out or going to sleep. You remain alert to your experience without analyzing it. This casual attitude is contrasted with active concentration, which occurs when you fix your attention on certain aspects of your experience and have an interest and goal-directed investment in it. Active concentration is essential for such things as preparing a new recipe or fixing a car. Passive concentration is required for relaxation.

You will not be able to maintain perfect passive concentration at first. Your mind will wander. That's natural. When you find this happening, just return to the formula as soon as possible. In addition, you may experience some initial symptoms known as "autogenic discharges," which are normal but distracting. For example, you may sense a change in your weight or temperature, tingling, "electrical currents," involuntary movements, stiffness, some pain, anxiety, a desire to cry, irritability, headaches, nausea, or illusions. At times you may experience fascinating insights or feelings of bliss. Whether you have pleasant or unpleasant experiences, just note them and return to your AT formulas. Remember that these experiences are transitory, they are not the purpose of AT, and they will pass as you continue to practice.

When you are ready to stop an AT session, say to yourself, "When I open my eyes, I will feel refreshed and alert." Then open your eyes and breathe a few deep breaths as you stretch and flex your arms. Be sure that you are not still in a trancelike state when you go on to your regular activities.

Read the helpful hints and cautionary notes in the Special Considerations section at the end of this chapter before you begin to practice AT.

Autogenic Verbal Formulas for Normalizing the Body

Set 1
My right arm is heavy.
My left arm is heavy.
Both of my arms are heavy.
My right leg is heavy.
My left leg is heavy.
Both of my legs are heavy.
My arms and legs are heavy.

Set 2
My right arm is warm.
My left arm is warm.
Both of my arms are warm.
My right leg is warm.
Both of my legs are warm.

Set 3
My right arm is heavy and warm.
Both of my arms are heavy and warm.
Both of my legs are heavy and warm.
My arms and legs are heavy and warm.
It breathes me.
My heart is calm and regular.

Set 4
My right arm is heavy and warm.
My arms and legs are heavy and warm.
It breathes me.
My heartbeat is calm and regular.
My solar plexus is warm.

Set 5
My right arm is heavy and warm.
My arms and legs are heavy and warm.
It breathes me.
My heartbeat is calm and regular.
My solar plexus is warm.
My arms and legs are warm.
My forehead is cool.

Autogenic Formulas for Calming the Mind

These formulas focus on mental rather than physical functions. They are intended to reinforce the effects of the autogenic verbal formulas for the six standard themes previously mentioned. Here is a list of examples:

I am calm and relaxed.

I feel quite quiet.

My whole body feels quiet, heavy, comfortable, and relaxed.

My mind is quiet.

I withdraw my thoughts from the surroundings and I feel serene and still.

My thoughts are turned inward and I am at ease.

Deep within my mind, I can visualize and experience myself as relaxed and comfortable and still.

I feel an inward quietness.

You may add one or more these phrases for calming the mind at the end of each set of autogenic verbal formulas. But for best results, intersperse them throughout each set. For example, the first set could be rewritten as follows:

My right arm is heavy.

I am calm and relaxed.

My left arm is heavy.

I am calm and relaxed.

> *Both of my arms are heavy.*
>
> *I am calm and relaxed.*
>
> *My right leg is heavy.*
>
> *I am calm and relaxed.*
>
> *My left leg is heavy.*
>
> *I am calm and relaxed.*
>
> *Both of my arms are heavy.*
>
> *I am calm and relaxed.*

Autogenic Modification Exercises

You can practice autogenic modification by making up what Schultz called "organ specific formulae" to deal with specific problems after you have mastered the six basic autogenic themes. For example, you can develop an indirect formula such as, "My feet are warm" or, "My shoulders are warm" each time you feel an embarrassing blush coming on. This allows you to passively attend to something other than the problem. At the same time, you move some of the blood from your head that would contribute to the blushing. You might also use a direct formula such as, "My forehead is cool."

When you experience persistent muscle pain or tension in a specific part of your body, use the autogenic verbal formulas to become generally relaxed. Then passively concentrate on the persistently tense or painful area and project the sensation of comfortably warm relaxation into that area. Repeat to yourself, "My [tense or painful area] is warm and comfortably relaxed."

If you have a headache, concentrate on the area that tends to tighten up most at the beginning of a headache. For instance, if it is the shoulders or neck or back of the head, passively concentrate on that area and project the sensation of warm relaxation into it, repeating to yourself, "My [tense area] is warm and comfortably relaxed." Occasionally intersperse the formula, "My forehead feels comfortably cool." Never make the suggestion, "My forehead feels warm," because that would stimulate vasodilatation to the area, which could result in pain.

When you are troubled by a cough, you may want to use the formula, "My throat is cool, my chest is warm." To cope with asthma, use the same formula and add, "It breathes me, it breathes me calm and regular."

When you are in a very relaxed state toward the end of an AT session, you are highly suggestible. This is a good time to use what Schultz called "intentional formulae." In other words, tell yourself to do things that you are having difficulty with. For example, if you want to stop smoking, say something over and over again such as, "Smoking is a dirty habit, and I can do without it." If you want to eat less, say, "I have control over what I eat. I can eat less and be more attractive." The special intentional formulas should be believable, persuasive, and brief.

Special Considerations

1. When practicing the six basic autogenic themes, start with your dominant arm: if you write with your left hand, begin with your left arm. Repeat, "My left arm is

heavy" four times and then go on to the next phrase, "My right arm is heavy," and repeat it four times, and so on.

2. If you have trouble experiencing the physical sensations suggested by the verbal formulas, try imagery. Contemplate being in a nice warm shower or bath, or having your hand submerged in a comfortably warm pan of water. Feel yourself sitting in the warm sun, or holding a nice warm mug of your favorite hot drink in your hand. Think about blood flowing gently through the fingertips of your hands and through your toes. Imagine lying under a comfortably heavy warm blanket or lying under the warm heavy sand at the beach. Recall a cool breeze or washcloth on your forehead.

3. Perhaps 10 percent of all people experimenting with AT never experience the basic sensations of heaviness or warmth. This does not matter. The formulas describing warmth and heaviness are used only to bring about a functional change in the body, which you may or may not feel. Just focus on doing the formulas correctly, and within two weeks of regular practice you should experience feelings of relaxation.

4. Some people experience a paradoxical response when they first practice the autogenic verbal formulas. For example, they feel light as they repeat the verbal formulas for heaviness, or they feel cool as they say the formulas for warmth. This is a sign that the body is responding to the formulas and will in time relax.

5. If you feel stuck or are experiencing unpleasant side effects while practicing one of the themes, move on to the next one and come back to the formula that is difficult for you at the end of your training.

6. If you have trouble becoming aware of your heartbeat, lie on your back with your right hand resting over your heart. If you experience any discomfort or distress while becoming aware of your heartbeat, move on to another theme and come back to this one at the end of your training, or skip it.

7. Skip the verbal formula, "My solar plexus is warm" if you have ulcers, diabetes, or any condition involving bleeding from abdominal organs. If you notice dizziness or lightheadedness when you practice the verbal formula, "My forehead is cool," practice it lying down.

8. If you think you would benefit more from having an audiotape during your AT practice, see chapter 11.

Further Reading

Coleman, D., and J. Green, eds. 1993. *Mind Body Medicine: How to Use Your Mind for Better Health.* Yonkers, N.Y.: Consumer Reports Books.

Linden, W. 1990. *Autogenics: A Clinical Guide.* New York: Guilford Press.

Pelletier, K. R. 1977. *Mind as Healer, Mind as Slayer.* New York: Delta.

————. 1984. *A Holistic Approach to Preventing Stress Disorders.* New York: P. Smith.

Peurifory, R. Z. 1992. *Anxiety, Phobias, and Panic: Taking Charge and Conquering Fear.* Citrus Heights, Calif.: Life Skills.

Brief Combination Techniques

10

In this chapter you will learn to:

☐ Tailor relaxation techniques to fit your specific needs

☐ Combine techniques for a more powerful effect

The relaxation exercises presented in this chapter are based on the work of many different therapists. They are creative blends of some of the techniques you have already learned. Learning several brief combination techniques can greatly benefit you for three reasons. First, when you put two or more relaxation approaches together, the combination can have a synergistic effect. This means that the sum relaxation effect of the combined techniques is far greater than what you would achieve if you did each relaxation procedure individually. As you experiment with the material presented in this chapter, you'll learn which techniques are best at activating each other and combining for the most powerful effect. The second reason that combination techniques are often more powerful is because the sequence is set up to draw you deeper into the relaxation experience. Each technique builds progressively upon the one before. For example, the relaxation you experience from visualizing a pleasant beach scene is more profound if you precede the visualization with some deep breathing. And if you follow the deep breathing and the beach scene with autogenic themes of heaviness and warmth, you have a sequence of techniques that build one upon the other toward a deeper relaxation response. The third advantage to using the combination techniques presented in this chapter is their brevity. You can easily do any of these combination sequences during a ten-minute coffee break. Any time you have a few minutes to spare, they can help you center yourself and regain a sense of calmness.

The combination techniques presented here are merely suggestions. While each one has been tested and proven useful, feel free to be inventive. Try your own unique combinations. Experiment with a different sequence. Since you are a unique person with unique needs and patterns of responses, it is important that you add, delete, and modify until you have a brief relaxation sequence that really works for you.

Symptom Effectiveness

The brief combination techniques presented here have been proven effective in the treatment of fight-or-flight symptoms and stress-induced physiological disorders. They are particularly helpful when stress is work-related and requires brief but frequent booster sessions during the day to help you cope with mounting tensions.

Time to Master

If you have mastered the component techniques presented in earlier chapters, these combination approaches can be immediately and effectively applied. Otherwise, allow one to two weeks to successfully use these combined approaches.

Instructions

1. *Stretch and Relax*

A. Take a big stretch. Tighten your arms and pull them back so that you stretch your chest and shoulders. Stretch and tighten your legs at the same time by first pulling your toes up toward you and then pushing them out straight.

B. Place one hand on your abdomen, just above your belt. Inhale slowly and deeply through your nose into your abdomen. Push up your hand as much as feels comfortable. Take four more deep breaths using the same procedure.

C. Suspend a pencil by its point over a desk or table or the floor. Tell yourself that when you are deeply relaxed the pencil will drop. The sound of the dropping pencil will be your signal to enter a healing, five-minute trance. (You could also omit the pencil and proceed with step C from here.) Close your eyes and say to yourself the key word or phrase that you have found most helpful in self-hypnosis. Tell yourself that you will become more and more relaxed with each number as you count backward from ten to zero. After the countdown, repeat to yourself these four phrases, over and over, in any order: "I am drifting deeper and deeper, deeper and deeper. . . . I am more and more drowsy, peaceful, and calm. . . . I am drifting and drowsy, drowsy and drifting. . . . I am drifting down, down, down, into total relaxation." If your pencil has not already dropped by this time, let it go deliberately and remind yourself that you will now enjoy five minutes of peaceful self-hypnosis.

D. While in trance, visit your special place and enjoy the uniquely relaxing qualities of that environment. Really experience the sights, sounds, and sensations of your special place. When it feels that you've been there long enough, count up from one to ten. Suggest that you are becoming more and more alert, refreshed, and wide awake as you count.

2. *Autogenic Breathing*

A. Begin by taking slow, deep breaths as described in 1B. Become aware of the growing feeling of relaxation as each deep breath expands your diaphragm.

B. Visualize a beach. See the waves rolling up the sand, the seagulls wheeling overhead, a few puffs of fleecy clouds. Hear the roar of waves, and then the quiet. Hear the alternating roar, quiet, roar, quiet. Over the ocean sound you can hear the seagulls calling. Now feel the warm sand. Imagine it covering your body, warm and heavy. Really feel the weight of the sand on your arms and legs. Feel surrounded by warmth and comfort.

C. While visualizing the sand, continue to breathe as deeply as feels comfortable. Notice the rhythm of your breath. As you breathe in, say the word "warm" to yourself. Try to feel the warmth of the sand around your body. As you breathe out, say the word "heavy." Experience the weight of the sand on your limbs. Continue your deep breathing, thinking "warm" as you inhale and "heavy" as you exhale. Continue for at least five minutes. (Note: If after a time you feel more comfortable shifting to shallower breathing, let yourself do so.)

3. *Stop and Breathe*

A. Whenever you notice disturbing or anxiety-provoking thoughts, internally shout "stop" to yourself (for more information about this technique, see chapter 12). Imagine hearing a voice with a great deal of sharpness and authority. If shouting "stop" to yourself doesn't interrupt the flow of thoughts, put a rubber band around your wrist and snap it as you shout "stop."

B. Shift your attention to your breathing. Begin taking slow, deep breaths into your belly. Place a hand over your abdomen to make sure it is expanding with each breath.

C. Now start counting your breaths. As you exhale, count one. As you exhale again, count two. Keep counting up to four. Each time you reach four, start over again at one. Try to keep your mind as empty as possible as you focus on counting each breath. Continue the procedure until you feel relaxed. Repeat the exercise each time anxiety-provoking thoughts occur.

4. *Changing Channels*

A. Use the thought-stopping procedure described in 3A, above.

B. As soon as you have interrupted the stressful cognition, use a prerehearsed visualization to block the return of any unwanted thoughts. Make sure the visualization is something you can elicit easily without struggle. Use an exciting sexual fantasy, images of success from some important achievement, scenes from an anticipated vacation, or images of your special place. The common thread of all these suggestions is to see yourself doing something that feels really good, and is easy to imagine. (Helpful hint: Try visualizing scenes you already use for daydreaming.)

C. If visualization doesn't work, try these alternatives: put on your favorite music, go out for a jog or some other strenuous aerobic exercise, start counting things (each Chevrolet you see, each person wearing a hat, how many families have children on your block), pick up a book or magazine, or sing and whistle. What matters is that the activity be arresting enough to divert attention away from stressful thoughts for a time.

D. Use a coping mantra. This is a reminder that you're basically safe and okay and can handle any stress that comes along. Some coping mantras are general affirmations such as, "I am well. . . . I am safe and calm. . . . I trust my ability to cope. . . . I am surrounded by support and love. . . . I can relax my body and my mind. . . . I can plan and decide later, now I'll relax." Other mantras require the development of a coping statement about a specific situation: "These are just stomach cramps and I'm not going to worry about them. . . . Tests show my heart is strong and healthy. . . . This is the same old neck pain, it always passes. . . . I can always get a loan. . . . I can set limits, I'll just tell her no. . . . I can ask for help with my problem. . . . I can make mistakes. . . . I don't have to finish everything on time. . . . I can disappoint sometimes and we'll still love one another. . . . I have a plan I can implement tomorrow. . . . These are just fight or flight symptoms, they'll pass soon. . . . I did the best I could, we'll see what happens." Use your coping mantra whenever the stressful thought threatens to take hold again. Repeat your mantra as often as necessary.

5. *I Am Grateful*

This exercise is particularly helpful as the day is wearing on and your sense of stress and frustration is rising. It is also an excellent sequence for relaxing and putting yourself in a pleasant frame of mind before you drift off to sleep.

A. Use the short form for progressive muscle relaxation outlined in chapter 4. (1. Curl fists, tighten biceps. 2. Wrinkle forehead and face like a walnut. 3. Arch back, take a deep breath. 4. Pull feet back, curl toes while tightening calves, thighs, buttocks.)

B. Reflect back over your day so far and select three things you feel grateful for. These do not have to be major events. For example, you may be grateful for the warm shower you took this morning, a co-worker helping you, your child giving you a hug and telling you he loves you, a lovely sunrise, and so on. Take a moment to relive and enjoy these experiences.

C. Continue to think back over your day. Recall three things you did that you feel good about. Remember that these don't have to be major feats. For example, you may feel good about saying no to something you really didn't want to do, taking time for yourself to exercise or relax, or being supportive to someone you like. Take a moment to re-experience those positive moments.

6. *Deep Affirmation*

A. Put your hand over your abdomen and begin taking slow deep breaths, as described in 1B.

B. Close your eyes and continue to breathe deeply as you scan your body for tension. Start with your toes and move up your body. Notice any tension in your calves, thighs, and buttocks. Explore areas of tension in your back, abdomen, or chest muscles. Notice your shoulders and neck, your jaw, cheeks, and forehead. Check for tension in your biceps, forearms, and hands. Whenever you discover a tense area, exaggerate the tension slightly so that you can become more aware of it. Notice exactly which muscles in your body are tense and then say to yourself, "I am tensing my [insert the name of the muscle you're working with]. I am hurting myself . . . I am creating tension in my body . . . I will let go of that tension starting now."

C. Use the self-hypnosis exercise outlined in 1C.

Select an affirmation to use while in trance. The following is a list of suggested affirmations reprinted from *Visualization for Change* by Patrick Fanning.

I can relax at will.

Tension is draining from my muscles.

I'm filled with peace, calm, and serenity.

I can turn my tension down like the volume on a radio.

Relaxation floods my body like healing, golden light.

I am in touch with my peaceful center.

I can look inward and find peace.

Relaxation is always within my grasp.

When you have relaxed long enough, count back up from one to ten. Suggest as you count that you are feeling more and more refreshed, alert, and wide awake.

7. *The Tension Cutter*

A. Take four deep breaths as described in 1B.

B. Close your eyes. Visualize your tension by giving it a color or a shape. Now change the shape and color of your tension. Make it bigger or smaller, lighter or darker. Now see yourself picking it up. Look at it in your hands. Toss it up and down once or twice as though it's a ball. Now see yourself rearing back in slow motion to throw your tension away. Go ahead and throw it. See it slowly leave your hand and move farther and farther away. Watch until it disappears out of your awareness.

C. Now imagine your body filled with lights. See red lights for tension and blue lights for relaxation. Imagine the lights changing from red to blue in all the tension areas of your body. Be aware of any physical sensation you experience while you change to the blue light of relaxation. See all the lights in your body as blue and see that color blue becoming darker and darker. Feel yourself relaxing further with each shade of blue you experience.

D. Now it's time for a mini-vacation. Here are two itineraries—use them as a model to create your own mini-vacation.

Vacation 1. Picture yourself in a forest. The light is bright in places and mottled in others. You feel safe and comfortable as you take a long pleasant walk. The air around you is cool and refreshing. You enjoy the bright spots of sunshine on the ground where the sun has filtered down through the leaves. You are walking barefoot. The leaves and moss feel soft and cool on your feet. You hear the bird sounds and the soft rustle of wind through the trees. The sounds make you happy and comfortable. As you walk your muscles feel more and more loose, heavy, and relaxed. The forest carpet of leaves and moss feels so comfortable that you want to lie down and close your eyes to rest. Now you see a small stream making a soft, bubbly noise. Next to the stream is a patch of tall, soft grass, lit and warmed by sunlight. It's a lovely place to rest and you sink down to your knees and roll gently over onto the soft, warm grass. You hear the bubbling stream, the birds' song, and the gentle wind. You are so deeply relaxed that every part of your body from your toes to the top of your head is loose and heavy.

Vacation 2. Picture yourself alone in a beach house with a view of the sea. The first rays of sun light up the wall of your bedroom as you sink deeper into the warm, soft bed. You take a deep breath and notice how relaxed your muscles are. Outside you hear the sounds of seagulls and the rhythmic crashing of the waves. The waves roll in and out, in and out. Each wave makes you more and more deeply relaxed. In and out, in and out. Drowsy, heavy, and calm. You can feel the cool salt air coming through the open window and you roll over to see the sand and the waves and the blue sky. You take deep breaths of the air and the relaxation deepens with each breath. You feel safe and yet very free, unhurried, aware that the day ahead is full of possibilities.

8. *Breath Counting*

A. Have in mind a brief affirmation (see the list in 6D) or coping mantra (see the list in 4D). Try to make sure that the affirmation or coping mantra is no longer than seven or eight words. Make up a statement that feels right for you and your unique situation.

B. To begin the relaxation process, use the short form of progressive muscle relaxation found in chapter 4.

C. Take four deep breaths, as described in 1B.

D. Now let your breathing go back to a normal rate. Focus on each breath, and as you exhale count the breath. When you get to the fourth breath, instead of counting four, say your affirmation or coping mantra: "One, two, three, I can make mistakes and be okay, one, two, three, I can make mistakes and be okay," and so on.

9. *Taking Control*

A. Get comfortable, close your eyes, and begin noticing your breathing. Try to notice each breath and nothing else. As you exhale, say to yourself the word "one." Keep saying "one" with each exhalation.

B. When you feel sufficiently relaxed, turn your attention from your breathing to a situation you find stressful or difficult. See yourself handling that stressful situation successfully and confidently. See yourself saying and doing the appropriate thing to succeed. See yourself smiling, standing, or sitting erectly. Now visualize yourself hesitating or making a small error, uncertain for a moment. But then you go on, confidently finishing the task, looking satisfied. You remind yourself, "I can handle this, I'm in control."

10. *Accepting Yourself*

A. Use the body-scanning procedure described in 6B.

B. Continue to relax by doing several minutes of autogenic breathing as described in 2C.

C. When you feel deeply relaxed, make these suggestions to yourself: "I let go of 'shoulds'. . . . I accept myself for all my humanness. . . . I breathe, I feel, I do the best I can." Rewrite this mantra in any way that feels more authentic or true for you. Anything will work, as long as it carries the basic message that you accept yourself.

11

Recording Your Own
Relaxation Tape

In this chapter you will learn to:

☐ Create a personalized tape tailored to your needs

One of the best ways to develop a complete relaxation regime is to make your own audiotape. A tape of twelve to twenty minutes can become a "relaxation workout" that incorporates many of the important techniques described in this book.

There are many relaxation tapes on the market, including some that we've recommended in this book. But there are advantages to making your own. First, you can delete segments that don't work for you while retaining and emphasizing techniques that you find particularly effective. Second, you can combine as many or as few relaxation techniques as you want for a long, medium, or short relaxation workout. Third, you can be creative. You can develop your own approach, create special relaxation or coping mantras, or visualize images that you find uniquely peaceful or calming. Fourth, using your own voice can make the tape feel especially intimate and friendly. Finally, you may use any accompanying music or sound effects that you wish, or leave the background entirely silent.

Relaxation tapes are also a big help when you're feeling passive and want to be told what to do. It's a lot easier to put on a tape and follow instructions than it is to figure out each step of a relaxation procedure yourself.

Symptom Effectiveness

Tapes can be effective for almost any symptom of stress or stress-related illness. A taped relaxation procedure can be especially helpful when you are low in energy or motivation. If you commit yourself to playing the tape at specific times during the day, you are more likely to follow your relaxation program consistently.

Time to Master

You will probably need to make several relaxation tapes before your voice and phrasing and the techniques you've selected feel right to you. Let yourself experiment. Over the course of a week, you should be able to develop a tape that works sufficiently well for you to get real benefit. From then on, you may periodically change the tape, rewriting, adding, and deleting certain parts as ideas occur to you. Make an effort to listen to your tape at least twice a day, morning and evening.

Instructions

The first thing to work on is your voice. Speak at normal volume, in a flat, almost monotonous tone. An uninflected voice on the tape will help keep your focus inward so that you can pay attention to your body and the exercise rather than to any distracting qualities of the voice. Speak slowly. Give yourself time to actually take a deep breath, tense or relax your arms, or form a visualization. Rushing through a relaxation tape defeats its purpose. When you wish to give special emphasis to an important word or instruction, simply say the words slower, drawing out the vowel sounds. "Your muscles are looose and relaxed . . . take a deeeeep breath . . . your forehead is smooooth as silk."

Many people enjoy hearing music in the background of a relaxation tape. However, there are two problems with adding musical background. First, you can't stop recording in order to fix mistakes. If you do, the background music will skip each time you stop the tape. Second, few rooms are acoustically suited for recording music. Your selection is apt to sound tinny or have a slight echo effect. But if music is important to you, go ahead and experiment. Try moving your microphone closer or farther away from the speaker; try different volumes for the music. If you enjoy New Age music, artists such as George Winston, Will Ackerman, Shadowfax, Steve Halpern, and Andreas Vollenweider can provide a very peaceful background. If you prefer classical music, the following pieces have been recommended by the Institute for Music and Imagery (their address, if you'd like to order from them, can be found at the end of the chapter).

Respighi, *Fountains of Rome* ("The Fountain of Valle Giulia at Dawn," "The Villa Medici Fountain at Sunset")

Debussy, *Danses Sacred and Profane*

Bach, *Passacaglia and Fugue in C Minor*

Pachelbel, *Canon in D*

Hadyn, *Cello Concerto in C* ("Adagio")

Glinka, *Life of the Tsar* ("Susanin Aria")

Sibelius, *Swan of Tuonela*

Boccherini, *Cello Concerto in B* ("Adagio")

Mantras and Affirmations

When you relax, you're in a suggestible state. Listening to your tape is an ideal time to remind yourself of important affirmations, coping strategies, and new attitudes that you are striving to remember. These affirmations and reminders may change daily. Or, you may want to repeat an important basic truth each time you listen to the tape so that it gradually finds its way into your subconscious beliefs.

Here are some examples of helpful affirmations that you may wish to use while listening to the tape.

Each day I become more and more relaxed.

I accept my body, every feeling, every sensation.

I can relax away stress.

I breathe deeply and calmly when I feel stress.

I can be direct and clear with my boss.

I am expressing my needs and feelings to my wife.

I am responsible for making myself feel good.

My stomach is loose and calm.

The knots in my shoulders are dissolving.

I am loving and good.

I can stop unloving thoughts.

I will succeed in my physics course.

Whenever I feel stress, I'll fill my body with peaceful light.

Affirmations can involve specific relaxation instructions, suggestions for behavioral change, imagery for healing, suggestions for improved self-esteem, mantras for success, reminders for attitudinal change, and assertions that everything, in the end, will turn out okay. If you want to change something, write an affirmation that will remind you to do so. Make the affirmation positive, and be certain it describes exactly what you want to achieve.

Mantras and affirmations work best if they are combined with an image, a mental picture of the change you want to create. If you want your stomach to be loose and calm, see braided strands untwisting. If you wish to express your needs and feelings to your wife, see yourself talking to her intimately and earnestly. If you wish to succeed in the physics course, see the report card with a B+ or an A.

Constructing Your Relaxation Script

The relaxation script below is divided into sections. Each section is a discrete component that can be included or deleted from your tape. Read through the entire script first and mark the sections that feel appropriate to include. Over the next few weeks you may rerecord your tape several times, adding or subtracting sections as you learn more about what works best for you.

Relaxation Script

Deep breathing. *Close your eyes. Put your hand over your abdomen* [just above the belt]. *Take a deep breath, way down into your belly.* [Pause.] *Let go and hear the air* *whoosh out through your lips. [Pause.] When you're ready, take another deep breath. You can feel your belly rise slowly as the air comes in. Let it out with a whooshing sound, like the wind, as you blow through your lips. Each breath leaves you more and more relaxed. Each breath purifies and relaxes your whole body and mind. Take another deep breath down into your belly. Feel your belly push out. As you relax, the air goes gently out your lips. Imagine with your next deep breath that clean, pure, white air is coming in through the soles of your feet. See it spread throughout your whole body, collecting the debris of tension and stress. The air gets darker as it takes the stress and tension from your body. Imagine the dark air being expelled through your lips, leaving your whole body clean and fresh and relaxed. Now take a deep purifying breath and feel it cleaning your body of stress and tension. See the tension leaving your body with the breath. Relax and enjoy the feeling of peace and calm that has spread throughout your body with each deep breath. Imagine one more breath coming in through the soles of your feet, pure and white. It is removing the last bit of tension from your body. As you exhale you feel your body clean and relaxed, deeply relaxed.*

Counting your breath. *Now let your breathing slow down and become automatic. Each breath continues to relax you. You are breathing quietly, peacefully. You're breathing in an easy and natural way. Each time you exhale, say silently to yourself, "one." Continue to breathe in and out, saying "one" each time you exhale. Whenever thoughts or perceptions take your attention away from your breathing, let go of them and return to saying "one." Breathe naturally, calmly, saying "one" as you exhale. [Leave one to two blank minutes on the tape to really enjoy this exercise.]*

Active progressive relaxation. *Now, while keeping the rest of your body relaxed, clench your right fist, tighter and tighter. [Pause five seconds.] Now relax. Notice the contrast between a tight muscle and a loose one. Notice a pleasant sort of burning that occurs when the muscle relaxes. Now try to relax your arm even more. Let the chair hold your arm up as you let go of the last bit of muscular tension. Now tighten your left fist, tighter and tighter. [Pause five seconds.] Relax and enjoy the feeling of looseness in your left arm. Really give yourself a chance to feel a difference between tension and relaxation. [Pause.]*

Now bend your elbows and tense your biceps. Tense them as much as you can and observe the feeling of tautness. [Pause five seconds.] Relax, straighten out your arms. Let the relaxation develop and feel the difference. [Pause.]

Now turn your attention to your head and wrinkle up your forehead as tight as you can. [Pause five seconds.] Now relax and smooth it out. Let yourself imagine your entire forehead and scalp becoming smooth and relaxed. [Pause.] Now frown and notice the strain spreading throughout your forehead. Feel the tension and the tightness. [Pause.] Now let go, allow your brow to become smooth again. Notice the difference between tension and relaxation in your forehead. [Pause.] Now clench your jaw, bite hard, and notice the tension throughout your jaw. [Pause five seconds.] Relax your jaw. When the jaw is relaxed, your lips will begin to part. Really feel and appreciate the contrast between tension and relaxation in your jaw. Notice how it feels to relax your lips and tongue.

Now shrug your shoulders. Keep the tension as you hunch your head down between your shoulders. [Pause five seconds.] Relax. Drop your shoulders and feel the relaxation spreading through your neck, throat, and shoulders. Pure relaxation, deeper and deeper. Feel how loose and easy your neck feels balanced on your shoulders.

Give your entire body a chance to relax. Feel the comfort and the heaviness. Take a deep breath and let it fill your abdomen. [Pause.] *Now exhale, letting the air out with a whooshing sound. Continue relaxing, letting your breath come freely and gently. Now, tighten your stomach and hold. Note the tension.* [Pause five seconds.] *Relax. Place your hand on your stomach. Breathe deeply into your belly, pushing your hand up. Hold.* [Pause.] *Relax. Feel the contrast with the tension as the air rushes out.*

Now concentrate on your back. Arch it very slightly, without straining. Focus on the tension in your lower back. Feel the tension. [Pause.] *Relax. Imagine loosening the lower back and pelvic muscles, feel yourself sinking deeper into the chair or bed. Focus on letting go of all the tension in the muscles of your lower back and pelvis and abdomen. Feel yourself sinking heavier and heavier into the chair or bed as your abdomen and back relax more and more deeply.* [Pause.]

Now tighten your buttocks and thighs. Hold the tension and notice how it feels. [Pause five seconds.] *Relax and notice the contrast between tension and looseness. Really experience what it feels like to relax your buttocks and thighs.* [Pause.] *Now curl your toes downward, making your calves tense. Study the tension.* [Pause five seconds.] *Relax. Feel and enjoy the relaxation.* [Pause.] *Now bend your toes toward your face, creating tension in your shins.* [Pause five seconds.] *Relax again, enjoying the feeling of peace and heaviness that spreads everywhere in your legs.*

Feel the heaviness in your body as the relaxation deepens. Feel yourself heavier and heavier, more and more deeply relaxed. More and more heavy, peaceful and calm.

Passive progressive relaxation. *Now you can scan your body for any last bit of tension. Let your arms become heavy and relaxed. Heavier and heavier, more and more deeply relaxed. Your arms are heavy, heavy, letting go of the last bit of muscle tension. More and more deeply relaxed. Letting go, letting go of all muscle tension.*

Now your face too can relax. Your forehead becomes smooth as silk, smooth and relaxed, letting go of all the tension and the worry. Smooth and relaxed. Your cheeks become smooth and relaxed, completely free of tension. Your cheeks and forehead are smooth and relaxed. And your jaw too lets go of the last bit of tension. Your jaw hangs loose and relaxed, loose and relaxed. Your tongue and lips are relaxed. And as your jaw becomes completely loose and relaxed, your lips begin to part, very slightly. They begin to part as you let go of the last bit of muscle tension. Your jaw is loose and relaxed.

Your neck and shoulders can now let go. Your shoulders droop and relax, droop and relax. Your neck is loose and easy. Your neck and shoulders are relaxed, you feel safe and calm. Your shoulders droop and you let go of the last bit of muscle tension.

Now you can take another deep breath, way down into your belly. Your belly pushes up as you inhale. [Pause.] *Let go now, making the whooshing noise with your lips. Feel the relaxation spread throughout your abdomen and chest and back. Take another deep breath, and as you do feel the air relax your chest and abdomen and back. Exhale with a whooshing noise, and feel the last bit of muscular tension leave your lower body.* [Pause.]

Now focus on your legs. Let them become heavier and heavier, more and more deeply relaxed. Heavier and heavier, letting go of the last bit of muscular tension. Letting go, letting go of tension, more and more deeply relaxed as your legs become heavier and heavier. You can imagine your legs as lead pipes, so heavy and relaxed.

Now you feel a relaxation throughout your entire body. Every cell is relaxed, calm, and quiet. Your legs and arms are heavy and relaxed, your face is smooth and relaxed, your jaw hangs loosely, loosely. Your neck and shoulders are relaxed, your shoulders droop and relax. Take another deep breath. [Pause.] As you do, your entire body will be filled with peace, calm, and relaxation.

Special place. *Now imagine a place where you feel peaceful, calm, and relaxed . . . a place where you are secure and safe. See whether it is outdoors or indoors, whether it is a place from your past or your present or a place you've never really seen. This is your special place, a retreat and a haven. You're going there now. You can see the shapes and colors of your special place. You see every detail like a picture. [Pause.] Now you can begin to hear the sounds of your special place . . . see and hear. [Pause.] Now you are able to feel your special place. You can feel it against your skin. You feel bathed in peace and a deep sense of contentment in your special place. Take a deep breath as you let the peace and tranquility of your special place spread throughout your entire body. Enjoy your place for a while. Let it nourish and relax you. [Pause one to two minutes.]*

Autogenics theme. *Take a deep breath, way down into your belly. As you breathe in, say the word "warm" to yourself. And as you breathe out, say the word "heavy." [Pause.] Take another deep breath and think to yourself, "warm." [Pause.] Let it go and think, "heavy." Now breathe deeply, at your own pace, thinking "warm" on the inhale and "heavy" on the exhale. Feel the warmth and heaviness in your arms and legs. With each breath let the feeling spread throughout your entire body, relaxing every muscle as you feel more and more heavy, warm, and relaxed. [Pause ninety seconds.]*

Coping imagery. *Notice the feeling of peace and relaxation. Imagine carrying this feeling into your everyday life. See yourself confident, relaxed, talking calmly. See yourself smiling with friends, co-workers, family. Your manner is easy as you state your needs and concerns. You see yourself standing comfortably and calmly with your boss, with people you barely know, with strangers. You see yourself smiling and enjoying the conversation. You are able to speak what is in your mind. You say what you feel and think clearly, in such a way that you are appreciated and understood. Your posture is relaxed yet straight. You feel strong and capable.*

Affirmation. *Now is the time to remember your affirmation. Say it to yourself slowly while focusing on any accompanying imagery. Give yourself time to let your affirmation really sink in, repeating as often as feels appropriate. [Pause twenty seconds.]*

Anchoring. *Now feel the relaxation in every part of your body. Notice the feeling of heaviness and peace in your arms and your legs. Feel the looseness in your jaw, the relaxation in your neck and shoulders. Take a deep breath, and as you exhale the last bit of tension will leave your body. [Pause.] Experience the feeling of being completely at rest.*

Now, while staying very aware of what relaxation feels like in your body, place your right hand over your left wrist. Grasp your wrist gently, but firmly. Whenever you hold your wrist in this way it will be your cue to relax. Any time you hold your left wrist with your right hand you will recover the deep feelings of relaxation you have right now.

Take a deep breath. Feel it cleansing and refreshing your body. Feel the healing energy of relaxation flowing through your arms and throughout your body. When you link your hand and wrist, it completes a circuit so the healing energy flows freely and reaches every part of your body. From now on, whenever you wish to relax, you will hold your left wrist with your right hand.

Using Your Tape

Now it's time to try out your tape. As you experiment by including or omitting different segments, you will discover which procedures work best for you. You may want to try writing some of your own script. Certain breathing exercises, visualizations, or meditation procedures may be more effective for you than some of the techniques on this sample script. The only rule to follow is: Do what works. This applies not just to the omission or inclusion of techniques. It means that you should order the techniques in any sequence that feels good to you, experiment with your voice and inflection, and try recordings of wind chimes, waterfalls, babbling brooks, or any other background noises or sound effects that seem appropriate.

Buying Tapes

If you prefer relaxation tapes based on a single specific technique, the following tapes were made to accompany this book and can be ordered from New Harbinger Publications, 5674 Shattuck Avenue, Oakland, CA 94609:

Progressive Relaxation and Breathing

Body Awareness and Imagination

Autogenics and Meditation

Self-Hypnosis

Thought Stopping

The Institute for Music and Imagery also has tapes available:

Fort Townsend, WA 94368
Box 173

Refuting Irrational Ideas

Man is not disturbed by events, but by the view he takes of them.

—Epictetus

In this chapter you will learn to:

☐ Recognize how your thoughts influence your feelings, physical sensations, and behavior

☐ Assess your distressing thoughts

☐ Counteract your needless distressing thoughts

Almost every minute of your conscious life you are engaging in self-talk, your internal thought language. These are the sentences you describe and interpret the world with. If the self-talk is accurate and in touch with reality, you function well. If it is irrational and untrue, you experience stress and emotional disturbance. Here is an example of irrational self-talk: "I can't bear to be alone." No physically healthy person has ever died merely from being alone. Being alone may be uncomfortable, undesirable, and frustrating, but you can live with it and live through it.

Another example of irrational self-talk is, "I should never be cruel to my wife. If I am, I know I'm a rotten person." The words "should never" allow no possibility of flaw or failure. When the inevitable fight occurs, you indict yourself as entirely rotten—all on the basis of a single incident.

Irrational ideas may be based on outright misperceptions ("When the airplane's wing shakes, I know it's going to fall off") or perfectionistic shoulds, oughts, and musts ("I ought to keep quiet rather than upset anyone"). Inaccurate self-talk such as "I need love" is emotionally dangerous compared to the more realistic "I want love very much, but I don't absolutely need it, and can survive and feel reasonably happy without it." "How terrible to be rejected" is fear-producing in comparison to, "I find it unpleasant and momentarily awkward, and feel regretful when I am rejected." Imperatives such as, "I've got to be more helpful around the house" can be converted to more rational statements, such as, "There would probably be more peace and compatibility if I did a greater share of the work."

Albert Ellis developed a system to attack irrational ideas or beliefs and replace them with realistic statements about the world. He called his system "rational emotive therapy" and first introduced it, with co-author Harper, in *A Guide to Rational Living* in 1961. Ellis' basic thesis is that emotions have nothing to do with actual events. Between the event and the emotion is realistic or unrealistic self-talk. The self-talk produces the emotions. Your own thoughts, directed and controlled by you, are what create anxiety, anger, and depression. The chart below shows how it works.

Feedback Loop

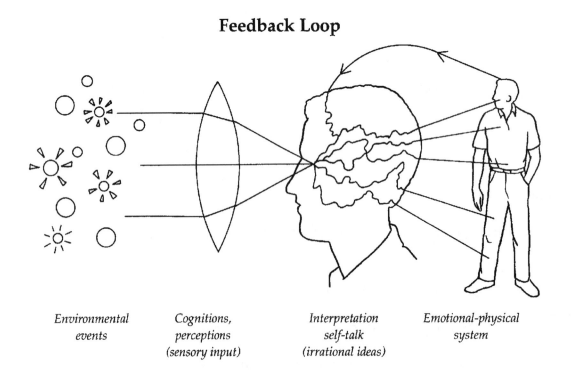

| Environmental events | Cognitions, perceptions (sensory input) | Interpretation self-talk (irrational ideas) | Emotional-physical system |

Example

A. Facts and events

A mechanic replaces a fuel pump he honestly believed was malfunctioning, but the car's performance doesn't improve. The customer is very upset and demands that he put the old fuel pump back.

B. Mechanic's self-talk

"He's just a grouch—nothing would please him."

"Why the hell do I get all the tough jobs?"

"I ought to have figured this out by now."

"I'm not much of a mechanic."

C. Emotions

Anger and resentment

Depression

The mechanic may later say to himself, "That guy really made me mad." But it is not the customer or anything that the customer has done that produces the anger—it is the mechanic's own self-talk, his interpretation of reality. This irrational self-talk can be changed and the stressful emotions changed with it.

Symptom Effectiveness

Rimm and Litvak (1969) found that negative self-talk produced substantial physiological arousal. In other words, your body tenses and becomes stressed when you use such irrational syllogisms as:

People seem to ignore me at parties.

It's obvious that I'm either boring or unattractive to them.

How terrible!

The emotional results of irrational self-talk are anxiety, depression, rage, guilt, and a sense of worthlessness. Rational emotive therapy has been shown to be effective in decreasing the frequency and intensity of these emotions.

Time to Master

Assessment of your irrational beliefs, plus homework sufficient to refute one of these beliefs, can take approximately twenty minutes a day for two weeks. Rational emotive imagery, the process by which you work directly on changing your emotions, also takes about two weeks if you practice ten minutes a day.

Instructions

Assessment

The following Beliefs Inventory is designed to uncover particular irrational ideas that contribute to unhappiness and stress. Take the test now, score it, and note the sections where your scores are highest.

Note that it is not necessary to think over any item very long. Mark your answer quickly and go on to the next statement. Be sure to mark how you actually think about the statement, not how you think you should think.

Beliefs Inventory

Agree	*Disagree*	*Score*	*Belief*
• ☐	☐	_____	1. It is important to me that others approve of me.
• ☐	☐	_____	2. I hate to fail at anything.
• ☐	☐	_____	3. People who do wrong deserve what they get.
•• ☐	☐	_____	4. I usually accept what happens philosophically.
•• ☐	☐	_____	5. If a person wants to, he can be happy under almost any circumstances.
• ☐	☐	_____	6. I have a fear of some things that often bothers me.
• ☐	☐	_____	7. I usually put off important decisions.
• ☐	☐	_____	8. Everyone needs someone he can depend on for help and advice.
• ☐	☐	_____	9. "A zebra cannot change his stripes."
• ☐	☐	_____	10. I prefer quiet leisure above all things.
•• ☐	☐	_____	11. I like the respect of others, but I don't have to have it.
••	☐	_____	12. I avoid things I cannot do well.
• ☐	☐	_____	13. Too many evil persons escape the punishment they deserve.
•• ☐	☐	_____	14. Frustrations don't upset me.
•• ☐	☐	_____	15. People are disturbed not by situations but by the view they take of them.
•• ☐	☐	_____	16. I feel little anxiety over unexpected dangers or future events.
•• ☐	☐	_____	17. I try to go ahead and get irksome tasks behind me when they come up.
• ☐	☐	_____	18. I try to consult an authority on important decisions.
• ☐	☐	_____	19. It is almost impossible to overcome the influences of the past.
•• ☐	☐	_____	20. I like to have a lot of irons in the fire.
• ☐	☐	_____	21. I want everyone to like me.
•• ☐	☐	_____	22. I don't mind competing in activities in which others are better than I.

Agree	Disagree	Score	Belief
• ❑	❑	_____	23. Those who do wrong deserve to be blamed.
• ❑	❑	_____	24. Things should be different from the way they are.
•• ❑	❑	_____	25. I cause my own moods.
• ❑	❑	_____	26. I often can't get my mind off some concern.
• ❑	❑	_____	27. I avoid facing my problems.
• ❑	❑	_____	28. People need a source of strength outside themselves.
•• ❑	❑	_____	29. Just because something once affects your life strongly doesn't mean it need do so in the future.
•• ❑	❑	_____	30. I'm most fulfilled when I have lots to do.
•• ❑	❑	_____	31. I can like myself even when many others don't.
•• ❑	❑	_____	32. I like to succeed at something, but I don't feel I have to.
• ❑	❑	_____	33. Immorality should be strongly punished.
❑	❑	_____	34. I often get disturbed over situations I don't like.
•• ❑	❑	_____	35. People who are miserable have usually made themselves that way.
•• ❑	❑	_____	36. If I can't keep something from happening, I don't worry about it.
•• ❑	❑	_____	37. I usually make decisions as promptly as I can.
• ❑	❑	_____	38. There are certain people whom I depend on greatly.
•• ❑	❑	_____	39. People overvalue the influence of the past.
•• ❑	❑	_____	40. I most enjoy throwing myself into a creative project.
•• ❑	❑	_____	41. If others dislike me, that's their problem, not mine.
• ❑	❑	_____	42. It is highly important to me to be successful in everything I do.
•• ❑	❑	_____	43. I seldom blame people for their wrongdoings.
•• ❑	❑	_____	44. I usually accept things the way they are, even if I don't like them.
•• ❑	❑	_____	45. A person won't stay angry or blue long unless he keeps himself that way.
• ❑	❑	_____	46. I can't stand to take chances.

Agree	Disagree	Score	Belief
• ☐	☐	_____	47. Life is too short to spend it doing unpleasant tasks.
•• ☐	☐	_____	48. I like to stand on my own two feet.
• ☐	☐	_____	49. If I had had different experiences I could be more like I want to be.
• ☐	☐	_____	50. I'd like to retire and quit working entirely.
• ☐	☐	_____	51. I find it hard to go against what others think.
•• ☐	☐	_____	52. I enjoy activities for their own sake, no matter how good I am at them.
• ☐	☐	_____	53. The fear of punishment helps people be good.
•• ☐	☐	_____	54. If things annoy me, I just ignore them.
• ☐	☐	_____	55. The more problems a person has, the less happy he will be.
•• ☐	☐	_____	56. I am seldom anxious over the future.
•• ☐	☐	_____	57. I seldom put things off.
•• ☐	☐	_____	58. I am the only one who can really understand and face my problems.
•• ☐	☐	_____	59. I seldom think of past experiences as affecting me now.
•• ☐	☐	_____	60. Too much leisure time is boring.
•• ☐	☐	_____	61. Although I like approval, it's not a real need for me.
• ☐	☐	_____	62. It bothers me when others are better than I am at something.
• ☐	☐	_____	63. Everyone is basically good.
•• ☐	☐	_____	64. I do what I can to get what I want and then don't worry about it.
•• ☐	☐	_____	65. Nothing is upsetting in itself—only in the way you interpret it.
• ☐	☐	_____	66. I worry a lot about certain things in the future.
• ☐	☐	_____	67. It is difficult for me to do unpleasant chores.
•• ☐	☐	_____	68. I dislike having others make my decisions for me.
• ☐	☐	_____	69. We are slaves to our personal histories.

Agree	Disagree	Score	Belief
• ❑	❑	_____	70. I sometimes wish I could go somewhere and take it easy forever.
• ❑	❑	_____	71. I often worry about how much people approve of and accept me.
• ❑	❑	_____	72. It upsets me to make mistakes.
• ❑	❑	_____	73. It's unfair that "the rain falls on both the just and the unjust."
•• ❑	❑	_____	74. I am fairly easygoing about life.
• ❑	❑	_____	75. More people should face up to the unpleasantness of life.
• ❑	❑	_____	76. Sometimes I can't get a fear off my mind.
•• ❑	❑	_____	77. A life of ease is seldom very rewarding.
• ❑	❑	_____	78. I find it easy to seek advice.
• ❑	❑	_____	79. Once something strongly affects your life, it always will.
• ❑	❑	_____	80. I love to lie around.
• ❑	❑	_____	81. I have considerable concern with what people are feeling about me.
• ❑	❑	_____	82. I often become quite annoyed over little things.
•• ❑		_____	83. I usually give someone who has wronged me a second chance.
• ❑	❑	_____	84. People are happiest when they have challenges and problems to overcome.
•• ❑	❑	_____	85. There is never any reason to remain sorrowful for very long.
•• ❑	❑	_____	86. I hardly ever think of such things as death or atomic war.
• ❑	❑	_____	87. I dislike responsibility.
•• ❑	❑	_____	88. I dislike having to depend on others.
• ❑	❑	_____	89. People never change basically.
• ❑	❑	_____	90. Most people work too hard and don't get enough rest.
•• ❑	❑	_____	91. It is annoying but not upsetting to be criticized.

Agree	Disagree	Score	Belief
•• ☐	☐	_____	92. I'm not afraid to do things which I cannot do well.
•• ☐	☐	_____	93. No one is evil, even though his deeds may be.
•• ☐	☐	_____	94. I seldom become upset over the mistakes of others.
•• ☐	☐	_____	95. Man makes his own hell within himself.
• ☐	☐	_____	96. I often find myself planning what I would do in different dangerous situations.
•• ☐	☐	_____	97. If something is necessary, I do it even if it is unpleasant.
•• ☐	☐	_____	98. I've learned not to expect someone else to be very concerned about my welfare.
•• ☐	☐	_____	99. I don't look upon the past with any regrets.
• ☐	☐	_____	100. I can't feel really content unless I'm relaxed and doing nothing.

Scoring the Beliefs Inventory

A. Single-dot items

If the item has one dot (•) and you checked the **Agree** box, give yourself one point in the space provided next to the item.

B. Double-dot items

If the item has two dots (••) and you checked the **Disagree** box, give yourself a point in the space provided next to the item.

C. Tally your points

Add up your points for items 1, 11, 21, 31, 41, 51, 61, 71, 81, and 91, and enter the total here: _____. The higher the total, the greater your agreement with the irrational idea that *it is an absolute necessity for an adult to have love and approval from peers, family, and friends.*

Add up your points for items 2, 12, 22, 32, 42, 52, 62, 72, 82, and 92, and enter the total here: _____. The higher the total, the greater your agreement with the irrational idea that *you must be unfailingly competent and almost perfect in all you undertake.*

Add up your points for items 3, 13, 23, 33, 43, 53, 63, 73, 83, and 93, and enter the total here: _____. The higher the total, the greater your agreement with the irrational idea that *certain people are evil, wicked, and villainous, and should be punished.*

Add up your points for items 4, 14, 24, 34, 44, 54, 64, 74, 84, and 94, and enter the total here: _____. The higher the total, the greater your agreement with the irrational idea that *it is horrible when things are not the way you would like them to be.*

Add up your points for items 5, 15, 25, 35, 45, 55, 65, 75, 85, and 95, and enter the total here: _____. The higher the total, the greater your agreement with the irrational idea that *external events cause most human misery—that people simply react as events trigger their emotions.*

Add up your points for items 6, 16, 26, 36, 46, 56, 66, 76, 86, and 96, and enter the total here: _____. The higher the total, the greater your agreement with the irrational idea that *you should feel fear or anxiety about anything that is unknown, uncertain, or potentially dangerous.*

Add up your points for items 7, 17, 27, 37, 47, 57, 67, 77, 87, and 97, and enter the total here: _____. The higher the total, the greater your agreement with the irrational idea that *it is easier to avoid than face life's difficulties and responsibilities.*

Add up your points for items 8, 18, 28, 38, 48, 58, 68, 78, 88, and 98, and enter the total here: _____. The higher the total, the greater your agreement with the irrational idea that *you need something other or stronger or greater than yourself to rely on.*

Add up your points for items 9, 19, 29, 39, 49, 59, 69, 79, 89, and 99, and enter the total here: _____. The higher the total, the greater your agreement with the irrational idea that *the past has a lot to do with determining the present.*

Add up your points for items 10, 20, 30, 40, 50, 60, 70, 80, 90, and 100, and enter the total here: _____. The higher the total, the greater your agreement with the irrational idea that *happiness can be achieved by inaction, passivity, and endless leisure.*

Irrational Ideas

At the root of all irrational thinking is the assumption that things are done to you: "That really got me down. . . . She makes me nervous. . . . Places like that scare me. . . . Being lied to makes me see red." Nothing is done to you. Events happen in the world. You experience those events (A), engage in self-talk (B), and then experience an emotion (C) resulting from the self-talk. *A* does not cause *C*—*B* causes *C*. If your self-talk is irrational and unrealistic, you create unpleasant emotions.

Two common forms of irrational self-talk are statements that "awfulize" and "absolutize." You awfulize by making catastrophic, nightmarish interpretations of your experience. A momentary chest pain is a heart attack, the grumpy boss intends to fire you, your mate takes a night job and the thought of being alone is unthinkably terrible. The emotions that follow awfulizing self-talk tend themselves to be awful—you are responding to your own description of the world.

Irrational self-statements that "absolutize" often include words such as "should," "must," "ought," "always," and "never." The idea is that things have to be a certain way, or you have to be a certain way. Any deviation from that particular value or standard is bad. The person who fails to live up to the standard is bad. In reality, the standard is what's bad, because it is irrational.

Albert Ellis suggested ten basic irrational ideas, which are listed below. To these we have added some additional common self-statements that are highly unrealistic. Based on your scores on the Beliefs Inventory, and your knowledge of the situations you characteristically experience stress in, place a check mark next to the ones that seem to apply to you.

❑   **1. It is an absolute necessity for an adult to have love and approval from peers, family, and friends.** In fact, pleasing all the people in your life is impossible. Even those who basically like and approve of you will be turned off by some behaviors and qualities. This irrational belief is probably the single greatest cause of unhappiness.

❑   **2. You must be unfailingly competent and almost perfect in all you undertake.** The results of believing that you must behave perfectly are self-blame for inevitable failure, lowered self-esteem, perfectionistic standards applied to mate and friends, and paralysis and fear at attempting anything.

❑   **3. Certain people are evil, wicked, and villainous and should be punished.** A more realistic position is that they are behaving in ways that are antisocial or inappropriate. They are perhaps stupid, ignorant, or neurotic and may need to change their behavior.

❑   **4. It is horrible when people and things are not the way you would like them to be.** This might be described as the spoiled-child syndrome. As soon as the tire goes flat the self-talk starts: "Why does this happen to me? Damn, I can't take this. It's awful, I'll get all filthy." Any inconvenience, problem, or failure to get your way is likely to be met with such awfulizing self-statements. The result is intense irritation and stress.

❑   **5. External events cause most human misery—people simply react as events trigger their emotions.** A logical extension of this belief is that you must control the external events in order to create happiness or avoid sorrow. Because such control has limitations and we are at a loss to completely manipulate the wills of others, a sense of helplessness and chronic anxiety results. Ascribing unhappiness to events is a way of avoiding reality. Self-statements interpreting the event caused the unhappiness. While you may have only limited control over others, you have enormous control over your emotions.

❑   **6. You should feel fear or anxiety about anything that is unknown, uncertain, or potentially dangerous.** Many describe this as, "a little bell goes off and I think I ought to start worrying." They begin to rehearse their scenarios of catastrophe. Increasing the fear or anxiety in the face of uncertainty makes coping more difficult and adds to stress. Saving the fear response for actual, perceived danger allows you to enjoy uncertainty as a novel and exciting experience.

❑   **7. It is easier to avoid than to face life's difficulties and responsibilities.** There are many ways of ducking responsibilities: "I should tell him I'm no longer interested— but not tonight. . . . I'd like to get another job, but I'm just too tired on my days off to look. . . . A leaky faucet won't hurt anything . . . . " If this way of thinking applies to you, write down your standard excuses to avoid responsibility:

Area of responsibility   *Method of avoidance*

_____   _____

_____   _____

_____   _____

_____   _____

❑ **8. You need something other or stronger or greater than yourself to rely on.** This belief becomes a psychological trap in which your independent judgment and your awareness of your particular needs are undermined by a reliance on higher authority.

❑ **9. The past has a lot to do with determining the present.** Just because you were once strongly affected by something does not mean that you must continue the habits you formed to cope with the original situation. Those old patterns and ways of responding are just decisions made so many times they have become nearly automatic. You can identify those old decisions and start changing them right now. You can learn from past experience, but you don't have to be overly attached to it.

❑ **10. Happiness can be achieved by inaction, passivity, and endless leisure.** This is called the Elysian fields syndrome. There is more to happiness than perfect relaxation.

Other irrational ideas

❑ **11. You are helpless and have no control over what you experience or feel.** This belief is at the heart of much depression and anxiety. The truth is we not only exercise considerable control over interpersonal situations, but also control how we interpret and emotionally respond to each life event.

❑ **12. People are fragile and should never be hurt.** This irrational belief results in failure to openly communicate important feelings, and in self-sacrifice that gives up what is nourishing and pleasurable (Farquhar and Lowe 1974). Since everything you need or want seems to hurt or deprive someone else, you feel frustration, helplessness, and depression. Relationships become full of dead space where conflicts developed and nothing was said.

❑ **13. Good relationships are based on mutual sacrifice and a focus on giving.** This belief rests on the assumption that it is better to give than to receive. It is expressed in a reluctance to ask for things and the anticipation that your hidden needs will be divined and provided for. Unfortunately, constant self-denial usually results in bitterness and withdrawal.

❑ **14. If you don't go to great lengths to please others, they will abandon or reject you.** This belief is a by-product of low self-esteem. You usually run less risk of rejection if you offer others your true unembellished self. They can take it or leave it. But if they respond to the real you, you don't have to worry about slacking off, letting down your guard, and being rejected later.

☐ **15. When people disapprove of you, it invariably means you are wrong or bad.** This extremely crippling belief sparks chronic anxiety in most interpersonal situations (Farquhar and Lowe 1974). The irrationality is contained in the generalization of one specific fault or unattractive feature to a total indictment of the self.

☐ **16. Happiness, pleasure, and fulfillment can only occur in the presence of others, and being alone is horrible.** Pleasure, self-worth, and fulfillment can be experienced alone as well as with others (Farquhar and Lowe 1974). Being alone is growth-producing and desirable at times.

☐ **17. There is a perfect love, and a perfect relationship.** Subscribers to this belief often feel resentful of one close relationship after another. Nothing is quite right because they are waiting for the perfect fit, which never comes.

☐ **18. You shouldn't have to feel pain; you are entitled to a good life.** The realistic position is that pain is an inevitable part of human life. Pain frequently accompanies tough, healthy decisions and the process of growth. Life is not fair, and sometimes you will suffer no matter what you do.

☐ **19. Your worth as a person depends on how much you achieve and produce.** A more rational assessment of your real worth would depend on such things as your capacity to be fully alive, feeling everything it means to be human (Farquhar and Lowe 1974).

☐ **20. Anger is automatically bad and destructive.** Anger is frequently cleansing and can be an honest communication of current feelings, without attacking the personal worth and security of others (Farquhar and Lowe 1974).

☐ **21. It is bad or wrong to be selfish.** The truth is that no one knows your needs and wants better than you, and no one else has as great an interest in seeing them fulfilled. Your happiness is your responsibility. Being selfish means you are accepting that responsibility.

You could probably add other irrational ideas to this list. Please do. The best way to uncover your irrational ideas is to think of situations in which you experience anxiety, depression, anger, guilt, or a sense of worthlessness. Behind each of these emotions, particularly if they are chronic, is irrational self-talk.

Your other irrational ideas:

_____

_____

_____

Much of the difficulty in uncovering irrational self-talk results from the speed and invisibility of thoughts. They may be lightning quick and barely on the edge of awareness. You will rarely be conscious of a complete sentence, as in the irrational statements above. Because self-talk has a reflexive, automatic quality, it is easy to keep the illusion that feelings arise spontaneously from events. However, once the thoughts are slowed down like a slow-motion film, frame by frame, the millisecond it takes to say, "I'm falling apart" is exposed for its malignant influence. The thoughts that create your emotions may frequently appear in a kind of shorthand: "No good . . . crazy . . . feeling sick . . . dumb," and so on. That shorthand has to be stretched out into the original sentence it was extracted from. The sentence can then be challenged with methods you'll learn in the section on refuting irrational ideas.

Rules to Promote Rational Thinking

Evaluate your self-statements against these six rules, or guidelines, for rational thinking (from David Goodman's *Emotional Well-Being Through Rational Behavior Training*).

It doesn't do anything to me.
The situation doesn't make me anxious or afraid. I say things to myself that produce anxiety and fear.

Everything is exactly the way it should be.
The conditions for things or people to be otherwise don't exist. To say that things should be other than what they are is to believe in magic. They are what they are because of a long series of causal events, including interpretations, responses from irrational self-talk, and so on. To say that things should be different is to throw out causality.

All humans are fallible creatures.
This is inescapable. If you haven't set reasonable quotas of failure for yourself and others, you increase the prospects for disappointment and unhappiness. It becomes all too easy to attack yourself and others as worthless, bad, and so on.

It takes two to have a conflict.
Before beginning a course of accusation and blame, consider the 30 percent rule. Any party to a conflict is contributing at least 30 percent of the fuel to keep it going.

The original cause is lost in antiquity.
Trying to discover who did what first is a waste of time. The search for the original cause of chronic painful emotions is extremely difficult. The best strategy is to make decisions to change your behavior now.

We feel the way we think.
This is the positively stated principle behind the first statement in this list. This statement reinforces the idea that events don't cause emotions—our interpretations of events cause emotions.

Refuting Irrational Ideas

There are five steps (A through E) to disputing and eliminating irrational ideas. Start by selecting a situation that consistently generates stressful emotions in you.

A. Write down the facts of the event as they occurred at the time you were upset. Be certain to include only the objective facts, not conjecture, subjective impressions, or value judgments.

B. Write down your self-talk about the event. State all your subjective value judgments, assumptions, beliefs, predictions, and worries. Note which self-statements have been previously described as irrational ideas.

C. Focus on your emotional response. Make a clear one- or two-word label such as "angry," "depressed," "felt worthless," "afraid," and so on.

D. Dispute and change the irrational self-talk identified at step B. Here's how it is done, according to Ellis:

1. **Select the irrational idea** that you wish to dispute. As an illustration, we will use the irrational idea, "It's not fair that I have to suffer with such a problem."

2. **Is there any rational support for this idea?** Since everything is as it should be, given long chains of cause and effect, the answer is no. The problem must be endured and dealt with because it happened. It happened because all the conditions existed necessary to make it happen.

3. **What evidence exists for the falseness of this idea?**

   a. There are no laws of the universe that say I shouldn't have pain or problems. I can experience any problem for which the necessary conditions exist.

   b. Life is not fair. Life is just a sequence of events, some of which bring pleasure and some of which are inconvenient and painful.

   c. If problems occur, it is up to me to solve them.

   d. Trying to keep a problem from developing is adaptive, but resenting and not facing it once it exists is a dangerous strategy.

   e. No one is special. Some go through life with relatively less pain than I do. This is due to one of two things: luck of the draw, or decisions I have made that contributed to the necessary conditions for my problems.

   f. Just because I have a problem doesn't mean I have to suffer. I can take pride in the challenge of a creative solution. This may be an opportunity to increase my self-esteem.

4. **Does any evidence exist for the truth of this idea?** No, my suffering is due to my self-talk, how I have interpreted this event. I have convinced myself that I should be unhappy.

5. **What is the worst thing that could happen to me** if what I want to happen doesn't, or what I don't want to happen does?

   a. I could be deprived of various pleasures while I deal with the problem.

   b. I might feel inconvenienced.

   c. I might never solve the problem and experience myself as ineffective in this particular area.

   d. I might have to accept the consequences of failure.

    e. Others might not approve of how I am behaving or I might be rejected as incompetent.

    f. I might feel more stress and tension.

6. What good things might occur if what I want to happen doesn't, or what I don't want to happen does?

    a. I might learn to tolerate frustration better.

    b. I might improve my coping skills.

    c. I might become more responsible.

E. Substitute alternative self-talk, now that you have clearly examined the irrational idea and compared it with rational thinking.

1. There's nothing special about me. I can accept painful situations when they emerge.

2. Facing the problem is more adaptive than resenting it or running away from it.

3. I feel what I think. If I don't think negative thoughts, I won't feel stressful emotions. At worst I will experience inconvenience, regret, and annoyance—not anxiety, depression, and rage.

Homework

To succeed in your war against irrational ideas, you need a daily commitment to homework. Use the homework sheet one page 123 as a model, and fill out one at least once a day, spending at least twenty minutes on it. When possible, do the homework right after the event has occurred. Use a separate sheet for each event, and save them as a record of your growth.

First read the example of a homework sheet on page 122, completed by a woman who had a date with a friend canceled:

Special Considerations

If you have difficulty making headway with rational emotive therapy, one of three factors may be at influence:

1. You remain unconvinced that thoughts cause emotions. If this is the case, confine your work initially to the technique outlined on page 124, under rational emotive imagery. If you then find that changes in your self-talk can push you toward less stressful emotions, the assumption that thoughts cause emotions may become more believable.

2. Your irrational ideas and self-talk are so lightning swift that you have difficulty catching them. If this is the case, try keeping a journal while you undergo intense emotions. Put down everything that flows through your mind: scenes, images, single words, vague half-formed thoughts, names, sounds, sentences, and so on.

3. You have difficulty remembering your thoughts. If this is the case, don't wait until after the fact. Use a journal to write everything down just as it is happening.

Homework Sheet

A. Activating event:

A friend canceled a date with me.

B. Rational ideas:

I know he's under a lot of time pressure right now . . . I'll do something by myself.

Irrational ideas:

I'll feel terribly alone tonight . . . The emptiness is setting in . . . He doesn't really care for me . . . No one really wants to spend time with me . . . I'm falling apart.

C. Consequences of the irrational ideas:

I was depressed . . . I was moderately anxious.

D. Disputing and challenging the irrational ideas:

1. Select the irrational idea:

I'll feel terribly alone tonight . . . I'm falling apart.

2. Is there any rational support for this idea?

No.

3. What evidence exists for the falseness of the idea?

Being alone is not as pleasurable as having a date, but I can find pleasure in an alternative activity.

I usually enjoy being alone, and I will tonight as soon as I face the disappointment.

I'm mislabelling frustration and disappointment as "falling apart."

4. Does any evidence exist for the truth of the idea?

No, only that I've talked myself into feeling depressed.

5. What is the worst thing that could happen to me?

I could continue to feel disappointed and not find anything really pleasurable to do tonight.

6. What good things might occur?

I might feel more self-reliant, and realize that I do have inner resources.

E. Alternative thoughts:

I'm OK. I'll get out my detective novel. I'll treat myself to a good Chinese dinner. I'm good at being alone.

Alternative emotions:

I feel quiet, a little disappointed, but I'm anticipating a good meal and a good book.

Homework Sheet

A. Activating event:

_____

_____

B. Rational ideas:

_____

_____

Irrational ideas:

_____

_____

C. Consequences of the irrational ideas:

_____

_____

D. Disputing and challenging the irrational ideas:
   1. Select the irrational idea:

   _____

   _____

   2. Is there any rational support for this idea?

   _____

   _____

   3. What evidence exists for the falseness of the idea?

   _____

   _____

   4. Does any evidence exist for the truth of the idea?

   _____

   _____

   5. What is the worst thing that could happen to me?

   _____

   _____

   6. What good things might occur?

   _____

   _____

E. Alternative thoughts:

_____

_____

Alternative emotions:

_____

_____

Rational Emotive Imagery

Dr. Maxie Maultsby (1971) introduced rational emotive imagery. This will help you develop strategies to change stressful emotions. The technique works as follows:

1. Imagine an event that is stressful and usually accompanied by unpleasant emotions. Notice all the details of the situation: sight, smell, sound, how you are dressed, what is being said.

2. As you clearly imagine the event, let yourself feel uncomfortable. Let in the emotions of anger, anxiety, depression, worthlessness, or shame. Don't try to avoid the emotion—go ahead and feel it.

3. After experiencing the stressful emotion, push yourself to change it. You can fundamentally alter this emotion so that anxiety, depression, rage, and guilt are replaced with keenly felt concern, disappointment, annoyance, or regret. If you think you can't do this, you are only fooling yourself. Everybody can push themselves to change a feeling, if only for a few moments.

4. Having contacted the stressful feeling and pushed it, however briefly, into a more appropriate emotion, you can examine how you did it. What happened inside your head that altered your original depression, anxiety, or rage? You told yourself something different about yourself, or others, or the situation.

5. Instead of saying, "I can't handle this . . . this will drive me crazy," you might now be saying, "I've dealt successfully with situations like this before." You have changed your beliefs, your interpretations of experience. Once you know how you changed the stressful emotion to a more appropriate one, you can substitute the new, adaptive beliefs any time you want. Become deeply aware of how the new beliefs lead you away from stress and produce more bearable emotions.

For example, rational emotive imagery was practiced by a housewife who became depressed whenever her husband turned on the television in the evening. During the day, she conjured up the situation in her imagination: her husband wiping his mouth, getting up from the table, taking the plates to the sink, and leaving the room. She could imagine a few moments later the sound of the television coming on, the changing of channels, voices from his favorite sitcom. As she went through the sequence, she sank into despondency.

After coming fully in contact with the stressful emotion, she pushed herself to change the feeling into one of disappointment and irritation. This felt like shoving a huge rock, and it took fifteen minutes of effort before she could get even momentary contact with the more appropriate emotions. Practicing at hourly intervals, she was soon able to push the depression into irritation or disappointment for several minutes.

She was ready to examine how she had changed her thoughts (self-talk) in order to change her emotions. She found she could change depression into irritation by saying, "I don't have to feel helpless. If he wants to spend his time with TV, I can do something that feels good to me." Other thoughts included: "It's his life. He can waste it if he wants to. I'm not going to waste mine. There are people that I don't visit because I think I should stay home with him. I'm going to take care of myself. He may be displeased if I don't stay home, but this is not fulfilling for me."

Developing Alternative Emotional Responses

Here is a list of sample situations and alternative emotional responses:

Situation	Stressful Emotion	Appropriate Emotion
Fight with mate	Rage	Annoyance, irritation
Failure to meet work deadline	Anxiety	Concern
Cruelty toward your child	Intense guilt	Regret
Something you enjoy very much is canceled	Depression	Disappointment
Criticized	Worthless	Annoyance, concern
A public mistake	Shame	Irritation

Now fill in your own stressful situations, including the stressful emotions you feel and the more appropriate emotions you would like to feel.

Situation	Stressful Emotion	Appropriate Emotion
_____	_____	_____
_____	_____	_____
_____	_____	_____
_____	_____	_____
_____	_____	_____
_____	_____	_____

You can use rational emotive imagery in each of these situations. If the stressful emotions do not change right away, let yourself keep feeling them until they do change. You *can* alter these emotions by merely pushing yourself to do so; this is certain. Afterward, you will isolate the key thoughts and phrases that made the new, more appropriate emotion possible. Changing your self-talk to include these more adaptive thoughts, beliefs, and ideas will make it increasingly easy for you to change the emotion you're working with. For best results, practice this technique ten minutes a day for at least two weeks.

Insight

Recognize that there are three levels of insight necessary to change:

1. Knowledge that you have a problem, and awareness of some of the events that may have caused the problem.

2. Seeing clearly that the irrational ideas you acquired early in life are creating the emotional climate you live in now, and that consciously or unconsciously you work fairly hard to perpetuate them.

3. The strong belief that after discovering these two insights, you will still find no way of eliminating the problem other than steadily, persistently, and vigorously working to change your irrational ideas.

Without a commitment to this last insight, you will experience difficulty altering your habitual emotional responses.

If you think this technique could be useful to you but you are unable to master it, contact a rational emotive therapist or center for consultation.

Further Reading

Beck, A. T. 1979. Cognitive therapy: Nature and relation to behavior therapy. In *Behavior Therapy*. New York: NAL/Dutton.

———. 1989. *Love Is Never Enough: How Couples Can Overcome Misunderstandings, Resolve Conflict, and Solve Relationship Problems with Cognitive Therapy*. New York: Harper-Collins.

Burns, D. D. 1990. *Feeling Good Handbook*. New York: NAL/Dutton.

Ellis, A. 1980. *Growth Through Reason*. Palo Alto, Calif.: Science and Behavior Books.

———. 1975. *A New Guide to Rational Living*. North Hollywood, Calif.: Wilshire Books.

———. 1986. *Anger: How to Live with and without It*. New York: Carol Publishing Group.

———. 1988. *Anger: How to Stubbornly Refuse to Make Yourself Miserable about Anything—Yes, Anything*. New York: Carol Publishing Group.

Farquhar, W., and J. Lowe. 1974. A list of irrational ideas. In *Youth Toward Personal Growth, a Rational Emotive Approach*, by D. J. Tosi. Columbus, Ohio: Charles E. Merrill.

Lazarus, A. A. 1996. *Behavior Therapy and Beyond* (Master Work Series). New York: Jason Aronson.

Maultsby, M. 1971. Rational emotive imagery. *Rational Living* 6:16–23.

Rimm, D. C., and S. B. Litvak. 1969. Self-verbalization and emotional arousal. *Journal of Abnormal Psychology* 74:181–7.

13

Thought Stopping

In this chapter you will learn to:

☐ Eliminate useless reoccurring distressing thoughts

Background

Thought stopping is a fun, quick, and easy-to-learn technique that can help you overcome everyday, nagging worry and doubt. It can also help you reduce phobic thoughts. There are two kinds of thought stopping. First, there is traditional thought stopping, which utilizes the imperative command "Stop!" to replace a negative thought. This form of thought stopping was first introduced by a man named Bain in 1928 in a little book called *Thought Control in Everyday Life*. In the late 1950s, it was adapted by Joseph Wolpe and other behavior therapists for the treatment of obsessive and phobic thoughts. There are three explanations for the success of this form of thought stopping: (1) The command "stop" serves as a punishment, and behavior that is consistently punished is likely to be inhibited. (2) The command "stop" acts as a distractor, and the imperative self-instruction is incompatible with obsessive and phobic thoughts. (3) Thought stopping is an assertive response and can be followed by thought substitutions of reassuring or self-accepting statements. For example, you say, "These big 747s are awfully safe," instead of, "Look at that wing shake, I bet it's ready to come off."

The second form of thought stopping was developed from the pioneering work of Francine Shapiro on Eye Movement Desensitization and Reprocessing (EMDR) and is called Eye Movement Technique (EMT). This method may interrupt negative thoughts by sequentially stimulating opposite sides of the brain. Shapiro discovered that when a person moves their eyes rapidly back and forth while vividly imagining a stress-inducing event, painful patterns of thinking can be broken and associated distress relieved.

Not all worry is bad. Worry can motivate you to be well prepared for an upcoming presentation or test, and it can spur you to work hard to meet a deadline or solve a problem. But worry is a real nuisance when it is unrealistic, distressing, unproductive, and repetitive. Worries often have a flavor of self-doubt, such as, "Did I lock the front door or not?" or "If my house is not perfectly clean and neat, people will think I'm a lazy slob," or "I'm just too plain to date." A useless worry tends to be a pessimistic forecast of the future that crowds out more likely, sunnier outcomes: "I don't care what the doctors say. I think this pain in my stomach is cancer," or "If they raise my rent, I'll have to move," or "I will never be able to do this job right," or "John's late ... I wonder if he's had an accident and is lying bleeding to death in the gutter." Either form of thought stopping can help with these types of distressing, improbable worries.

Phobias are irrational fears about specific objects or situations that you find so frightening that you want to avoid them if at all possible, or you endure them with considerable distress. Phobic thoughts are also anxiety producing: "I couldn't stand it if I got trapped in an elevator," or "What if they think I'm stupid or boring? I can't go to the party." The frequency of phobic thouts such as these can be reduced with thought stopping techniques.

It has been well documented that negative and frightening thoughts invariably precede negative and frightening emotions. If the thoughts can be controlled, overall stress levels can be significantly reduced.

Symptom Effectiveness

Thought stopping has proved effective with a wide variety of obsessive and phobic thought processes: color naming, sexual preoccupation, hypochondriasis, obsessive thoughts of failure, sexual inadequacy, obsessive memories, and frightening reoccurring impulses leading to chronic tension and anxiety attacks. While thought stopping is only effective in approximately 20 percent of cases involving compulsive ritual behavior, it is more than 70 percent effective at reducing anxiety associated with phobias such as fear of snakes, driving, the dark, elevators, someone lurking in the house at night, fear of insanity, and so on. Thought stopping is recommended when the problem behavior is primarily cognitive, rather than acted out, and when specific thoughts or images are repeatedly experienced as painful or leading to unpleasant emotional states.

Eye movement technique has proven very effective and simple to learn when used in conjunction with other anxiety-reducing techniques, such as exposure therapy and progressive or cue-controlled relaxation exercises. Using EMT as an auxiliary tool of stress reduction, approximately two out of three people are successful in blocking negative thoughts and lowering their anxiety and stress levels (Smyth 1996).

Time to Master

For effective mastery, thought stopping must be practiced conscientiously throughout the day for three days to one week.

Thought Stopping Instructions

Step 1. List Your Stressful Thoughts

On a blank piece of paper, write down several distressing, irrational, useless thoughts that have become habits and are hard to stop.

Ask yourself these questions about each of the stressful thoughts you have written down: Is the thought unrealistic? Is the thought counterproductive? Is the thought self-defeating? Is the thought hard to control? Does it interfere with my concentration and what I really want to be doing? Does it cause me a lot of discomfort? Would I be a happier, more relaxed person without this thought? If you answered Yes to all these questions for one of your distressing thoughts, thought stopping is likely to be a powerful technique for you.

Thought stopping requires consistent motivation. Decide now if you really want to eliminate this stressful thought over the next week. Do not work on more than one stressful thought at a time.

Step 2. Imagine the Thought

Close your eyes and bring into imagination a situation in which the stressful thought is likely to occur. Try to include normal as well as obsessive thinking. In this way, you can interrupt the stressful thoughts while allowing a continuing flow of healthy thinking.

Step 3. Thought Interruption

Thought interruption can be accomplished initially by using one of two "startler" techniques:

Set a stopwatch, egg timer, or alarm clock for three minutes. Look away, close your eyes, and ruminate on your stressful thought as described above in step 2. When you hear the ring, shout "Stop!" You may also want to snap a rubber band you can wear loosely around your wrist, pinch yourself, or snap your fingers. Let your mind empty of all but the neutral and nonanxious thoughts. Set a goal of about thirty seconds after the stop, during which your mind remains blank. If the upsetting thought returns during that time, shout "Stop!" again.

Tape-record yourself loudly exclaiming "Stop!" at intermittent intervals (for example, three minutes, two minutes, three minutes, and one minute). You may find it useful to repeat the taped stop messages several times at five-second intervals. Proceed the same way as with the stopwatch, egg timer, or alarm clock. The tape recording shapes and strengthens your thought control.

Step 4. Unaided Thought Interruption

Now take control of the thought stopping cue without the timer or tape recorder. While ruminating on the unwanted thought, shout "Stop!" and snap your rubber band or pinch yourself.

When you succeed in extinguishing the thought on several occasions with the shouted command, begin interrupting the thought with a "Stop!" in a normal voice.

After succeeding in stopping the thought by using your normal speaking voice, start interrupting the thought with "Stop!" verbalized in a whisper.

When the whisper is sufficient to interrupt stressful thoughts, use a subvocal command. Imagine hearing "Stop!" shouted inside your mind. Tighten your vocal chords and move your tongue as if you were saying "Stop!" out loud. Success at this stage means that you can stop thoughts alone or in public without making a sound or calling attention to yourself.

Step 5. Thought Substitution

The last phase of thought stopping involves thought substitution. In place of the obsessive thought, make up some positive, assertive statements and/or images that are appropriate in the target situation. For example, if you are afraid of flying, you might say to yourself, "Flying commercial airlines is the safest mode of transportation. I can lean back and relax." Develop several alternative assertive statements to say to yourself, because the same response may lose its power through repetition. Imagine arriving at your destination and having a perfect vacation or productive business meeting.

Example of Successful Thought Stopping

A business executive who did a great deal of traveling developed a fear of sleeping in strange places. He was aware that his obsessive worrying about having to take overnight trips had begun about the time of his divorce. When preparing for bed in the motel, he would think about people entering the room by passkey while he slept. While planning his next business trip at home, he would become very tense anticipating the anxiety he would feel in the strange motel.

Utilizing thought-stopping techniques, he allowed himself to visualize unpacking in a strange motel, thinking about plans for the next day, and anticipating going to bed. He imagined lying in darkness with the feeling that the door might be swinging slightly ajar. In the middle of these thoughts the egg timer went off, so he shouted "Stop!" and simultaneously snapped his fingers. If the thought recurred before thirty seconds were up, he shouted "Stop!" again.

After succeeding with the shout, he began saying "Stop!" in a normal voice, and then a whisper. Finally, he was able to shout "Stop!" silently inside his head. He noted that he had repeated each phrase five or ten times before feeling that he could go on to the next one. After interrupting his fear thought with "Stop," he used a thought substitution: "I am and will be perfectly safe." During the next three days, he shouted "Stop!" subaudibly at the very beginning of each phobic thought. Occasionally he reinforced the command by snapping a rubber band that he kept around his wrist. The thoughts decreased in frequency and only lasted a few moments when they occurred. He succeeded in markedly decreasing stress on his next trip. He took his tape recorder and set it to say "Stop!" at intervals of five, ten, three, and eight minutes during the time he was preparing for bed. By the end of the trip, he was aware that he wasn't thinking about the terrors of sleeping in strange places, but was much more focused on the challenges of his business.

Special Considerations

1. Some people respond best to a visual image combined with the stop command. You may want to try visualizing a stop sign, or you can try visualizing your stressful cognition being blown up as you say "Stop!"

2. Failure with your first attempt at thought stopping may mean that you have selected a thought that is very difficult to extinguish. In this situation, select an unwanted thought that is either less intrusive or less frightening than your initial choice. Becoming proficient at the technique before tackling more stressful obsessive or phobic thoughts is helpful.

3. If the subvocalized "Stop!" is not successful for you and you find it embarrassing to say "Stop!" aloud in public, simply snap your rubber band or pinch yourself when unwanted thoughts occur. Or you might try pressing your fingernails into the palms of your hands to stop unwanted thoughts.

4. Stopping a thought takes time. The thought will return and you will have to interrupt it again. The main effort is to stifle each thought just as it begins and to concentrate on something else. The thoughts will return less and less readily in most cases, and will eventually cease to be a problem.

5. See chapter 10, Brief Combination Techniques, for two variations on thought stopping: Stop and Breathe, and Changing Channels.

6. Another variation on thought stopping involves dropping the last word of the sentence you are attempting to eliminate and replacing it with the word "Stop!" Keep repeating the sentence, replacing the last word of it with "Stop!" until the only word is "Stop!" (For example, "I'm going to fail" becomes "I'm going to stop," which becomes "I'm going stop," which becomes "I'm stop," which becomes "Stop!")

7. See the chapter called Refuting Irrational Ideas for tools to help you decide if your distressing thoughts are irrational.

8. See the chapter called Worry Control for additional powerful techniques to manage your worry.

Eye Movement Technique Instructions

Eye movement technique is an especially useful thought-stopping tool that can help you manage or control anxiety that is caused by recent or past events. Once you are familiar with EMT, you can successfully use it for all types of stress—from chronic anxiety to event-specific fears. The technique is simple and can be inconspicuous, allowing you to use it even when you're in a crowded room. An example of how one individual utilized and benefited from using this technique follows the five steps of EMT below.

Step 1: Identify a Stressful Thought

Focus on a recurring thought, image, or memory that distresses you.

Step 2: Rate Your Stress Level

On a scale of 0 to 10, with 0 indicating complete relaxation and 10 implying extreme distress or terror, rate your level of stress while focusing on the stressful thought. For EMT to be most effective, your stress level should be rated around a 5 or 6, but not higher. A rating of 5 to 6 implies you are experiencing a moderate level of stress that causes unpleasant discomfort, but doesn't cause any major heart-palpitating fear.

If your initial rating is higher than a 6, try reducing your stress level before beginning EMT. To do this, engage in one of the relaxation exercises you learned in chapter 7 until your stress level is between 5 and 6.

If your initial rating is less than 5, focus intently on the stressful event and vividly add or imagine specific details and circumstances, until you reach a stress level of 5 or 6. You can raise your anxiety level by thinking about the "what ifs" or "oh, nos!" associated with the stressful event. Again, don't allow your reaction to raise beyond a 6 rating.

Step 3: Rapid Eye Movement

Once your stress level is between 5 and 6, keep your head still and rapidly move your eyes back and forth between two predetermined points twenty to twenty-five times. You can rapidly move your eyes between two corners of a room or window, between one hand resting on each of your knees, or between two sides of a table. As soon as you start moving your eyes, stop concentrating on the stressful event and let your mind go.

There may be situations in which moving your eyes rapidly back and forth is too conspicuous or uncomfortable to do in public situations. Although it may be a little more difficult to do, EMT is also effective if you move your eyes from side to side when your eyelids are closed. In this way, any observer may believe your eyes are closed simply because you are in deep thought or resting.

Step 4: Rerate Your Stress Level

As soon as you've finished rapid eye movement, rerate your stress level between 0 and 10. EMT commonly will block—or significantly diminish—your ability to focus a thought or image. Your rating should diminish to 4 or less. Additional sessions of EMT will reduce it further.

Step 5: Repeated Exposure

Repeat steps 1 through 4 whenever the stressful thought recurs. Each time you use EMT, its thought-stopping effect tends to get more powerful. Whenever a target unwanted thought returns, zap it again with EMT. In the beginning, you might have to do this at ten-minute intervals, but soon you'll likely get much longer periods of relief. So don't hesitate to use EMT multiple times, because it can only get more effective. For decidedly stressful thoughts and situations, you may want to commit to doing an EMT session as needed throughout the day for one week. After reassessing your progress, you can renew your commitment for another week, and so on. When you are familiar with the process, you can use EMT to reduce your anxiety in the moment (or as close to the moment as possible) that a stressful thought, image, or memory is taking place. As you repeatedly engage in EMT, your overall level of anxiety should generally decrease.

Example

Trent was the director of a downtown office complex. He enjoyed his job tremendously and felt especially good about his relationships with the people who rented office space in his building. One night, as Trent was leaving the offices very late, he was held up at gunpoint, physically assaulted, and robbed of his wallet, keys, and car.

Fortunately, Trent only suffered minor physical injuries from which he rapidly recovered. More difficult to heal, however, was the stress and fear Trent carried with him for months after the event. Thoughts and flashbacks of the experience continually interrupted his day. And, although he still appreciated his relationships with his tenants, Trent's stress level and fear made him uneasy and suspicious of most people.

To manage his stress, Trent was working with a psychologist and was regularly engaging in relaxation exercises. Once a day, usually after work, he turned on the answering machine and did progressive muscle relaxation; four to five times a day he did cue-controlled exercises (see chapter 7).

After a few months, Trent felt better. He was still unhappy, however, with unbidden thoughts and images about the assault. Although Trent was skeptical, he decided to try EMT. His first step was to imagine the robbery. He pictured himself walking toward his car and seeing the man who assaulted him standing by the trash dumpsters. Trent felt his fears begin to escalate, so he didn't push himself to imagine the scene any further. He rated his anxiety on a scale of 0 to 10, and determined it was about 6.

Sitting comfortably on a chair, Trent placed a hand on each of his knees. He let go of the robbery images as he smoothly moved his eyes laterally back and forth twenty-five times between his two knees. When he completed the rapid eye movement, he took a deep breath and rerated his anxiety. To his surprise, he rated it between 3 and 4.

Interestingly, Trent found that he was unable to evoke really clear images of the robbery right after the EMT. With a reduced stress rating, Trent was hopeful. Within ten minutes, he did two more EMT sessions. At the end of the last session, Trent's stress rating was down to 1, and the robbery image seemed vague and far away.

Further Reading

Nelson, J. 1988. *Understanding*. Rocklin, Calif.: Prima Publishing.

Smyth, L. 1996. *Treating Anxiety Disorders with a Cognitive-behavioral Exposure Based Approach and the Eye-movement Technique: The Manual*. Baltimore: Red Toad Company.

Wolpe, J. 1992. *The Practice of Behavior Therapy*. Needham Heights, Mass.: Allyn & Bacon.

Worry Control

In this chapter you will learn to:

☐   Accurately evaluate your worries

☐   Use worry exposure to overcome your worst fears

☐   Identify and change behavior that contributes to worry

Background

Worrying is a natural response to many life circumstances. Whether you're worried about your child's safety or you're concerned that you'll be passed up for a promotion, everybody has similar worries from time to time. However, if your worries become all consuming and you find yourself making choices and decisions based on fears rather than on logic or reason, your relationship with worry may be problematic.

You have a serious problem with worry if you:

- are chronically anxious about future dangers or threats,

- consistently make negative predictions about the future,

- often overestimate the probability or seriousness of bad things happening,

- can't stop repeating the same worries over and over,

- escape worry by distracting yourself or avoiding certain situations, and/or

- find it difficult to use worry constructively to produce solutions to problems.

(McKay, Davis, and Fanning 1997)

Symptom Effectiveness

The techniques offered in this chapter have been found to be effective in reducing the excessive worry that is the chief feature of generalized anxiety disorder (O'Leary, Brown, and Barlow 1992). Worry-behavior prevention has also been found to be helpful in curbing ritual, preventive, and checking behaviors that tend to perpetuate worry.

Time to Master

You should feel, within one to two weeks, stress-reduction benefits from deep breathing, progressive muscle relaxation, and cue-controlled relaxation exercises (see chapters 2, 3, and 7, respectively). During this time, you can begin learning to accurately assess your risks, schedule and honor worry appointments, engage in worry exposure, and learn to reduce worry behavior. Although you will experience some benefits from all of these techniques almost immediately, you will begin to feel positive long-term results within ten to twelve weeks (White 1999).

Instructions

Distinguishing Healthy versus Unhealthy Worry

Contrary to what many believe, not all worry is negative. In fact, some types of worry are healthy. The determining factor for healthy versus unhealthy worry is whether your main focus is on catastrophic thinking or problem solving. Unhealthy worry leads you to continually examine an endless list of all the potentially negative (that is, catastrophic) "what if" outcomes of a situation.

Healthy worry, on the other hand, is focused on effective problem solving. You brainstorm alternative solutions, evaluate possible outcomes, make a decision, develop action steps, and form a timetable. Any thought about possible problems, pain, or catastrophe is merely a signal to start the search for a solution.

Following are two examples to strengthen the distinction between healthy and unhealthy worry. Remember, the main difference is whether the worrier is engaged in catastrophic "what if"-type thinking or future-oriented problem solving.

1. *Tamara hopes to be promoted to vice president of a magazine's creative-content department. This position would allow her to utilize the knowledge she acquired while earning her master's degree in communication and the skills she has learned from being a freelance writer and editor for more than fifteen years. Her interview is scheduled for next Wednesday. Tamara worries that she will not be promoted, even though she believes she is the best candidate for the position. Her main concern is that she won't be articulate during the interview. She finds herself continually asking: What if my mind goes blank? What if I'm freaked out and can't articulate strong answers to their questions? What if I get defensive? What if my daughter becomes ill and it's impossible to find daycare so that I can attend the interview? What if I forget my portfolio of writing samples? Oh no!*

This is a clear example of unhealthy worry. Although Tamara is highly qualified for the job, her main concerns focus is low-probability "what ifs." Tamara isn't using her worries to better prepare for the interview. There's no planning or problem solving—just catastrophizing.

2. Weather permitting, Tyler's son, Justin, is going to experience his first unassisted skydive two weeks from Thursday. So far, Justin has only skydived tandem with an instructor. For his first solo attempt, he would like his father to come watch as he jumps from a plane that is thousands of feet in the air. Secretly hoping that the weather will be bad and the jump canceled, Tyler agrees to support his son. In the meantime, he worries that he will be unprepared for an emergency if it should arise. As a result, he makes a note to be sure his cellular phone battery is charged, just in case he needs it. Also, Tyler is concerned with how he will pass the time waiting for his son without becoming a nervous wreck. Before he forgets about this worry, he places a couple of magazines and a pair of binoculars in the trunk of his car—one will be a distraction and the other will help him look for his son in the sky. Who knows, he thinks, maybe I'll do some bird-watching while I'm at it—and he adds a bird book to the pile of stashed magazines in the trunk.

This is an example of healthy worry. Although Tyler has a deep desire to be a supportive father, he cannot deny that he is worried about his son's safety. His worry, however, is healthy, as it helps him to create solutions that better prepare him to cope and distract himself.

Worry into Problem Solving

Here is a step-by-step plan for turning worry into problem solving, adapted from the *Worry Control Workbook*, by Mary Ellen Copeland (1998). Each step is followed by an example of how a young entrepreneur used the problem-solving process to deal with worries about starting her business.

1. Write down one situation that is really worrying you. *I really want to start a business of my own, but my financial resources are very limited. I'm worried that I don't know enough to avoid the pitfalls and I'll end up losing everything.*

2. Brainstorm for solutions. Make a list of possible things you can do to improve or correct the situation.

- *Talk to other entrepreneurs about their experiences in starting their businesses.*

- *Research organizations that support entrepreneurial efforts and people.*

- *Research the possibility of acquiring a small-business loan or other capital available for small start-up businesses.*

- *Join a couple of small business and entrepreneurial organizations.*

- *Find investors among friends and family.*

- *Start the business out of my home to save overhead and protect me financially*

- *Work an extra job for a couple of years to earn more money.*

- *Stay at current place of employment while starting my own company part-time.*

3. Evaluate each idea. Which ones are not possible? Put an X next to those. Which ones would be difficult to implement? Put a question mark next to those. Which ones could you do right now? Put a Y next to those.

Y Talk to other entrepreneurs about their experiences in starting their businesses.

Y Research organizations that support entrepreneurial efforts and people.

Y Research the possibility of acquiring a small-business loan or other capital available for small start-up businesses.

? Join a couple of small business and entrepreneurial organizations.

Y Find investors among family and friends.

? Start the business out of my own home to save overhead.

X Work an extra job for a couple of years to earn more money.

X Stay at current place of employment while starting the company part-time.

4. Set specific dates. Make a contract with yourself to do all the *Y* things.

By April 1, I will talk to other entrepreneurs about their experiences in starting their businesses.
By April 15, I will research organizations that support entrepreneurial efforts and people.
By May 1, I'll have canvassed family and friends for possible investors.
By May 15, I will research the possibility of acquiring a small-business loan or other capital available for small start-up businesses.

5. When you have completed the *Y* things, go on to the more difficult *?* things. Make a contract with yourself to do those.

By June 15, I will join a couple of small business and entrepreneurial organizations.
By July 1, I'll decide whether I should clear out a back bedroom to create a home-based business office.
By July 15, I will apply for all available capital that I find during my initial research.

6. Now maybe some of the *X* things don't look so hard. If there are any you think you could manage, make a contract with yourself to take that action.

By August 15, if other options have not worked out, I will start my company part-time while working full-time at my current place of employment.

Problem-Solving Worksheet

Use this space to apply the problem-solving technique for one of your worries.

1. Write down one situation that is really worrying you.

_____

_____

_____

_____

2. Brainstorm for solutions. Make a list of possible things you can do to improve or correct the situation.

_____

_____

_____

_____

_____

_____

3. Evaluate each idea. Which ones are not possible? Put an *X* next to those. Which ones would be difficult to implement? Put a question mark next to those. Which ones could you do right now? Put a *Y* next to those.

4. Set specific dates. Make a contract with yourself to do all the *Y* things.

   By _____ (date), I will _____

   By _____, I will _____

   By _____, I will _____

   By _____, I will _____

5. When you have completed the *Y* things go on to the more difficult *?* things. Make a contract with yourself to do those.

   By _____ (date), I will _____

   By _____, I will _____

   By _____, I will _____

   By _____, I will _____

6. Now maybe some of the *X* things don't look so hard. If there are any you think you could manage, make a contract with yourself to take that action.

   By _____ (date), I will _____

   By _____, I will _____

   By _____, I will _____

   By _____, I will _____

Four Steps to Managing Your Worry

The first step to managing worry is to deal with your physical stress level by practicing and utilizing the relaxation skills you have been learning in this book. Next, you'll address your worry-based thoughts by learning to assess risk, limit your worry time, and engage in worry exposure. Lastly, you'll manage your behavioral reactions by learning worry-behavior prevention. These steps are based on the effective worry-control process presented in the book *Overcoming Generalized Anxiety Disorder* (White 1999).

Step 1. Relaxation

By practicing relaxation daily, you can significantly affect or eliminate the fight or flight reactions that worry causes. Your first task in managing worry is to master the progressive muscle relaxation and cue-controlled relaxation exercises found in chapter 7,

Applied Relaxation Training. If you have not already read chapter 7, you should do that now.

Choose a specific time once a day to do the full progressive muscle relaxation procedure. Regardless of what else is going on in your schedule, you should do this relaxation exercise every day for the same amount of time. Do not skip or shorten your relaxation exercises. Experiencing a level of deep relaxation once a day is an important component of managing worry. If you skip your exercises one day, the benefits cannot be postponed or "made up" the next.

Next, commit to doing quick cue-controlled relaxation five times a day, at more or less regular intervals. This exercise is brief, and you can do it anywhere. Frequent relaxing moments will keep your overall level of physical stress under control.

Step 2. Risk Assessment

If you worry excessively, you most likely don't have the skills to appropriately assess risk. Some people worry excessively every time they plan to fly on an airplane or each time they drive their car on a highway. Others worry beyond reason about suddenly losing their job, even when there is no external circumstance that would warrant their unemployment.

The problem with overestimating risk is that it subtly increases your worry until it becomes a bigger problem than the dangers you worry about. Learning accurate risk-assessment skills can make a huge difference in your overall anxiety level.

Predicting Outcomes

Most chronic worriers focus their attention on catastrophic outcomes. Regardless of whether the event you're worrying about occurs, your fear is primarily based on the worst possible consequence. For instance, a woman who constantly worried about being abandoned thought her life had been destroyed when her husband told her he was leaving their marriage. But instead of being lonely and sad and single for the rest of her life, she became very social, physically active, and even fell in love with a more suitable partner—all before her divorce was final. Obviously, the catastrophic outcome she'd expected never came to be.

When you worry, you tend to forget that your capacity to cope with even the most serious disaster is quite remarkable. People survive—and sometimes even benefit from—situations that they originally perceive as catastrophic. In most instances, you, your friends, and your family will find a way to cope with whatever happens.

You can use the Risk Assessment form below to lower your anxiety by estimating accurate probabilities and making coping plans for catastrophe. On the first line, record one of your worries in the form of a feared event. Write down the worst possible version of your worry. For example, if you worry about your spouse, who is a traveling salesperson, imagine the worst: a disastrous plane crash over the Pacific Ocean, months of investigation that lead to no evidence, and none of the bodies ever being recovered. You never see your spouse again, and you end up in financial despair.

On the second line, write the worry thoughts that typically come up: "He'll die . . . the family will never be able to make it . . . I'll never sleep again . . . horrible . . . a nightmare beyond nightmares . . . " Jot down whatever comes to mind, even it is just an image or a fleeting word.

Next, rate your anxiety when considering this worst-case scenario. Use 0 for no anxiety and 100 for the worst fear you have ever experienced. Then rate the probability of this worst-case scenario coming to pass—from 0 percent for no likelihood at all to 100 percent for absolute inevitability.

The next four questions focus on catastrophic thinking. Assuming your biggest fear actually occurred, predict all the worst possible consequences. Then try to think of specific coping thoughts and actions that might help you manage in the face of the catastrophe. Once you have some ideas of how you would cope, go ahead and create a revised prediction of the consequences. Some things would now look a little less daunting because you have a coping plan. You'll recreate your anxiety after this process to see if there's been any change.

The next two questions address the issue of overestimation. List the evidence against the worst outcome happening. Figure the odds as realistically as you can. Then list all the alternative outcomes you can think of. Finally, rerate your anxiety and the probability of the event. You should find that both your anxiety and probability ratings have declined as a result of your making a full and objective risk assessment.

Here is an example of a filled-out Risk Assessment form from Paul, who is afraid of failure in general, and specifically worried about his entrance exam to law school.

Feared event: *Performing poorly on my law school entrance exams (LSAT).*

Automatic thoughts: *I'll score extremely low. My mind will freeze and I won't know any of the answers.*

Rate anxiety from 0 to 100: *95*

Rate probability of event from 0 to 100 percent: *90*

Assuming the worst happens:

Predict the worst possible consequences: *I'll score so low that I won't get into any law school. All my undergraduate work will be useless. I'll end up working at a job I detest.*

Possible coping thoughts: *If I don't do well the first time, I can take it again and learn from the experience. There are other appealing careers besides law, for example, I'm still very interested in publishing.*

Possible coping actions: *Study regularly. Take a class that will help me prepare for the exams. If I need to take the LSAT again, maybe I could find a study partner who is planning to take the entrance exams at the same time I am.*

Revised predictions of consequences: *I won't completely fail. If I do poorly the first time, I'll use that information to help me better prepare for the next opportunity to take the exams. Also, I really could consider an alternative career.*

Rerate anxiety from 0 to 100: *70*

Evidence against the worst possible outcome: *I am studying diligently and I typically receive higher-than-average scores on exams. I scored in the eighty-fifth percentile on my SATs.*

Alternative outcomes: *I may do just fine. I may do better than I expect. I may not do as well as I need to get into my first-choice law school, but my second choice is also a reputable institution. I may need to take it again and make a bigger commitment to preparation. In each case, I'd end up being a lawyer.*

Rerate anxiety from 0 to 100: *45*

Rerate probability of event from 0 to 100 percent: *35*

Fill out the Risk Assessment form each time you are confronted by a significant worry, or whenever you return to a worry more than once. It's important to do this exercise consistently. Each risk assessment helps you change old habits of catastrophic thinking. When you've completed a risk assessment, keep the form. You may wish to refer to it again when confronting a similar worry.

Risk Assessment Form

Feared event

_____

_____

_____

_____

Automatic thoughts

_____

_____

_____

_____

Rate anxiety from 0 to 100 _____

Rate probability of event from 0 to 100 percent _____

Assuming the worst happens:

Predict the worst possible consequences

_____

_____

_____

_____

Possible coping thoughts

_____

_____

_____

_____

Predict coping actions

_____

_____

_____

_____

Revised predictions of consequences

_____

_____

_____

_____

Rerate anxiety from 0 to 100_____

Evidence against the worst possible outcome

_____

_____

_____

_____

Alternative outcomes

_____

_____

_____

_____

Rerate anxiety from 0 to 100 _____

Rerate probability of event from 0 to 100 percent _____

Step 3. Scheduling Worry Time and Worry Exposure

Two important tools that will turn your tendency to worry into beneficial attributes are scheduling worry time and worry exposure. As previously discussed, worrying is not necessarily unhealthy. When used appropriately, worry often produces beneficial outcomes, such as increased productivity, efficient preparation for future events, and more. You'll find respite from your tendency to worry excessively once you learn to limit and focus the amount of time you worry and the topics you choose to worry about.

Scheduling Worry Time

By learning to worry only at specific times, you can limit the impact of worry on your life. Toward this end, set aside thirty minutes each day in which you will do nothing but worry. Be sure to actually schedule this thirty-minute "worry appointment" on your daily calendar to assure yourself the space and time to worry. Once your appointment is scheduled, your commitment should be to worry *only* during your scheduled time. If you find yourself starting to worry at times other than your official worry appointment, remind yourself that you have an appointment to worry later in the day and let go of the subject. It's not always easy, but it usually helps reduce some of your anxiety. If it helps, you can make notes about what you are worried about and then refer to these notes during your allotted worry time. Be very rigid about the amount of time you've scheduled: Do not worry for more (or less!) than thirty minutes a day.

Worry Exposure

You can, when you are ready, use your scheduled worry time to practice worry exposure. This is a technique that helps you concentrate on and extinguish your worries—first minor worries and then, increasingly, more distressing ones. During worry exposure, you flood your mind with fearful images of all the worst possible outcomes in a situation. By imagining the catastrophic details of your worries again and again, even your most upsetting thoughts eventually become overly familiar and boring, making them easier to deal with and less upsetting.

Worry exposure is effective because it focuses your worrying. When you simply worry on your own at random times throughout the day, you gain none of the benefits of structured worry because you don't spend enough time dwelling exclusively on the worst possible outcomes. Instead, you distract yourself or try, in some other fashion, to escape from your worrisome thoughts. The result: the worry isn't concentrated enough to become dull and boring.

Worry exposure consists of eight simple steps:

1. List Your Worries. Write a list of things you worry about. Include worries about success and failure, relationships, performance anxiety, physical danger, career, health, rejections, shame, and so on.

2. Rank Your Worries. Put your worries in order from the least to the most anxiety provoking. Here is a sample list of Trish's worries.

- Being seen as cold and aloof by the support staff at work.

- Our credit-card debt.

- My son's lack of interest and attention to his studies.

- My high cholesterol readings.

- Fear that I won't be able to lure new business clients.

- My husband's health problems.

- Breaking down on the freeway and being mugged while waiting for help.

3. Relax. You will begin by working with the first worry on your list. Get into a comfortable position, breathe deeply, and begin cue-controlled relaxation. Close your eyes and let the tension drain from your body.

4. Visualize a Worry. Vividly imagine the item from your list of worries. Picture in your mind the worst-case scenario again and again. Focus on the worst possible outcome and concentrate on the sights, sounds, smells, and the sensations as if they were really happening. Be sure to imagine that you are actively participating in the horrific event.

Do not allow your mind to wander away from the worrisome event for a full twenty-five minutes. You may want to set a timer to keep track of the minutes. Do not stop focusing on the scene early—even if you're bored or your anxiety is high.

Here's an example of Trish doing worry exposure on her second worry item, credit-card debt. She imagined huge sums owed on the monthly statements. She imagined opening them one after another. So many bills. Huge interest rates. No way to pay them off. She imagined nasty collection letters, notices canceling her cards. She saw herself in stores and restaurants with no way to make a purchase . . . the filing for bankruptcy . . . the humiliation as people found out. They wouldn't be able to move or buy a house for seven years. Stuck. Helpless. And then she'd have to forget the holidays—no money for gifts. And forget vacations, too.

When Trish reached the end of her worst imaginings, she just started over. She kept the images coming for the full twenty-five minutes, going over and over them and adding details. She resisted imagining any alternative scenarios until the twenty-five minutes were up.

If you find that your anxiety level is much lower than you believe you would normally experience in the actual situation, you may be having difficulty creating vivid images. Some people are better with sounds, textures, or smells. For example, Rich didn't feel very anxious using visual images of his welding equipment catching fire and burning down his home. But, when he switched to other senses and imagined the smell of burning wood, the crackle of breaking equipment, and screeching fire-engine sirens, his anxiety skyrocketed to a rating of 95 out of 100.

5. Rate Your Peak Anxiety from 0 to 100. As you are engaged in visualizing your worry, rate your highest anxiety level. You may want to jot down numbers throughout your twenty-five-minute session. You can do this without opening your eyes. Use a rating of 0 for no anxiety and a rating of 100 for the worst you've experienced.

At first Rich rated his anxiety at 60. Ten minutes later, however, his imagination made him extremely anxious, and he raised the rating to 95.

6. Imagine Alternative Outcomes. After a full twenty-five minutes of imagining the worst possible situation, allow yourself to visualize alternative, less stressful outcomes. Don't start early. Spend just five minutes imagining an outcome that is not as bad as your worst scenario. For example, after a full twenty-five minutes of anxiety, Trish imagined that she cut up a few of her cards and consolidated the debt with a lower interest home-owner's loan.

7. Rerate Anxiety from 0 to 100. After spending five minutes focusing on alternative outcomes, rerate your anxiety. It will probably be lower. Rich's final rating was 30.

8. Repeat. Repeat steps 3 through 7 with the same worry until your peak anxiety is 25 or less. Then do the procedure with the next item on your worry list. Complete at least one session a day. If you have the time and can tolerate it, you can do several sessions a day. By the time you have worked through your entire list, you should find your general worry level to be significantly reduced.

Trish needed a little more than a month to complete her entire worry list, averaging one and a half sessions a day. During that period, she worried a lot less. Whenever she started to worry, she told herself that she could postpone the worry until her next scheduled worry appointment. Even after she stopped doing regular worry exposure, Trish found that her fear of making mistakes and forgetting things was significantly reduced. When she would start to worry, she would remember her exposure sessions and think, "I've worried about this enough already." She usually was able to stop worrying soon or at least switch to a more balanced assessment of alternative outcomes.

Step 4. Worry-Behavior Prevention

You may notice that you have certain habits or rituals based on your worries. Worry behavior most often involves checking (to see if something bad has happened), avoidance (to stay away from something that makes you nervous), or utilizing "lucky charms." For instance, Ann is always worried that a phone call is going to bring bad news. Before answering the phone, she always takes a moment, looks at the ceiling, and says out loud, "Master of the Universe, we all deserve love and peace." Harold, on the other hand, has been concerned ever since his wife died about a break-in during the night. Before going to bed, he spends nearly an hour testing and retesting the locks, then watching the street for suspicious strangers.

Although these types of behaviors can seem as if they are helpful, they actually do not serve much purpose beyond perpetuating your worry. They hold absolutely no power in preventing bad things from happening. In fact, most often, worry-induced behaviors and rituals significantly reinforce your worry rather than prevent bad things from occurring.

You can prevent worry behavior by following these five steps:

1. Record Your Worry Behavior. Write down the activities you do to prevent the things you worry about from happening. For example, Eric was constantly worried that he would be perceived as inadequate and a slacker. He identified three worry behaviors:

- Arriving at work at least an hour earlier than expected.

- Producing numerous reports and paper trails to document the progress of work projects.

- Always volunteering for committees and projects, even when his available time is limited.

Your key worry behaviors:

_____

_____

2. Pick the Easiest Behavior to Stop and Predict Consequences of Stopping It. Choose the worry behavior that would be easiest to stop and write it here. Then write down the predicted consequences. Eric picked arriving at work an hour earlier than expected. He predicted, "I will not be as productive and, therefore, will not be able to meet the department's timelines and will be labeled a 'slacker.'"

Behavior   Consequence

_____   _____

_____   _____

_____   _____

3. Stop the Easiest Behavior and/or Replace It with a New Behavior. This step is the most difficult. To learn if your prediction/worry will come true, you have to experiment. The next time you start worrying, commit to refraining from your chosen behavior. For example, Eric decided that for the entire length of his next assignment, he would not arrive at work before at least one other person was in the office. He resolved to sit in his car and read the newspaper if he had to, but he was not going to be the first to arrive. As he got further into his project, Eric felt an urgency to get to work earlier and earlier, but he resisted the temptation. Instead, he tried to schedule his time in the office as efficiently as possible.

Sometimes even the "easiest" behavior is not so easy to stop doing. In this case, you need to create a hierarchy of replacement behaviors that allows you to taper off from your worry behavior. For example, Lee's eighteen-year-old son was a stunt actor at Universal Studios Theme Park. Lee worried incessantly about his safety. She called her son each night and even listened to the news to see if there had been any accidents at Universal. When her son visited, Lee would inquire about each of his body parts individually, asking if he felt any pain in his arm, in his leg, in his heart, on his head, and so on. Regardless of his answers, she was not ever fully convinced that he was 100 percent okay.

Although Lee knew her worry behavior was excessive, she couldn't stop cold turkey. She created the following hierarchy:

- Stop listening to radio news.

- Stop watching TV news.

- Check in with my boy every other night.

- Check in every third night.

- Check in once a week.

- Stop asking about his body and his health entirely.

Lee worked her way through each step of her hierarchy. For each step, she predicted dire consequences and experienced high anxiety. At each step, the consequences failed to appear and she gained confidence in the next step. Eventually she was able to eliminate her compulsive behaviors. The relationship she had with her son improved because she wasn't always questioning him. Although it was always a possibility that her son would be hurt doing live stunts, she ultimately was able to pursue her own life without focusing exclusively on his safety.

4. Assess Your Anxiety Before and After. When you wanted to perform your old behavior but knew you were not going to do it, how anxious were you? Rate your anxiety from 0 to 100, with 0 standing for no anxiety. Now, after performing your new behavior, or the cut-down version of your old behavior, how anxious are you? Rate your anxiety again from 0 to 100. Has your anxiety diminished?

Eric, the employee who habitually showed up for work earlier than everyone, rated his anxiety of not completing his projects on time as a full 100. After he experimented with arriving to work later than usual, he reduced his rating to 25.

Also, assess the consequences. What actually happened as a result of your reduced or new behavior? Did your dire predictions come true? In Eric's case, his prediction did not come true. He finished his project on time, was not perceived as a slacker, and even was able to read the newspaper before work on a couple of mornings.

5. Repeat Steps 2 through 4 with the Next-easiest Behavior. From your initial list, pick the worry behavior that is the next easiest to stop, and repeat the steps: predict the consequences of stopping the behavior, stop it or replace it with a new behavior if appropriate, then assess your anxiety level before and after the experiment.

For example, Trevor's experience with worry control shows how all four steps fit together. Trevor constantly worried about failure—failure to succeed, failure in his marriage, failure as a father, failure as a provider. As he worried incessantly about failure, he desperately tried to convince himself that if he could only make enough money, everything else would be okay. As manager of his own stock portfolios, Trevor continually worried he would lose all of his family's money and, ultimately, lose his family. He would brood over his fears, constantly seeking reassurance and support from his wife. Trevor's worry caused him to be emotionally volatile and insecure. Some days he would be angry and wouldn't talk to anyone; other days he would try to make up for his behavior by being overly loving. Everyone in his family—including himself—began to resent his fears and his behavior.

Trevor learned progressive muscle relaxation and did it every morning before he took a shower. He also mastered cue-controlled relaxation; he set the alarm on his computer to go off every three hours so that he would remember to stop and relax and take a few deep breaths every day. This helped him reduce his ongoing arousal level so that the chronic worries in the back of his mind didn't build as much throughout the day.

As Trevor learned relaxation skills, he worked on filling in the Risk Assessment form. Once he assessed the true risk of losing his family's entire financial nest egg and, hence, losing his whole family, he realized a couple of important things: First, regardless of how much money he lost, he would not use any of the money from his retirement or his children's college accounts. Secondly, his wife and children loved him deeply and would not leave him just because he had financial troubles.

After discussing his needs with his wife, Trevor took out his calendar and scheduled thirty-minute worry appointments with himself for each day of the week. He chose a time of day when it was less likely that he would be distracted—after the stock market closed and near the time of day when his daughter was napping. For comfort, Trevor placed next to his computer a pad of paper with the word "worries" written on it. He committed to writing down anything he was worried about, but only worrying during his daily thirty-minute worry appointment.

Next, Trevor made a hierarchical list of his failure-based thoughts to use in worry exposure. He started with his mildest worry, that he would oversleep and miss the early morning hours of trading. This scene quickly became boring after a couple of sessions. Trevor went on to eliminate his reaction to exposure scenes that included being distracted by his two young children, being unable to emotionally contribute to the family, not staying current with relevant and always-changing computer technology, losing a substantial amount of money, and, finally, being abandoned by his wife and children.

Trevor concluded his worry-control treatment with two kinds of worry-behavior prevention. First, he scheduled another daily appointment. In addition to concentrating on his worry for thirty minutes each day, he spent a minimum of one hour with his family. He promised himself that he would not discuss the trade market during this time. In fact, Trevor's goal for this sixty minutes was to exclusively support his wife and children and talk about the events in their lives. Although this time was limited, he found that it contributed to better family dynamics and greatly increased the love and joy in his home.

To change his behavior of continually relying on his wife for support and reassurance, Trevor decided to hire a business coach with whom he could discuss his business vision, hopes, and concerns. He stopped sharing his catastrophic fears with his wife.

Further Reading

Brown, T. A., R. M. Hertz, and D. H. Barlow. 1992. New developments in cognitive-behavioral treatment of anxiety disorders. In *American Psychiatric Press Review of Psychiatry*, Vol. 2, edited by A. Tasman. Washington, D.C.: American Psychiatric Press.

Copeland, M. E. 1998. *The Worry Control Workbook*. Oakland, Calif.: New Harbinger Publications.

McKay, M., M. Davis, and P. Fanning. 1997. *Thoughts and Feelings*. Oakland, Calif.: New Harbinger Publications.

O'Leary, T. A., T. A. Brown, and D. H. Barlow. 1992. The efficacy of worry control treatment in generalized anxiety disorder: A multiple baseline analysis. Paper presented at the Meeting of the Association for Advancement of Behavior Therapy, Boston.

White, J. 1999. *Overcoming Generalized Anxiety Disorder: Client Manual*. Oakland, Calif.: New Harbinger Publications.

Coping Skills Training

15

In this chapter you will learn to:

☐ Feel calmer and more capable when anticipating stressful events

☐ Relax before and during stressful situations

☐ Counteract irrational anxious and angry thoughts in stressful situations

Background

Donald Meichenbaum (1977), one of the principal developers of coping skills training, suggests that the fear response involves the interaction of two main elements: (1) physiological arousal and (2) thoughts that interpret your situation as threatening or dangerous and attribute your physiological arousal to the emotion of anxiety or fear. The actual stressful situation has little to do with your emotional response. Your evaluation of the danger and how you label your body's response are the real forces that determine what emotional response you will have. This accounts for why the same person who loves the "feelings of exhilaration" he experiences when skydiving leaps to a chair shaking and screaming in mortal terror when he sees a pet mouse on the floor and at his birthday party gets angry when his girlfriend serves him chocolate cake. In all three situations he is experiencing the fight or flight response. In the first case he views jumping out of an airplane as a thrilling adventure and he labels his physical sensations as excitement; they actually serve to heighten the pleasure of his experience. In the second situation he sees the mouse as his mortal enemy because of some prior adverse learning, and he interprets his physiological arousal as fear, which further confirms to him that the situation is dangerous. In the third instance, he believes his girlfriend is being thoughtless because he had told her before that he is allergic to chocolate; his physiological arousal affirms to him how unreasonable her behavior is.

With coping skills training, you learn to relax at the first sign of the stress response and counter your anxious or angry thoughts with coping thoughts when faced with a challenging situation. This training doesn't assume that you will master anxiety or anger so that it will never come back. Rather, it gives you effective coping strategies so you develop confidence in your ability to handle any situation, no matter how upsetting it may feel at first.

Coping skills training involves five steps:

1. Relaxation skills. You have probably already begun to master the relaxation procedures described in other chapters in this book that you will need for coping skills training: diaphragmatic breathing, progressive relaxation, progressive relaxation without tensing, and cue-controlled relaxation.

2. Stressful-events hierarchy. In order to apply coping skills training to your life, you will construct a personal hierarchy, or list, of your stressful situations, ranging from the least distressing to most distressing situation.

3. Coping thoughts. You will create your own list of coping thoughts. These will be used to get you through times when you feel anxious or angry and are likely to be saying to yourself something such as, "This is impossible . . . I can't do this . . . I'm too weak . . . it isn't fair . . . how dare they make me do this."

4. Imago coping skills. Using your imagination, you can call up each stressful situation in your hierarchy, feel the tension and distressing emotions associated with it, and then relax away tension and counter your stressful thoughts with coping thoughts. This rehearsal in imagination prepares you to reverse the stress response when you're under fire in real life.

5. In vivo coping skills. Having completed the first four steps, you begin to apply them in challenging situations in your daily life. Eventually, self-relaxation procedures and stress-coping thoughts become automatic in any stressful situation.

Symptom Effectiveness

Coping skills training has been shown to be effective in the reduction of anxiety in specific situations such as before and during interviews, speeches, and tests. It is useful in the treatment of phobias, particularly the fear of heights. The control of specific and generalized anxiety has long-term effects: two-year follow-ups of hypertense, postcardiac patients showed that 89 percent were still able to achieve general relaxation using coping skills training, and 79 percent were able to fall asleep sooner and sleep more deeply. Novaco (1975), Hazaleus et al. (1986), and Deffenbacher et al. (1987) have demonstrated in numerous studies the effectiveness of stress-coping statements and relaxation exercises for anger control.

Time to Master

You can master the key relaxation techniques for coping skills training within a month. Writing out a stressful-events hierarchy takes a few hours, typically spread over a few days. You can successfully go through your stressful events hierarchy in your imagination using your relaxation procedures and coping thoughts in a week or less. With regular practice for two to six months in real life, these coping skills can become automatic and be used whenever you feel anxious or angry.

Instructions

Coping Skills for Anxiety

Step One: Learn to Relax Efficiently

The foundation stone of coping skills training is knowing how to relax. The skills you will need are all in this book:

- Diaphragmatic breathing (chapter 3)

- Progressive relaxation (chapter 4)

- Relaxation without tension (chapter 7)

- Cue-controlled relaxation (chapter 7)

- Special-place visualization (chapter 6)

You will need to overlearn these relaxation techniques so that (1) you can use them at a moment's notice and (2) you can achieve deep relaxation in a minute or two. You want to be able to relax with the same unconscious coordination with which you ride a bike or write your name. Begin practicing these relaxation techniques immediately. You can complete Steps 2 and 3 while you are learning to relax, but don't go beyond step 3 until you have mastered each of these relaxation techniques.

Step 2: Make a Stressful-Events Hierarchy

Pick a theme in your life you feel anxious about (for example, participating in groups, driving, heights, health, family, deadlines). On a piece of paper, list all the things you could do that might trigger anxiety about this theme. Try to include only stressful situations that you are likely to encounter in the relatively near future. Be specific, including the setting and the persons involved. Get as close to thirty items on your list as possible, and let them run the full gamut from very mild discomfort to your most dreaded experiences. These items should be things you would like to do if you were free of your fear.

At the top of another piece of paper write the least anxiety-provoking item you imagined. At the bottom of the page write the item that would make you the most anxious. Now select between six to eighteen items of graduated intensity that you can fill in between your lowest and highest anxiety scenes. Each item on the list should represent an increase in stress over the preceding item, and the increases should be in approximately equal increments.

For help with this, you can use the Wolpe et al. (1966) rating system called subjective units of distress, or SUDs. Total relaxation is 0 SUDs, while the most stressful situation on your hierarchy should be rated at 100 SUDs—the highest stress you can imagine. All the other items on your hierarchy should fall somewhere between 5 and 99 SUDs. Assign SUDs scores to each of your items, based on your subjective impression of where each situation falls relative to your most relaxed or most anxious states.

For instance, Ann has a fear of heights and her most stressful item is, "A five-hour flight to New York for my daughter's wedding," which she ranks at 100, while her least stressful item is, "standing on a low stool," which she rates as a 5. "Driving over a suspension bridge" she ranks at 70, and "walking over an overpass" she ranks at 45. You are the expert on how you react to each situation, and you therefore must decide where each stressful event fits, relative to the others. For a list of twenty items, try to separate them all by increments of five SUDs. In that way, the items on your hierarchy will progress in relatively equal steps from one to twenty.

Zack, a college student, constructed the following hierarchy for his social anxiety:

Hierarchy Worksheet

Theme: Social Anxiety

SUDs Rank	Item
5	Make eye contact and smile at classmates I happen to see around campus.
10	Make eye contact, smile, and say "hello" to classmates I see around campus.
15	Make small talk for five minutes before class.
20	Join a classmate during a break in the cafeteria and make small talk.
25	Join a small group of classmates during a break in the cafeteria and make small talk.
30	Attend a family Fourth of July picnic.
35	Ask a classmate to work on a class project with me.
40	Call on the phone to inquire about a summer job.
45	Attend a party with friends and strangers.
50	Volunteer to answer the teacher's questions in class.
55	Ask questions in class.
60	Volunteer my opinion during a class discussion.
65	Make eye contact, smile, and say "hello" to a very attractive woman.
70	Join a very attractive woman in the cafeteria and make small talk.
75	Give a five-minute presentation in class.
80	Give a twenty-minute presentation in class.
85	Invite a very attractive woman to join me for coffee after class.
90	Ask a very attractive woman out to dinner.

| 95 | Interview for a summer job. |
| 100 | Be best man at a friend's wedding and toast the bride and groom. |

Here is a blank Hierarchy Worksheet. Make several copies of it to work on.

Hierarchy Worksheet

Theme:_____

SUDs Rank	Item

Step 3: Create Stress-Coping Thoughts

Stress-coping thoughts can put a stop to or least soften painful emotions. To understand how they work, consider the four components of an emotional response, continuing with the example of Zack, the socially anxious college student:

1. **The stimulus situation:** He is giving a five-minute presentation in front of his class.

2. **Physical reactions:** His aroused autonomic nervous system produces cotton mouth; cold, clammy, tremulous hands; butterflies in his stomach; tightness in his throat; sweaty armpits; rapid heartbeat; and lightheadedness.

3. **Behavioral response:** He fights the impulse to bolt out of the room, gets up, and gives a stiff presentation that he reads very softly and quickly, avoiding eye contact.

4. **Thoughts:** How he interprets the situation, what his self-evaluations are, and what he predicts will happen are what create his emotions. He says to himself: "I can't do this. . . ." *(prediction);* " I'm a nervous wreck. . . ." *(self-evaluation);* "I'm going to go blank and nothing is going to come out of my mouth. . . ." *(prediction);* "Everyone is going to be looking at me and thinking I'm a complete idiot. . . ." *(interpretation).*

Zack's emotional response is high anxiety and his behavior is inhibited. The feedback loop from thoughts to physical reactions to behavioral choices to more negative thoughts can spiral on and on. Fortunately, your thoughts don't have to intensify your fear response. Instead, they can serve to calm your body and neutralize your feelings of high anxiety. According to McKay, Davis, and Fanning (1997), the feedback loop can work for you as well as against you. Stress-coping thoughts tell your body there is no need for arousal—it can relax. Before and during any stressful situation, you can begin saying to yourself a series of fear-conquering statements such as, "Take a deep breath and relax. . . . You've given lots of successful class presentations before. . . . Calm down. . . . It's natural to be a little nervous. . . . Nobody is going to think less of you for it. . . ."

The more attention you give to your coping monologue, the faster you will experience relief from the fight or flight response.

Meichenbaum and Cameron (1974) suggest four times when you can use stress-coping statements:

1. When you are preparing to do something anxiety provoking and you are having thoughts that trigger anticipatory anxiety.

2. When you confront the stressful situation and you are having anxiety-provoking thoughts that interfere with your ability to concentrate and cope comfortably in the moment.

3. When you feel tension and need to be reminded to relax.

4. When you have completed an anxiety-provoking activity and want to acknowledge that you succeeded in getting though the stressful event using your coping skills.

1. Preparation

There's nothing to worry about.

I'm going to be all right.

I've succeeded with this before.

What exactly do I have to do?

I know I can do each one of these tasks.

It's easier once you get started.

I'll jump in and be all right.

Tomorrow I'll be through it.

Don't let negative thoughts creep in.

2. Confronting the stressful situation

Stay organized.

Take it step by step, don't rush.

I can do this, I'm doing it now.

I can only do my best.

Any tension I feel is a signal to use my coping exercises.

I can get help if I need it.

If I don't think about fear, I won't be afraid.

If I get tense, I'll take a breather and relax.

It's okay to make mistakes.

3. Coping with fear

Relax now!

Just breathe deeply.

There's an end to it.

Keep my mind on right now, on the task at hand.

I can keep this within limits I can handle.

I can always call _____.

I am only afraid because I decided to be. I can decide not to be.

I've survived this and worse before.

Do something and the fear will lessen.

4. Reinforcing success

I did it!

I did all right. I did well.

Next time I won't have to worry so much.

I am able to relax away anxiety.

I've got to tell _____ about this.

It's possible not to be scared. All I have to do is stop thinking I'm scared.

How to Create Your Own Stress-Coping Thoughts

While many of the stress-coping thoughts listed above can work for you, the ones you create yourself will probably fit you best. For each one of the items on your hierarchy, select or create two or three stress-coping thoughts that will relax your body and reassure your mind.

- Visualize an item on your hierarchy in detail.

- Notice how you feel.

- Listen to what you are saying to yourself that is anxiety provoking.

- Write down these stressful thoughts for each item on your hierarchy.

- Examine each of your stressful thoughts. Typically, anxious thoughts are not completely accurate or rational. Questioning your anxious thoughts will tend to lead to stress-coping thoughts. Here are seven questions to ask when evaluating your anxious thoughts.

1. Can I really read people's minds?

2. Can I really predict the future?

3. Am I exaggerating how bad it is or will be?

4. If what I fear does happen, how long will I really have to endure it?

5. How likely is it that what I fear will actually happen?

6. What are some other things that could happen that are more probable?

7. What coping skills can I use to handle what I fear might happen (relaxation skills, ways to reassure myself, people I can call on to help me, things I can do, a plan)?

For example, here are some of the distressing thoughts that Zack, the anxious college student, had when he contemplated doing a couple of the activities he listed on his hierarchy. He used the seven questions above to challenge his anxious thoughts.

- Make eye contact and smile at classmates I happen to see around campus.

They'll think I'm weird and they won't want to have anything to do with me.

1. I can't read minds.

2. I can't predict the future.

3. I'm exaggerating. The worst thing that will happen is that they'll ignore me or make a rude remark.

4. If someone responds negatively, I can endure a few moments of rejection.

5. It's extremely unlikely. Most people are pretty friendly. Smiling at people is usually considered a friendly gesture. They'll probably think I'm just another friendly guy.

6. Most likely, most people will respond positively.

7. If someone responds negatively, I don't have to take it personally. Maybe he's just having a bad day. I'll just relax, make eye contact, and smile. I can keep track of how many people respond positively versus how many don't.

• Call on the phone to inquire about a summer job.

I'll go blank because I'm so nervous, and really blow it!

1. (not applicable to this situation)

2. I can't predict the future.

3. I'm exaggerating. I've never gone blank in my life. If it really happened, I'd excuse myself and call back later or call some other company.

4. I'd only have to endure it intensely for a few minutes at the most.

5. It is highly unlikely since I'm well prepared, am using coping skills, and have everything I want to ask written out in the event I forget something.

6. I'll do just fine. I'll make a few mistakes but still get the information I'm seeking in spite of being a little nervous.

7. I can relax before and during the call. I can refer to my notes if I need to. It's okay not to be perfect.

• Give a five-minute presentation in class.

I will feel panicky; I can't stand that.

1. (not applicable to this situation)

2. I can't predict the future.

3. I'm exaggerating. I don't like high anxiety, but I have handled it before and I survived.

4. My anxiety level will be high for no more than five minutes and drop as soon as I sit down after my presentation.

5. I know that I will be able to handle my anxiety and give my presentation using coping skills.

6. As I continue practicing my coping skills, I might even enjoy giving presentations.

7. Anxiety is my cue to relax and breathe. My notes are there if I need them. I can look forward to basketball practice after class.

Exercise

On a piece of paper, write the first item on your hierarchy. Then write down one of your anxious thoughts about that item. Finally, write down the number of the question(s) that you are answering along with your answer(s). Follow this format for each item on your hierarchy:

SUDs Rank: _____   Item: _____

Anxiety-Provoking Thought: _____

Question Numbers   My Answers:

_____   _____

_____   _____

_____   _____

_____   _____

_____   _____

_____   _____

_____   _____

_____   _____

_____   _____

Select two or three stress-coping thoughts for each of the items on your hierarchy that will relax your body and reassure your mind. To do this, star your best answers to question seven. Particularly powerful stress-coping thoughts are brief, accurate, realistic, believable, and positive. If you have difficulty coming up with your own stress-coping thoughts, refer to the general list of stress-coping statements on pages 160–161.

Step 4: Imago Coping Skills

A. Relax for ten or fifteen minutes or until you feel deeply relaxed, calm, and safe. Now briefly review your coping statements for the situation you plan to work with next.

B. Imagine you're in the situation. Try to make the scene come alive in your imagination. See the situation. Hear what is going on. Feel the mounting tension in your body. Remember your anxiety-provoking thoughts. When you can really feel the anxiety, proceed to C.

C. Start to cope. As soon as the imagined scene is clear in your mind and you can feel its effects, begin relaxing and using coping thoughts. Cue-controlled relaxation is the fastest stress-reduction technique and therefore is most ideal for this step. Keep saying your coping thoughts to yourself and relaxing while you continue to imagine the anxiety-provoking scene for about one minute.

D. Rate your anxiety. On a scale from 0 (no anxiety) to 10 (the most anxious you have ever felt), rate the anxiety you experienced in the scene just before you shut it off. If your anxiety is a 1 or 0, you can relax (step E) and move on to the next situation in your hierarchy. If your anxiety is 2 or more, relax (step E) and then repeat steps B and C using the same situation.

Review your coping thoughts. If any of them are ineffective, replace them with new ones of your own or go back to the general list of stress coping statements and try one or two others. Keep in mind that the ones you create yourself are likely to be the most powerful for you.

E. Always relax deeply between scenes. Use cue-controlled relaxation and spend time calming yourself in your special place. If you are having difficulty relaxing using these two techniques, use progressive relaxation or relaxation without tension before re-entering the scene.

Continue imagining and coping with scenes until you have finished the most difficult item in your hierarchy. Practice daily for best results. Your first practice session should be about fifteen to twenty minutes. Later you may want to extend your session to as long as thirty minutes. If you get tired and have trouble visualizing a scene, it's better to postpone practice until you are more alert. Expect to master one to three hierarchy items during each practice session. Always go back to the last scene you successfully completed when starting a new practice session. This helps consolidate your gains before you face more anxiety-provoking items.

When you have mastered all the items on your hierarchy using imagery and coping skills, you will have a better awareness of how and where tension builds in your body. You will be able to use the early signs of tension as your signal to relax. Mastery of those items with the highest SUDs provides a degree of confidence that stress reduction is possible—even in the most threatening situations.

Example

Zack, the socially anxious college student, began his imago coping skills sessions with ten minutes of relaxation. When he tried to visualize the first stressful situation (5 SUDs), he had difficulty recalling the details of the scene and he didn't experience any anxiety. Since learning to relax in the face of fear requires that each scene be vivid and real, he waited until the following morning just before class to study the sights, sounds, and smells of the busy halls of his college. He closed his eyes and described to himself the scene, using all of his senses. Then he opened his eyes and added to his description the things that he had missed the first time. He described to himself how he felt and what he was thinking as he imagined himself making eye contact and smiling at his classmates hurrying by. That night he began his practice again with ten minutes of relaxation before he visualized the first item on his hierarchy. This time it was easy to imagine himself in the scene and he experienced some tension in his throat, chest, and stomach. He then used cue-controlled relaxation and coping thoughts as he continued to imagine being in the stressful scene for about one minute. He rated his level of anxiety at the conclusion of one minute as 0. He took a couple of minutes to relax in his special place, using cue-controlled relaxation, then went on to imagine the next item on his hierarchy.

Sometimes Zack had to visualize a situation six or more times before the image produced no anxiety. He scheduled his practice mornings and evenings for fifteen to twenty minutes. On the average, he was able to successfully relax away tension in three scenes per day, and in a week he completed the hierarchy.

Step 5: In Vivo Coping Skills

When you encounter stress in real life, your body tension is a cue to begin to relax. At that time, repeat to yourself stress-coping thoughts as you prepare for and confront the situation and limit the fear. Remember to praise yourself for meeting the challenge. Using coping skills in real life will probably be more difficult than relaxing away stress in the imagined scenes. Some setbacks are inevitable. Practice, however, will make relaxation and stress-coping thoughts so natural that eventually they will automatically begin at the first symptom of tension.

Zack was preparing for a job interview the next morning. Rather than staying up late worrying, he wrote down his stress-coping thoughts to use before, during, and after the interview. Then he spent twenty minutes practicing his stress-coping skills, using the coping thoughts that he found most powerful, just as when he was practicing his hierarchy.

1. Preparation

I've succeeded with this before.
I know what to do to succeed this time.
I'm prepared.
I can relax and get a good night's sleep.

2. Confronting

Focus on my goal.
It's okay to not know something.
Answer the questions so the interviewer learns my strengths.

3. Coping with fear

I can use my anxiety as a cue to relax.
Keep breathing from the belly and let go of the tension.
I can feel anxious and still deal with this situation.
I'll feel great when this is over.

4. Reinforcing success

I did it!
I was able to cope with my anxiety and do a good job.
It's getting easier to calm down and relax.
I can really relax now.

Zack typed a file card with the phrase, "Take a deep breath and let go of the tension," and taped it to the top of his computer monitor. Other signs went on the front page of his notebook, his refrigerator, and his car visor. On the way to the interview he practiced deep breathing and repeated the coping thoughts listed under Preparation. While he waited in the lobby to be called in by the interviewer he continued to relax and slowly read over all of his coping thoughts. He memorized several of them. In spite of all this preparation, when the interviewer came out for him, he thought, "Oh no, here we go!", and he felt his heart beat hard in his chest, his stomach knot, and his mouth go dry. He remembered the coping thought, "I can use my anxiety as a cue to relax," and immediately began consciously deep breathing and focusing on relaxing his jaw, shoulders, and stomach. As the interviewer began to question him, he repeated to himself, "Talk about my strengths . . . I can be anxious and still deal with this. . . ." When he was asked a question that he didn't know the answer to, his mind momentarily froze, until he thought, "Its okay not to know something . . . take a deep breath and relax." By the end of the interview, he was actually enjoying himself. When he left the interviewer's office, his first thought was, "I did it! I was actually able to cope with my anxiety and do a good job!"

When it came to dealing with spontaneous social interactions, at first he often forgot his training and was overwhelmed by the intensity of a situation. In time, he discovered that the key to real-life practice was to start using cue-controlled relaxation and stress-coping thoughts the moment he noticed any tension or anxiety. He gradually learned to spot stress coming, tune into his early warning signs of physical tension, and start coping skills early.

Coping Skills for Anger

Anger, like anxiety, is not automatic. Just because someone pelts you with hurtful, demeaning criticism or you almost have an accident when a weaving car cuts in front of you on the freeway doesn't mean you have to get instantly furious or fume for several hours. Your thoughts about painful and stressful events are what trigger anger. Thoughts that lead to anger typically involve (1) blaming others for deliberately and needlessly causing you pain and (2) judging others as breaking rules of appropriate or reasonable behavior. If you think someone is deliberately harming or attacking you or that you are the victim of their unreasonable behavior, your thoughts trigger the fight or flight response in your body and you feel angry. Raymond Novaco (1975) expanded coping skills training (also referred to as "stress inoculation training") to the treatment of anger. The five steps of coping skills training for anger control are the same as those for anxiety control.

Step One: Learn to Relax Efficiently

The fight or flight response is an important component of anger. While angry thoughts may trigger the response, often you are already in a high level of sympathetic nervous system arousal when something happens that provokes angry thoughts and further stimulates your physiological arousal, which in turn fuels your angry thoughts, and so on. An all-too-common example of this is when you are driving home from a long day at work in heavy traffic, suffering from a tension headache or stomachache and someone does something reckless. Already tense, you lash out. One way to intervene in your cycle of anger is to lower your overall sympathetic nervous system arousal through regular practice of deep relaxation techniques. This prepares you to relax rather than overreact at the first sign of stress and tension. (See step 1 under Coping Skills for Anxiety for more information.)

For example, Greg was a salesman with an anger problem that was contributing to his high blood pressure and chronic indigestion and quite possibly going to cost him his job. He worked long hours to support his wife and two children. He often felt at the mercy of thoughtless and self-centered people, which caused him to feel chronically annoyed and at times explode. At first it was difficult for him to make the time to practice his relaxation exercises because, "They're not productive" and "I've got so much else to do." But when he discovered that they temporarily lowered his blood pressure and calmed his stomach, he began practicing them twice a day.

Step Two: Make a Stressful-Events Hierarchy

On a piece of paper, list thirty situations that make you angry. Include situations that you are likely to encounter in the near future. The situations should range from those that only mildly annoy you to those that make you as mad as you ever get. Be specific and include the people and settings. If you find yourself getting angry in almost every situation, pick one theme or area to concentrate on. For instance, you could make a list of thirty situations that anger you at work, with family members, on the road, with authority figures, or with the public.

At the top of another piece of paper write the least anger-provoking item you recalled. At the bottom of the page write the item that makes you the most angry. Now select between six and eighteen items of graduated intensity that you can fill in between your lowest and highest angry scenes. Each item on the list should represent an increase in stress over the last item, and the increases should be in approximately equal increments. Again, you could use the SUDs scale (0 to 100) to help you with this. As described earlier, assign SUDs scores to each of your items, based on your subjective impression of where each situation falls relative to your most relaxed or most anger-provoking states.

To prepare for his hierarchy, Greg brainstormed a list of situations ranging from those that caused him mild annoyance all the way up to scenes that caused him to blow up. This proved to be a difficult task, because just thinking about some of the events sent his blood pressure soaring. He cut up his list of items so that there was only one item on each slip of paper. Then he spent some time rearranging the slips of paper so that the least annoying item was at the top and the most explosive item was on the bottom. He used the SUDs rating system to fit the rest of the items into the middle. Here is Greg's hierarchy:

Theme: Anger-Provoking Events

SUDs Rank	Item
5	My wife comes home late from a meeting.
10	A customer expects special treatment.
15	A customer criticizes me because his order is shipped a day late.
20	I order a rare steak in a restaurant and it comes well done.
25	My team loses the Super Bowl and I had $150 riding on them.
30	The kids leave their bikes in the driveway so I can't get in the garage . . . again.
35	A customer complains bitterly about a product I sold him at a deep discount.
40	A new policy requires that I complete time-consuming additional 4 paperwork on all my routine sales contracts.
45	My boss tells me to do something that he should be doing himself.
50	My mother guilt-trips me for not visiting her more often.
55	I'm given the finger when I don't let a car cut in front of me.

60	I get stuck in a traffic jam and I realize I'm going to miss an important meeting.
65	My friend borrows my new video camera and doesn't return it.
70	My flight is overbooked and I am bumped to the next flight, which leaves two hours later.
75	My neighbor has a loud party and won't turn down the music when I ask him to.
80	The airlines misplace my baggage and I'm stuck in New York for three days without a change of clothes.
85	A car on the freeway weaves in and out of traffic and almost sideswipes my car.
90	A driver cuts in front of me, causing me to slam on my breaks to avoid an accident.
95	My boss tries to cheat me out of part of my commissions.
100	My boss threatens to fire me if I don't get an "attitude adjustment."

Here is a blank Hierarchy Worksheet. Make several copies of it to work on.

Hierarchy Worksheet

Theme:_____

SUDs Rank	Item

Step 3: Create Stress-Coping Thoughts for Anger

According to McKay (1992), there are two kinds of thoughts that trigger anger: "should" statements and blaming statements.

"Should" Statements

"Should" statements are based on the assumption that someone has violated appropriate rules of behavior. There are two problems with this assumption. First, other people often do not agree with your definition of appropriate rules of conduct. They have their own rules, or at least their own interpretation of the rules that can leave them feeling blameless and justified in a situation where *you* think they are guilty of wrongdoing. Second, people are less inclined to do what they should do, and more likely to do what is in their self-interest to do. Shoulds are really nothing more than values and needs imposed on others who may very well have different values and needs. Here are some general coping responses to counter should statements:

- People do what they want to do, not what I think they should do.

- Forget the shoulds, they only get me upset.

- I may not like it, but they're doing the best they can.

- They are simply pursuing what they think is in their best interest.

Should statements often contain the notion of entitlement: "I want something, therefore I should have it. My need justifies my demanding others to provide it. If I don't get what I need, someone is deliberately depriving me." The problem with these statements is that they confuse desire with obligation. Just because I want something doesn't mean others should be obligated to give it to me. Here are some coping statements to replace statements of entitlement:

- I am free to want, and you are free to say no.

- I have a right to say no and so do you.

- My desire doesn't obligate you to meet it.

Should statements frequently include the idea of fairness: "There is an absolute standard of correct and fair behavior that people should understand and live up to." Unfortunately, no two people can agree on what is fair. What is fair is based on subjective judgment that reflects a person's beliefs, expectations, needs, and wants. Here are some coping statements to counter statements about fairness:

- Our needs are equally important.

- Nobody is right and nobody is wrong. We just have different needs.

- Each need is legitimate—we can negotiate.

Should statements sometimes spring from the belief that you can change people if you apply enough pressure. Unfortunately, people change only when they see it in their interests to change and when they are capable of making the change. No amount of cajoling, nagging, or threatening will cause people to change if they don't want to. Here are some coping statements to combat statements about changing others:

- People change only when change is reinforced and they are capable of changing.

- People only change when they want to.

- Nobody is bad; people do the best they can.

- While I don't agree with them, I'm not going to waste my time trying to teach them a lesson.

Blaming Statements

Blaming statements are based on the concept that the pain you feel is there because *they* did it to you. Blaming is seductively appealing because it feels good to hold someone else responsible for your woes and to punish them, at least mentally. When you get stuck blaming others, you forget that you have the ability to make choices that will change the situation. Another problem with blaming is that people are moving through life trying to make the best choices they can to insure that their own needs are met. When you blame others for their actions, you are blaming them for taking care of themselves in the best way they know how to at the moment.

Here are some coping statements to help you with blaming:

- I may not like it, but they're doing the best they can.

- I'm not helpless—I can take care of myself in this situation.

- Blaming just upsets me. It doesn't solve the problem.

Blaming often involves assuming malicious intent. That is, you think that whatever has happened is a consequence of someone's deliberately trying to harm you. You never ask; you think you can read their minds. Unfortunately, by never asking, you never find out what the other person's true motives are. Here are some coping statements for this distortion:

- Nobody is a mind reader.

- Don't second-guess the motives of others.

- Check out every assumption.

- I don't have to jump to conclusions and assume the worst.

- They're not out to get me; they're just pursuing their self-interests.

- This is not personal.

Blaming often involves exaggeration. Magnifying the seriousness of a problem increases your anxiety as well as your anger and your sense of being victimized. You anticipate that something terrible is about to happen. You view events as awful: "I can't stand this horrendous news about the company downsizing!" You overgeneralize by using absolutes such as "always," "never," "all," or "nobody": "She's always late." "He never thinks of anybody but himself." When you exaggerate the problem, you feel deeply wronged. Coping statements for this distortion are:

- Accuracy, not exaggeration.

- Let the facts speak for themselves.

- Ban absolutes.

- I don't have to be a helpless victim in this situation . . . I can take care of myself.

Blaming statements frequently include global labels that indict the entire person. Rather than focusing on a particular behavior that you find disturbing, you make a sweeping negative judgment about the other person. So instead of saying to your partner, "You forgot to mail our income tax return today," you say, "You stupid, lazy, selfish screw-up. . . ." Coping statements for this distortion are:

- No one is bad—people do the best they can.

- No mean labels.

- Be specific.

General Stress-Coping Thoughts for Anger

Often the best coping thoughts simply remind you to stay calm and relaxed when faced with irritants. Consider using some of the following general coping thoughts when you deal with anger:

- Take a deep breath and relax.

- Getting angry won't solve this problem.

- Just as long as I keep my cool, I'm in control.

- Easy does it . . . there's nothing to be gained by getting upset.

- I'm not going to let them get to me.

- I can't change them with my anger; I'll just upset myself.

- I can find a way to say what I want to without anger.

- Stay calm . . . no sarcasm, no attacks.

- I can stay calm and relaxed.

- I can cope with this situation even though I don't like it.

- Keep an open mind, make no judgments.

- No matter what is said, I know I'm a good person.

- I'll focus on the facts and stay rational.

- Their opinion isn't important . . . I won't be pushed into losing my cool.

- It's just not worth it to get angry.

- This is funny if you look at it that way.

- Anger means it's time to relax and cope.

- Maybe they want me to get angry. I'm going to disappoint them.

- I can't expect people to act the way I want them to.

- Keep cool; take it easy.

- I can manage this; I'm in control.

- I don't have to take this so seriously.

- I have a plan to relax and cope.

The Principle of Self-Responsibility

According to Fanning and McKay (1993), a powerful antidote to anger is taking personal responsibility for yourself. After all, you are the one who knows and understands your needs the best. Likewise, other people know and understand best what they need. Each individual is charged with the responsibility of taking care of his or her own needs. Inevitably people's needs will conflict. Your overall satisfaction in life will depend on how effective your strategies are for satisfying your needs and avoiding pain. Rather than blaming or judging, some of the most effective coping strategies involve a specific plan for dealing with a situation: "I will negotiate the best deal I can get." "I will simply say 'no' calmly and firmly." "I will state my needs clearly." "I will demonstrate to him how his meeting my needs is in his interests too." "I will find another way to solve my problem that doesn't require their cooperation." "I will find new sources of support and appreciation." "I value this relationship so much that I am willing to let go of this need." "I value this need so much I am willing to let go of this relationship." When you have a good plan in which you take responsibility for meeting your own needs, you will feel more in control and will be less apt to feel angry.

While you may choose to use the stress-coping statements listed above to counter your angry thoughts, often the coping statements that you create for yourself are the most powerful ones for you.

On a piece of paper, write down your anger-provoking thoughts in the Stressful Thoughts column for each item on your hierarchy. In the Stress-Coping Thoughts column, write down at least two coping thoughts that will serve to calm your mind and remind you to relax your body. Use the following format:

SUDs Rank	Item	Stressful Thoughts	Stress-Coping Thoughts

Here are some suggestions, adapted from McKay et al. (1997), for identifying your anger-provoking thoughts and developing effective stress-coping thoughts: Visualize the first item on your hierarchy. Make it as vivid in your imagination as possible. Ask yourself these questions:

- What do you see?

- What do you hear?

- What do you feel in your body?

- What are you saying to yourself that is triggering your anger?

- Are you blaming someone for deliberately harming you?

- Are you accusing someone of breaking rules about appropriate or reasonable behavior?

Using what you have learned about blaming statements, should statements, and personal responsibility, counter each of your angry thoughts with less stressful, more accepting coping thoughts.

Here is a sample of angry and stress-coping thoughts from Greg's Hierarchy Worksheet:

SUDs Rank	Item	Angry Thoughts	Stress Coping Thoughts
5	Wife comes home late from a meeting.	*"She's inconsiderate. She should be on time or call if she's going to be late."*	I can't change her, but I can take care of myself. Getting upset won't help. We have different values about punctuality. I can relax and enjoy this time alone.
40	Another new policy requires that I complete time consuming paper work on all my routine sales contracts.	*"This is a stupid waste of my time."*	This is a good time to stay calm and relax. As soon as I get the hang of it, this paperwork will go fast. I can't expect the M.B.A.'s who create these policies to think as I do.
50	My mother guilt- trips me for not visiting her more often.	*"She's so manipulative. She has friends she doesn't visit and expects me to fill her social life."*	I know she's lonely; I can't make her get a life. Remember to breathe and stay calm. I can be compassionate and still set limits to take care of my needs.

75	My neighbor has a loud, late night party and doesn't turn down the music when I ask him to.	*"He's an inconsiderate S.O.B. for keeping the whole neighborhood awake."*	Stay cool, calm, and in control. I can't fix this with anger. If he doesn't turn down the music in 15 minutes, I can call the police.
90	A driver cuts in front of me, causing me to slam on my brakes to avoid an accident.	*"*@&$! You almost killed me! You need to be taught a lesson."*	Take a deep breath and relax. I can drive safely and get away from him. I'm not going to risk my neck teaching him a lesson . . . he's not worth it. I can listen to some calming music, relax my muscles, and forget about him.

Step 4: Imago Coping Skills

Here is how Greg applied anger-coping skills in his imagination:

A. Take ten or fifteen minutes to get relaxed. Greg practiced coping skills training twice a day for twenty minutes. First he relaxed for ten minutes using diaphragmatic breathing, progressive relaxation with and without tensing, visualization of a safe place, and cue-controlled relaxation.

B. Visualize the situation. Greg imagined the first item on his hierarchy that he planned to work on that day. He recalled the details of the scene, using all his senses. He remembered his anger-provoking thoughts. He reminded himself of the unfairness, the wrongness, the outrageousness of the offense. He felt the tension in his body.

C. Start to cope. Once Greg had the scene clearly in mind and was in touch with his anger he began to relax, using cue-controlled relaxation and repeating to himself his coping thoughts as he continued to imagine being in the anger-provoking situation for about another minute.

D. Rate your anger. Using the eleven-point rating system (0 being no anger and 10 being the worst rage he ever felt), Greg found that for certain items such as his work and his road rage he had to practice many times in order to bring down his anger. For these scenes, he found that changing some of his coping statements helped him calm his intense anger.

E. Always relax deeply between scenes. While Greg found cue-controlled relaxation and spending time in his special place effective ways to relax between practicing the easier items on his hierarchy, he needed to use progressive relaxation with and without tension before re-entering the scenes involving his work and driving.

Step 5: In Vivo Coping Skills

Since anger situations seem to occur spontaneously, you may assume that scheduling real-life practice for your new anger coping skills will be difficult. However, if you have included on your hierarchy situations that frequently or predictably occur, you will have ample opportunities to practice. You can have ready your well-rehearsed coping thoughts. You can be alert for the early signs of anger in your body and your mind. The sooner you intervene with cue-controlled relaxation and coping thoughts, the more likely you are to maintain control.

If you know that you are going to be in a situation that is likely to spark your anger, prepare your coping thoughts ahead of time and commit yourself to using them along with cue-controlled relaxation. With practice this will become easier to do, and in time it will become more automatic. If you forget to use your coping skills or start to use them but then give in to the heat of the moment, later visualize the scene and practice coping just as you did when you were working on your hierarchy. This will help you use your coping skills the next time a similar situation occurs.

When coping with anger in his daily life, Greg found cue-controlled relaxation and a handful of well-chosen general coping thoughts helpful in managing most irritating situations. He ended up successfully suing his boss for back commissions and getting a job with another company, which reduced the stressors in his life for a while.

When his new boss began reneging on agreements regarding commissions, Greg made an appointment to meet with him. He prepared a list of coping statements to use before, during, and after the meeting:

1. Preparation

People do what they want to do, not what I think they should do.
Forget shoulds . . . they only upset me.
Getting mad only hurts me and doesn't solve the problem.
I am responsible for protecting myself and taking care of my needs.
Take a deep breath and relax.

2. Confrontation

I will negotiate the best deal I can get.
I can find a way to say what I want to without anger.
I'll focus on the facts and stay rational.
Any sign of tension is a signal to relax.

3. Coping with anger

Easy does it . . . there is nothing to be gained by getting upset.
Let go of the tension and anger.
Stay calm . . . no sarcasm, no attacks.
I can manage this . . . I'm in control.

4. Reinforcing success

I did it!
I kept my cool and accomplished my goal!
I've got to tell my wife about this.
We will celebrate tonight!

Greg relaxed, visualized his appointment, and practiced his coping statements until he felt confident that he could calmly and firmly confront his boss without blowing up. He studied his coping statements on a three-by-five card just before his appointment and was able to use many of them during his meeting with his boss because he was so well prepared. Needless to say, his meeting went well.

After persistent practice on an almost daily basis, Greg was surprised at how effective his new coping skills were in eliminating his road rage. When he forgot to use his coping skills or they proved inadequate, he rehearsed the scene again and again in his mind, using his coping skills. He made a commitment to use his coping skills the next time he felt the first signs of anger, which for him was tightness in the gut and chest and elevated heart rate, along with judgmental and blaming thoughts. His hard work paid off with improved health and a general sense of well-being.

Special Considerations

1. If you have difficulty relaxing at the beginning of the session, you may want to record your relaxation routine and play it.

2. If you have difficulty imagining your scenes, reread chapter 6, Visualization. Be sure to use all of your senses. You might also try going to the real setting of one of your scenes to gather images and impressions and practice remembering the details. Close your eyes and describe the scene to yourself and then open your eyes and see what you missed. Keep this up, gradually adding sound, textures, smells, and temperatures until you have a vivid sense picture in your imagination.

3. If you can visualize your scenes clearly yet experience little or no anxiety, your first items need to be more challenging, or perhaps you need more variety in the content of your scenes. In either case, you may need to rewrite your hierarchy.

4. If you can visualize your scenes clearly and experience erratic levels of tension, you may need to rearrange your hierarchy. You also may need to rewrite some of your scenes so that you have a more even increase in the intensity of anger as you move down your hierarchy.

Further Reading

Deffenbacher, J. I., D. A. Story, R. S. Stark, J. A. Hogg, and A. D. Brandon. 1987. Cognitive-relaxation and social skills interventions in the treatment of general anger. Journal of Counseling Psychology 34(2):171–176.

Fanning, P., and M. McKay. 1993. *Being a Man: A Guide to the New Masculinity*. Oakland, Calif.: New Harbinger Publications.

Goldfried, M. R. 1973. Reduction of generalized anxiety through a variant of systematic desensitization. In *Behavior Change through Self-Control*, edited by M. R. Goldfried, and M. Merbaum. New York: Holt, Rinehart and Winston.

Hazaleus, S., and J. L. Deffenbacher. 1986. Relaxation and cognitive treatments of anger. *Journal of Psychological Record*. 15:501–511.

McKay, M. 1992 Anger control groups. In *Focal Group Psychotherapy*, edited by M. McKay and K. Paleg. Oakland, Calif.: New Harbinger Publications.

McKay, M., M. Davis, and P. Fanning. 1997. *Thoughts and feelings: Taking Control of Your Moods and Your Life*. Oakland, Calif.: New Harbinger Publications.

Meichenbaum, D. 1992. Self-Instructional Methods. In *Helping People Change*, edited by F. K. Kanfur and A. P. Goldstein. New York: Pergamon Press.

——. 1977. *Cognitive Behavior Modification*. New York: Plenum.

Meichenbaum, D., and R. Cameron. 1974. Modifying what clients say to themselves. In *Self-Control: Power to the Person*, edited by M. J. Mahoney and C. E. Thoresen. Monterey, Calif.: Brooks/Cole. Out of print.

Novaco, R. 1975. *Anger Control: The Development and Evaluation of an Experimental Treatment*. Lexington, Mass.: D. C. Health.

Suinn, R. M., and F. Richardson. 1971. Anxiety management training: A non-specific behavior therapy program for anxiety control. *Behavior Therapy* 2:498–510.

Wolpe, J., and A. A. Lazarus. 1966. *Behavior Therapy Techniques*. New York: Pergamon Press.

Goal Setting and Time Management

In this chapter you will learn to:

- ☐ Clarify values, define your goals, and develop a plan to reach your goals

- ☐ Assess how you are currently spending your time

- ☐ Reorganize your time to fit your priorities

- ☐ Combat procrastination

- ☐ Use shortcuts for time management

Background

Most people approach the subject of time management with one major question: "How can I get more done in less time?" If you are one of these people, you are probably wondering how you are going to fit some of the exercises described in the other chapters of this book into your already overloaded schedule. You may feel so pressured to take care of the demands and details in your life that you rarely have guilt-free time to do as you please. Or you may have loads of free time, yet never get around to doing the things that would give you the most satisfaction. Other problems associated with ineffective time management include:

- constant rushing

- frequent lateness

- low productivity, energy, and motivation

- frustration

- impatience

- chronic vacillation between alternatives

- difficulty setting and achieving goals

- procrastination

How is it that while we all have twenty-four hours in a day, some of us feel as though we have no time at all, while others manage to get their work done and still have enough time left over to enjoy themselves? People who effectively manage their time have learned to structure their lives so that they focus most of their time and energy on what is most important to them and minimize the time they spend on activities that they do not value. They realize that the quality of their lives is enhanced when they are able to do a few things well, instead of trying to find time to do a little of everything.

If you are thinking, "All of my responsibilities are important; I can't simply drop some of them to do what I please," consider the 80–20 principle. Vilfredo Pareto, an Italian economist, noted that 20 percent of what we do yields 80 percent of the results. Conversely, 80 percent of what we do yields 20 percent of the results. This principle can be applied to many areas of life. For example, about 20 percent of the newspaper is worth your while to read. You are better off just skimming the rest of it. A good 80 percent of most people's mail is junk and best not read at all. Just about 80 percent of your housework can wait almost indefinitely, while 20 percent of it, if not done, would soon make your home uninhabitable.

Symptom Effectiveness

Effective time-management skills can help with minimizing deadline anxiety, procrastination, and job fatigue.

Time to Master

You can begin to clarify what is most important in your life in as little as an hour and then return to this important task as additional ideas occur to you. Take at least a few more hours to define your goals. You can create an action plan for one of your goals in an hour. You will need at least three days to complete the time log. Take at least a few hours to compare how you are actually spending your time in terms of your priorities and goals and to decide how you want to change the way you are spending your time so that it more closely matches your ideals and goals. While you can put the tips to combat procrastination and organize your time more efficiently into practice in a week, you'll probably need several months of conscious effort before these techniques become habitual. If all this seems like a big investment, consider that the time you spend now will give you more free time in the future.

Instructions

In this chapter you will be asked to do six tasks:

1. Clarify your values.

2. Set goals.

3. Develop an action plan.

4. Evaluate how you spend your time.

5. Combat procrastination.

6. Organize your time.

Since each step builds on the previous steps, start with the first step and work your way through to the last.

Clarifying Your Values

The first step toward effective time management is deciding what is most worthwhile or desirable to you. People typically have priorities involving such things as career, health, home, family, spirituality, finances, leisure, learning, creativity, happiness, peace of mind, and communication. Knowing what is most valuable to you gives you direction in life. You can focus the majority of your time and energy on these values, rather than on things that are less important to you. When you have to choose between alternatives, you can look to your priorities to help you make your decision.

Identify Your Highest Priorities

The two brief guided fantasies that follow will help you identify your highest priorities.

1. Close your eyes, take a few deep breaths, and relax. Imagine yourself in a favorite place where you can take a few minutes to think. The time is many years from now. You have lived a long and full life. Reflect upon your life from this mature vantage point. What did you most enjoy experiencing and doing? What did you most appreciate accomplishing or having? Write your answers in this space or on a separate piece of paper.

_____

_____

_____

_____

2. Return to your relaxed position and imagine yourself again in your favorite place. This time, you are still your current age. You have just learned that you have a rare illness that has no symptoms but will kill you in six months. Given only half a year to live, what do you want to experience, do, accomplish, and have? Write your answers in this space or on another piece of paper.

_____

_____

_____

_____

_____

Compare your two sets of answers. Are they the same or different? Most people actually faced with a life-threatening illness find that their priorities change. Things once thought to be crucial seem less important, and things once overlooked take on new meaning.

Order Your Values

Take the list that you have developed and order your values from the most to the least important for you. You will find that this list will come in handy when you have difficulty choosing between two or more alternatives.

Here's how Alice, a single working parent, listed her values in order of importance.

l. Family	5. Nice home
2. Financial security	6. Friends
3. Health	7. Travel
4. Creativity	8. Honesty

Alice was troubled because her bosses pressured her to sign off on incomplete drafts of her designs. When she refused, they simply bypassed her signature. She vacillated between reporting her company's infractions to a government regulatory agency and remaining silent to avoid reprisal. In examining her values, she realized that not speaking out was a form of dishonesty. But she also realized that while honesty was important to her, it had the lowest priority of all her values, and that all her other values were being successfully fulfilled by her job. With this insight, she stopped criticizing herself and waited until she had found a job in another company to report her former employer's misconduct so that she did not jeopardize the other important aspects of her life.

Rank your values from the most to least important for you:

1.	5.
2.	6.
3.	7.
4.	8.

Setting Goals

The second step to effective time management involves setting goals. Values are ideals. They are the things, experiences, qualities, and principles that you would most like to have in your life. Goals are real and specific. Goals are objectives that you want to achieve, given the constraints of your time and other resources. Your fondest hope might be to become a champion race-car driver. Your goal might be to cross the Indianapolis 500 finish line in first place three years from now. To bring your life into closer alignment with what you consider most worthwhile, use your list of values to guide you in defining your goals.

Designing Effective Goals

Here are five crucial questions to ask yourself when designing effective goals:

1. **Is this a goal that you really want to devote a lot of time and energy to accomplish?** Or is it simply a dream of what you would like to have fall in your lap, but are not willing to work for? Many people think that they would like to travel around the world, but are not willing to save the money this would require.

2. **Is this goal consistent with your highest values?** One reason that you may not accomplish a goal is because it does not fit in with what is most important to you. If you value education and your goal is to finish college in the next year, but your highest priorities are family and socializing with friends, you may want to give yourself more time to complete this goal so that you won't have to neglect your family and friends.

3. **Is this goal achievable?** Is it specific enough so that you will know when you have achieved it? Is it achievable within a definite time frame that you can set for yourself? Do you have access to the resources necessary to achieve it? Rather than saying that you want to "retire on a comfortable income," set a date for retirement and specify an amount of money that you know you can realistically earn and save to support the lifestyle that you want to have. You can modify your goals as you get more information.

4. **Is this goal positive?** You are more likely to achieve goals that you are moving toward, rather than away from. Instead of setting yourself the negative goal of no longer overeating, give yourself the positive objective of eating three sensible, nutritious meals a day.

5. **Are your goals in balance?** Do most of your goals involve career and finances, while almost none of them have to do with health, relationships, or fun? Lack of balance is a major source of stress. If you spend your workday alone in front of a computer terminal, a short-term goal might be to get regular exercise outdoors with other people.

Balancing Your Goals

Do you have about an equal number of short-term, medium-term, and long-term goals? Some people plan on waiting until they retire to live their lives the way they really want to. Others can enjoy the here and now, but are handicapped when it comes to achieving goals that involve delayed gratification. A mixture of short-term, medium-term, and long-term goals can provide you with satisfaction in the here and now as well as offer you objectives that you find meaningful to work toward.

Are your short-term and medium-term goals compatible with your long-term goals? If you want to live to a ripe old age to travel the world with old friends, your short-term and medium-term goals need to include taking care of your health, cultivating friendships, and making money.

Do you periodically reassess your goals to make sure that they are still what you want? As you work toward your goals, you gain new information and insights. Part of balancing your goals involves adapting them to changes taking place in your life. Be flexible.

Here's how Eric, a forty-one-year-old manager in an electronics firm, used his list of values to guide him in setting his life goals. First he listed his values:

1. *Family:* To enjoy, take care of, and provide for them.

2. *Health:* To preserve the good health I have into my eighties.

3. *Financial security:* To have enough money to take care of family, leisure, travel dreams, and retirement.

4. *Professional success:* To become a vice president with my company.

5. *Nature:* To spend time in the wilderness every year; to learn more about animal behavior.

6. *Friends:* To enjoy them and help out.

7. *Spiritual:* To maintain my connection with my higher power and give my children an opportunity for this also.

8. *Travel:* To go as often and as far as time and money permit.

9. *Communication:* To be open and honest with others and feel that they are with me.

Here are the goals that Eric developed, based on his list of values.

Long-term goals (over five years):

1. Own and live in a house on the lake where I spent my summers as a child.

2. Optimize my health with regular exercise, diet, rest, and medical checkups.

3. Raise my three children and provide them with an education.

4. Save and invest enough money so that I can retire at fifty-five years old, live at the lake, and travel.

5. Publish a book on tracking based on my wilderness experience.

Medium-term goals:

1. Become a vice president for the company in four years.

2. Buy a new house to accommodate our growing family within two years.

3. Find a church that the whole family can agree on and become an active participant.

4. Listen to audiotapes on personal financial planning and investing when commuting.

5. Go on a backpacking trip with friends to the Lost Coast a year and a half from now.

Short-term goals:

1. Go camping with my wife alone for a long weekend in the next month.

2. Set up a weekly family night starting this Thursday.

3. Have a fun evening with friends at least once a week.

4. Jog three mornings a week and take a hike with family and friends at least once a month.

5. Meditate for fifteen minutes before leaving the office for home.

6. Remember to take a few deep breaths and relax my muscles when faced with a stressful event.

Write down one or more specific goals for each of your priorities. You may find it helpful to list your various goals under the following three categories:

1. Your long-term goals (goals that will take you over five years to accomplish).

_____

_____

_____

_____

_____

2. Your medium-term goals (goals that will take you between one and five years).

_____

_____

_____

_____

_____

3. Your short-term goals (goals that will take from one week to less than one year).

_____

_____

_____

_____

_____

_____

Developing an Action Plan

Your third step is to identify the specific steps that you need to take in order to achieve each of your goals. The most common reason that people do not attain their objectives is that they do not have an action plan that describes step by step how they are going to get from where they are now all the way to their goal. Without an action plan, your goal may seem too big and too remote. Without knowing what to do first, you never get beyond the dreaming stage.

An effective action plan includes:

- a well-thought-out and specific goal

- a description of all the resources that you will need and how you will access them

- each step you must take, in the correct order

- how you will monitor your progress

- the most likely reasons why you might procrastinate and how you will deal with this

- what rewards you will use to motivate yourself

Here are two alternative strategies to create an action plan.

1. **Imagine that you have already achieved your goal.** How would you feel, look, behave, and sound? How would people around you respond to you? Once you have a clear picture of what you want and are in touch with the good feelings that picture generates for you, begin to work backward from that fantasized image. Ask yourself what steps you must have taken to achieve your objective. Notice which resources you used. Did you need to develop new skills? Did you use outside resources or did you simply rely on your personal ones? How much time did it take? How did you deal with obstacles such as your fears and excuses and other people's demands on your time? How did you motivate yourself to keep going? Run a mental movie from where you are now all the way through to achieving your goal. Write down, in order, the steps you took.

Tom, a student in a college English class, used this approach. His goal was to receive an A on a paper for his creative writing class. First he visualized getting his paper back from his professor with an A on its cover. After relishing his pleasure and excitement and enjoying the imaginary congratulations of his friends, he went on to think through the steps he could have taken to reach that goal. Here's the original list of steps that he generated:

1. I take a walk by myself just to come up with a topic for my paper.

2. While walking, I come up with a great idea about writing a short story about salmon fishing in Alaska, which is how I earned extra money last summer. I reminisce about my experiences. I get excited about writing the paper.

3. I write an outline of my story.

4. I write a rough draft of my story.

5. I look over the rough draft and write a more polished version.

6. I have my friend read my paper. I am encouraged by her positive comments.

7. I review and incorporate many of my friend's suggestions.

8. I make the final copy of my paper.

9. I turn my paper in on time.

After thinking about his action plan, Tom realized that it didn't really deal with one familiar obstacle: his tendency to get sidetracked by his family and friends. He decided that his best strategy would be to reward himself with some time off once he had written a rough draft and then bring himself back to the project by again visualizing accomplishing his goal.

2. Brainstorm. A second way to create an action plan is to write your goal at the top of a blank sheet of paper and then randomly ask yourself questions about everything you need to know and do in order to achieve your objective. When you are finished brainstorming, rewrite the specific steps you need to take from where you are now all the way through to your goal.

Angela's goal was to establish an ongoing aerobic exercise program. She started by asking herself these questions:

Why do I want to exercise?

I want to feel and look healthy, fit, trim, and strong. One of my long-term goals is to be healthy into my old age.

How often and how long do I need to exercise aerobically to get the results I want?

I need to read more about exercise to answer these questions. I can talk to my friends about their experiences with exercise. I want to start out gradually and set more challenging goals as I become stronger.

What kind of exercise do I like? What kind am I capable of doing and have the time and resources to do?

Walking, swimming, jogging, biking, and working out to an aerobic dance videotape are all good candidates.

What do I need in order to exercise safely and have a hassle-free time?

I need an exercise that I can do without getting in my car and having to deal with traffic. (That rules out swimming and biking!) There's a safe trail near my house. I have a

VCR and I can buy an aerobic dance tape. Except for shoes, I already have plenty of clothes I can dance, walk, and jog in.

Which tape should I buy?
I can ask my friends for recommendations, or rent some tapes and see which I like best. I can go to the book, record, or video store and buy the ones I like best.

What kind of shoes should I get and where do I find them?
Go to the local sports store and ask the salesperson for help. I could read up on shoes, but I'd rather talk to my friends.

When am I going to exercise?
After work, when I first come home, before I do anything else.

How am I going to motivate myself to stick with this program?
I can jog with a friend. I can participate in local races. I can notice how much better I feel and look when I have been exercising regularly for a while. I can reward myself with new exercise clothes and tapes and gold stars. I can always do aerobic dance, even when the weather is bad or it's dark outside.

How am I going to monitor my progress?
I will keep track of my progress by reviewing the gold stars on my calendar every other week with my friend Stacey, who knows what I am trying to accomplish and is very supportive of me.

Here's the action plan that Angela developed after she had read through and reorganized her answers:

1. Define my specific exercise goal and keep in mind my purpose in exercising regularly.

2. Read more about aerobic exercise to find out how often and how long I need to exercise.

3. Talk to my friends about jogging, proper shoes, and aerobic dance tapes.

4. Find a jogging partner. (An optional step: not essential for me to start my program.)

5. Consult with a salesperson at local sports store and buy a comfortable pair of shoes to fit my needs.

6. Try out aerobic tapes by renting or borrowing them first.

7. Buy favorite aerobic tapes at local record, book, or video store.

8. Jog or do an aerobic dance tape when I first come home from work.

9. Monitor my progress by putting a gold star on the days of the week I exercise. I'll use the calendar in my kitchen, since I look at it every day.

10. Evaluate my progress with Stacey.

11. Reward myself by buying new exercise clothes, participating in local races, buying new tapes. I can look and feel great!

Evaluating Your Progress

Identifying a way to keep track of your progress should be a part of your action plan. One powerful approach is to plan to go over what you have accomplished toward your goal with a support person every couple of weeks. Choose a support person who understands and appreciates what you are trying to do. This person should be able to give you positive suggestions and encouragement, as well as point out when you are fooling yourself.

By the time of your second two-week progress evaluation, you should begin to see some positive results. Success can serve as a powerful reinforcer to continue your program, but don't let your first gains trick you into slacking off. Old habits don't die easily, and it can take three months to develop new ones.

If you are not seeing positive results, or you catch yourself making excuses for not following through on your plan, don't be too hard on yourself. Instead, reassess your original goal. Is this what you really want? If not, modify your goal. If it is something you want, consider how you can modify your action plan so that you can get moving toward your goal.

Writing a Self-Contract

You can formalize your goals and your action plan by writing a contract for yourself. In the contract, spell out your goals clearly and precisely. Include the details of how and when you are going to achieve them and how you plan to reward yourself for your efforts. Sign and date your contract. To ensure that you follow through on your self-contract, show it to the support person you have asked to sit down with you every other week for the next three months to evaluate your progress.

Here's the self-contract that Angela wrote for her exercise goal.

> *I, Angela Sanchez, am going to walk, jog, or exercise to an aerobic dance tape forty minutes per day, four days a week, starting this week. I will monitor my progress by giving myself a gold star every day that I exercise and by participating in local races. I will reward myself with a new T-shirt or shorts or aerobic tape at the end of each month I stick with my goal. I will evaluate my progress every two weeks for the next three months with Stacey by reviewing the gold stars on my calendar and discussing what it's like for me to be exercising regularly.*

> *Angela Sanchez*
> *June 1*

Evaluating How You Spend Your Time

Now you can begin the fourth step toward effective time management by keeping a daily log of your time. Do this in real time, rather than trying to estimate how much time you spent on the various activities that fill your day. Most people tend to grossly underestimate how long it takes to do things and to overlook or forget the unplanned activities that pop up during the day. If you really want to learn something new about yourself, stop once an hour during your waking day to record how long it took you to do each activity that you were involved in during that hour. At the very least, get out your notebook after

Sample Contract Form

I, _____ , am going to do _____
                (your name)   *(activity or goal)*

for or by _____ . I will monitor my progress by
                (how long, how often, by when)

_____ . I will evaluate my progress every
                (the method you will use)

_____ with my support person _____ .
                (how often)   *(name)*

I will reward myself with _____ .
                                    (something that will motivate you)

lunch and dinner and before bed and write down every activity you engaged in. Note the amount of time each one took. When you're through, the total amount of time for all activities should be fairly close to the total number of hours you were awake.

Keep this time inventory for at least three days. Categories of activities at work might include: paperwork, work-related and personal phone calls, socializing face-to-face, meetings, low-priority work, productive work, routine work, eating, and daydreaming. Typical activities not related to work are: personal hygiene, grooming, dressing, cooking, eating, naps, daydreaming, child care and parenting, shopping, household chores and maintenance, commuting, travel for errands, telephone calls, face-to-face conversations, television, hobbies, reading, participating in sports, exercising, and other recreation. Modify or add categories to suit yourself. Keep in mind that this time log is designed to help you break down and examine as carefully as you need to the various ways that you use your time, so that later you can decide if you want to spend more or less time engaged in each of these activities.

Samantha, a radio public-affairs interviewer, kept the following record on the first day of her three-day time assessment.

Sample Time Log

Activity Waking through lunch	*Time*
After lunch through dinner	
After dinner until sleep	

Samantha's Time Log

Activity	Time
Waking through lunch	
Lying in bed trying to get up	20 minutes
Shower	20 minutes
Grooming and dressing	25 minutes
Cooking breakfast	5 minutes
Eating breakfast and reading paper	10 minutes
Phone call (family)	10 minutes
Commute and listen to news	45 minutes
Morning staff meeting (10 minutes late)	40 minutes

Routine work - review and respond to:
    Phone messages
    Electronic mail
    Written memos
    Mail
	60 minutes

Daydreaming	5 minutes
Socializing (friend)	15 minutes
Meeting (15 minutes late)	45 minutes
Productive work (preparing for interview)	40 minutes
Lunch with friend (15 minutes late)	75 minutes
After lunch through dinner	
Productive work (preparing for interview)	95 minutes
Phone call (friend)	5 minutes
Daydreaming	10 minutes
Low-priority work (helping co-worker)	65 minutes
Socializing with co-worker	15 minutes
Phone call (work related)	30 minutes
Commute	45 minutes
Shopping	40 minutes
Mail	10 minutes
Phone call (personal)	25 minutes

Activity	Time
Neighbor visits	20 minutes
Phone (work related)	30 minutes
Cook while listening to news on TV	60 minutes
Eat	20 minutes
After dinner until sleep	
Clean up kitchen	15 minutes
Phone call (personal)	10 minutes
Television (documentary)	60 minutes
Reading novel	25 minutes
Turn off light (30 minutes late)	

Evaluating Your Time Log

Now that you know how you are actually spending your time, you are ready to compare the inventory you made with your real priorities. From there, you'll be able to go on to decide what changes you want to make to bring your current schedule into closer alignment with your most important values and goals. Here are some questions to guide you in making this comparison.

1. Which of the activities on your daily log are in line with your values and goals? Mark these activities with a star.

Samantha starred "reading the paper" and "listening and watching the news," since these activities reflected her priority of staying current with the news. She starred her productive time at work preparing for radio interviews because this reflected her priority to be a successful radio interviewer. She starred "phone calls with friends" since one of her priorities was to spend time with friends.

2. Which of the activities on your daily log are not in line with your values and goals?

Circle these activities.

Samantha was amazed to find that on this day she had spent three hours and fifteen minutes preparing, eating, and cleaning up after meals. She felt that over two hours on the phone and reading memos and mail for work was excessive. She also realized that she had wasted a half hour in the morning with extra time in bed and a long shower. She recognized that she allowed unexpected calls and socializing to get in the way of being on time. When she analyzed her work patterns, it became obvious that her most productive hours were at midday—and that lunch was a big interruption right in the middle of this time.

Look at the circled items on your list and write down how you would be willing to reschedule, reduce, or eliminate low-priority activities in your day.

_____

_____

_____

_____

3. Are any of your values being violated by any of the activities on your daily log? Mark these activities with an X.

Engaging in activities that run counter to your values can make you feel guilty, ashamed, anxious, depressed, resentful, or exhausted. Samantha's problem with tardiness ran counter to her priorities of peace of mind and being a successful radio interviewer. She felt rushed, anxious, guilty, and embarrassed when she arrived at meetings late.

Look at the items that you have marked with an X and write down how you would be willing to change your behavior so that it no longer violates your values.

_____

_____

_____

_____

4. Are some of your values and goals being neglected or ignored?

Activities that reflect these neglected values and goals may be the very ones that you need to expand or increase in order to bring balance to your life. On the other hand, these neglected values may actually have a lower priority at this time in your life than your other values, and you may realize that you feel okay about postponing activities associated with them.

Samantha noticed that her priorities having to do with friends, family, and health were underrepresented in how she spent her time. Except for brief phone calls, she didn't talk with her family. Since her parents and sisters lived in another state and she had recently visited them, this limited contact was okay with her for right now. She did want to spend more time with friends and take better care of herself physically. Her sedentary lifestyle and eating habits had caused her to gain weight.

Write down how you would be willing to change your behavior so that it would be consistent with the values and goals that you have been neglecting.

_____

_____

_____

_____

_____

Samantha decided that she was willing to make the following immediate changes in her use of time.

1. Eat a quick breakfast that does not require cooking.

2. Give being on time priority over unexpected phone calls and other low-priority activities.

3. Limit lunch to an hour and take it later in the day to take advantage of my most productive time of day.

4. Prepare simple dinners in half an hour.

5. Limit most work-related calls to ten minutes.

6. Skim written communication for "must know" and "must respond" information.

7. Give going to sleep on time priority over TV and reading.

8. Get up with the alarm and limit shower to ten minutes.

9. Go to the gym and work out with my friends four nights a week.

While it is unlikely that you would want to try to do something that reflects each one of your values and goals every single day, you can integrate all of your values and most of your goals into your activities if you plan your time on a weekly or even monthly basis. Continue using the tools you learned earlier in this chapter to clearly define your goals and prepare an action plan that lets you evaluate and reward yourself for the progress you have made.

Combating Procrastination

The fifth step toward effective time management is to get yourself unstuck. You have already learned several ways to combat procrastination in this chapter. What distasteful activity are you avoiding? Compare it with your values. Does it violate one of your priorities? If it does, are you ready to take a stand and declare that you are not going to do it? If not, what can you do to change your circumstances in the future so that you will no longer be violating one of your values? If you are avoiding an activity that is tied to one of your goals, review the section in this chapter on setting effective goals. If you don't know where to start, create an action plan. If you simply need to get better organized, refer to the sixth and final step in this chapter, which deals with organizing your time.

Here are ten additional suggestions to use when you find yourself procrastinating.

1. **Stop worrying.** You probably spend more time worrying about chores that you do not want to do than you would spend by simply doing them. To illustrate this point to yourself, keep track of how much time you take to complete each distasteful task.

2. **Start small.** Once you start doing an unpleasant task, you may find that it isn't as bad as you anticipated. Lead yourself into the cold water with a small but related task. If you have to mow the lawn, decide to go as far as filling the gas tank on the mower and wheeling it out to the edge of the lawn.

3. **Count the cost.** Make a list of all the unpleasant aspects of doing the activity that you are avoiding and then make a second list of the consequences of putting it off. Look squarely at the discomfort of doing it versus the cost of delay and ask yourself which list contains the greater degree of unpleasantness. Use this information to create enthusiasm for getting the job done.

4. **Look for the hidden rewards.** Look for any payoffs that you may be receiving for not getting the distasteful job done. For example, by procrastinating you may be avoiding feeling anxious or facing the possibility of failure. Also examine the advantages of avoiding whatever changes might follow from completing the task. For example, success might mean that you lose the attention that you now get from people who nag you or sympathize with your predicament.

5. **Confront negative beliefs.** Read chapter 12, Refuting Irrational Ideas, to confront beliefs that may be interfering with doing what you need to do. Are you making statements to yourself such as, "No way am I going to do this, it just isn't fair," "I must do it perfectly," "Life should be easy," "I can't stand the thought of giving a speech in front of a group of strangers," "What if I succeed? They'll expect even more out of me," or "I'll fail, so why try?"

6. **Double your resistance.** Exaggerate and intensify whatever you are doing that is putting off beginning a task. If you are staring at yourself in the mirror in the morning instead of getting to work, draw that stare out. Really study all your pores and go over each quadrant of your face minutely. Keep it up until you are really bored and getting to work seems like a more attractive alternative.

7. **Take responsibility for each delay.** You are the one wasting your precious time. Make a list of each procrastination or escape activity and note how long it took. Add up the total and list all the positive things you could have done with that time if you'd simply finished the job to begin with.

8. **Tie a distasteful activity to an activity that you know you will do.** For example, if you dislike exercise, find a gym you can go to on your way home from work or plan to exercise by walking to lunch in a restaurant twenty minutes from your office.

9. **Reward yourself for doing activities that are unpleasant to you.**

10. **Finish things.** Avoid beginning a new task until you have completed a specific segment of your current task. The experience of finishing something is itself a great reward.

Organizing Your Time

The sixth and final step toward more effective time management is to get better organized. Here are twelve suggestions to structure your time and focus your attention on creating the life of your choice.

1. **Purchase an organizer.** Find one that includes a daily, weekly, and monthly calendar and use it.

2. **Post copies of your written values, goals, action plans, and self-contracts in places where you will often be reminded of them.** Use brightly colored paper and ink to catch your eye. Try keeping a copy in your organizer or on a wall calendar or your bathroom mirror or any other place that you look at frequently.

3. **Make sure that your list of daily goals and your calendar reflect your long-term, medium-term, and short-term goals.** If you want to be physically fit and relaxed, schedule time each day for exercise and for practicing relaxation techniques. If spending quality time with a loved one is high priority, block off regular time on your calendar to do this and include that time on your daily to-do list. If you arrange your schedule of activities on a weekly or even monthly basis, you will find that you have time to work on all of your important goals.

4. **Plan for efficiency.** Combine activities that can be done at the same time, such as watching your favorite TV show while exercising, ironing, or washing dishes. Sequence activities to save time. Match tasks to your varying energy levels. Although you can usually predict your energy level at different points during the day and plan accordingly, occasionally you will run out of steam earlier than anticipated. If so, you may want to reschedule activities that require energy and alertness to a time when you can perform them with maximum efficiency.

5. **Minimize time wasters.** Cut back on TV, telephone interruptions, drop-in visitors, unproductive meetings, ineffective delegation of responsibilities, crises, activities that lack direction, and overly ambitious goals. Plan ways to avoid as many predictable time wasters as possible, but be realistic enough to schedule some time for unexpected interruptions.

6. **Learn to say no.** Set limits on how much you are willing to do for others. If you have difficulty with this, see chapter 17, Assertiveness Training.

7. **Make a list of things to do when you're waiting.** Good candidates include doing a relaxation exercise, planning tomorrow's list of goals, reviewing your priorities and goals, reading a book, or filing your nails.

8. **Set aside several short periods each day for quiet time.** Use this time to practice your deep relaxation techniques. This will help you stay in touch with what is most important to you, rather than rushing faster and faster in response to others' demands.

9. **When you are performing a high-priority activity, focus your full attention on it.** Make a list of your usual distractions and plan how you can block each one of them. For instance, if you often find yourself daydreaming when you should be working, schedule in a visualization session or some other way of using your imagination during one of your quiet times.

10. **Arrange your environment to support your values and goals.** If your priorities require focus and concentration, make sure that you have a quiet room or corner available for reading, writing, practicing deep relaxation, or just thinking through your plans.

11. **Don't waste time on decisions that involve equally attractive or inconsequential alternatives.** If you find yourself in a quandary over choices like this, just flip a coin and go with the winning call.

12. **Reward yourself for improving your time management.** One of the greatest rewards of effective time management comes from not having to rush to accomplish the important things in your life. By prioritizing and planning your activities, you can choose to move through your day at a more leisurely pace.

Organizing Your Day

Managing your time on a daily basis requires setting immediate priorities and sticking to them. At the beginning of each day, develop a to-do list that reflects your goals as well as necessary tasks. Each day's list should be prioritized by sorting activities into the following categories:

1. *Top drawer.* These are the most essential and most desired items.

2. *Middle drawer.* You could put these activities off for a while, but they are still important.

3. *Bottom drawer.* You can easily put these tasks off indefinitely with no harm done.

Go through your list and mark each item TD, MD, or BD according to its status. Now, as you start your day, you have a blueprint for how to apportion your time. Start with the top-drawer items first and work your way down the list. Only move on to the middle drawer when all of your top-drawer items have been completed. If you have too many top-drawer tasks to finish in a day, then you've given too many things a high priority. Only assign top-drawer status to tasks that absolutely cannot be put off and would result in negative consequences if they were.

Banish the bottom-drawer items from consideration unless you have completed all your higher priority items for the day. The definition of bottom-drawer items is that they can wait. Unless it's your boss who's asking, keep away from commitments that force you to spend time in the bottom drawer. Be prepared to say, "I don't have the time" to these requests. If circumstances force you to take on a bottom-drawer task, try to delegate it. Give it to your secretary, your housecleaner, or your children.

As you move through your day, stay focused on the high-priority tasks and make sure that you limit your opportunities for procrastination. Block off any escape routes that turn up by scheduling daydreaming for a later time, putting off socializing until a chunk of work is done, avoiding getting caught up in busywork or less important errands, and resisting the impulse to run out for ice cream or other tempting indulgences.

At the end of the day, review your to-do list. Check off the items that you completed as planned and give yourself a mental pat on the back. Add anything you did that was not on your original list. Note whether it was a high-, medium-, or low-priority item. Important things you did not finish can be moved to the next day. A good time to prepare a day's list of goals is the preceding evening or first thing in the morning. Either way, you start out fresh, on top of things, and in tune with your priorities.

Further Reading

Brinkman, R. 1993. *Life by Design: Making Lifestyle Choices That Contribute to Better Physical and Emotional Health.* Boulder, Colo.: Career Track Publications. (This is an audiotape and workbook set.)

Epstein-Shepherd, B. 1993. *Creating More Time in Your Life.* Boulder, Colo.: Career Track Publications. (This is an audiotape set.)

Griessman, B. E. 1994. *Time Tactics of Very Successful People.* New York: McGraw Hill.

Rechtschaffen, S. 1997. *Time Shifting: Creating More Time to Enjoy Your Life.* New York: Doubleday.

Scott, D. 1981. *How to Put More Time in Your Life.* New York: New American Library.

Stautberg, S. S., and M. L. Worthing. 1992. *Balancing Acts! Juggling Love, Work, Family, and Recreation.* New York: Master Midea.

Assertiveness Training

In this chapter you will learn to:

☐ Evaluate your current patterns of communication

☐ Differentiate between aggressive, passive, and assertive styles of communication

☐ Express your feelings and opinions, set limits, and initiate change

☐ Listen assertively

☐ Avoid manipulation

How you interact with people can be a source of major stress. Assertiveness training can reduce that stress by teaching you to stand up for your legitimate rights, without bullying others or letting them bully you.

Before reading any further, write down how you would typically respond to the following problem situations.

1. You finish shopping in the market, and after you walk out you discover that the change is five dollars short.

I would:

_____

_____

2. You order a steak rare and it arrives medium-well.

I would:

3. You're giving a friend a lift to a meeting. The friend keeps puttering around for half an hour and you realize that you will arrive late.

I would:

4. You have really been looking forward all week to seeing a particular movie, and your companion informs you that he or she wants to see a different movie.

I would:

5. You are relaxing with the paper after a long day. Your spouse pops in, list in hand, and says, "I thought you'd never get here. Quick, pick these up from the store."

I would:

6. While you wait for the clerk to finish with the customer ahead of you, another customer comes in and the clerk starts to wait on him before you.

I would:

_____

_____

_____

After you have written down what you would do in these problem situations, set your responses aside. They will be put to use shortly.

Background

Andrew Salter initially described assertiveness as a personality trait in 1949. It was thought that some people had it, and some people didn't, just like extroversion or stinginess. But Wolpe (1958) and Lazarus (1966) redefined assertiveness as "expressing personal rights and feelings." They found that nearly everybody could be assertive in some situations, and yet be totally ineffectual in others. The goal of assertiveness training is to increase the number and variety of situations in which assertive behavior is possible, and decrease occasions of passive collapse or hostile blowup.

You are assertive when you stand up for your rights in such a way that the rights of others are not violated. Beyond just demanding your rights, assertiveness implies that you can express your personal likes and interests spontaneously, you can talk about yourself without being self-conscious, you can accept compliments comfortably, you can disagree with someone openly, you can ask for clarification, and you can say no. In short, when you are an assertive person, you can be more relaxed in interpersonal situations.

Some people think that assertiveness training turns nice people into irascible complainers or calculating manipulators. Not so. It's your right to protect yourself when something seems unfair. You are the one who best knows your discomfort and your needs.

Investigators such as Jakubowski-Spector (1973) and Alberti and Emmons (1970) discovered that people who show relatively little assertive behavior do not believe that they have a right to their feelings, beliefs, or opinions. In the deepest sense, they reject the idea that we are created equal and are to treat each other as equals. As a result, they can't find grounds for objecting to exploitation or mistreatment. They likely learned as children traditional assumptions that implied that their perceptions, opinions, feelings, and wants were less important or correct than those of others. They grew up doubting themselves and looking to others for validation and guidance.

You did not have much choice about which traditional assumptions you were taught as a child. Now, however, you have the option of deciding whether to continue behaving according to assumptions that keep you from being an assertive adult. Each of these mistaken assumptions violates one of your legitimate rights as an adult:

Mistaken Traditional Assumptions	*Your Legitimate Rights*
1. It is selfish to put your needs before others' needs.	You have a right to put yourself first sometimes.
2. It is shameful to make mistakes. You should have an appropriate response for every occasion.	You have a right to make mistakes.
3. If you can't convince others that your feelings are reasonable, then the feelings must be wrong, or maybe you are going crazy.	You have a right to be the final judge of your feelings and accept them as legitimate.
4. You should respect the views of others, especially if they are in a position of authority. Keep your differences of opinion to yourself. Listen and learn.	You have a right to have your own opinions and convictions.
5. You should always try to be logical and consistent.	You have a right to change your mind or decide on a different course of action.
6. You should be flexible and adjust. Others have good reasons for their actions and it's not polite to question them.	You have a right to protest unfair treatment or criticism.
7. You should never interrupt people. Asking questions reveals your stupidity to others.	You have a right to interrupt in order to ask for clarification.
8. Things could get even worse, don't rock the boat.	You have a right to negotiate for change.
9. You shouldn't take up others' valuable time with your problems.	You have a right to *ask* for help or emotional support.
10. People don't want to hear that you feel bad, so keep it to yourself.	You have a right to feel and express pain.
11. When someone takes the time to give you advice, you should take it very seriously. They are often right.	You have a right to ignore the advice of others.

Mistaken Traditional Assumptions	*Your Legitimate Rights*
12. Knowing that you did something well is its own reward. People don't like show-offs. Successful people are secretly disliked and envied. Be modest when complimented.	You have a right to receive formal recognition for your work and achievements.
13. You should always try to accommodate others. If you don't, they won't be there when you need them.	You have a right to say "no."
14. Don't be anti-social. People are going to think you don't like them if you say you'd rather be alone instead of with them.	You have a right to be alone, even if others would prefer your company.
15. You should always have a good reason for what you feel and do.	You have a right not to have to justify yourself to others.
16. When someone is in trouble, you should help them.	You have a right not to take responsibility for someone else's problem.
17. You should be sensitive to the needs and wishes of others, even when they are unable to tell you what they want.	You have a right not to have to anticipate others' needs and wishes.
18. It's always a good policy to stay on people's good side.	You have a right not to always worry about the goodwill of others.
19. It's not nice to put people off. If questioned, give an answer.	You have a right to choose not to respond to a situation.

As you continue through this chapter, keep in mind that assertive communication is based on the assumption that you are the best judge of your thoughts, feelings, wants, and behavior. Nobody is better informed than you regarding how your heredity, history, and current circumstances have shaped you into a unique human being. Therefore, you are the best advocate for expressing your positions on important issues. Because of your uniqueness, there are many times when you differ with significant people in your life. Rather than overpowering the meek or giving in to the aggressive, you have the right to express your position and try to negotiate your differences.

Symptom Effectiveness

Assertiveness training has been found to be effective in dealing with depression, anger, resentment, and interpersonal anxiety, especially when these symptoms have been brought about by unfair circumstances. As you become more assertive, you begin to lay claim to your right to relax and take better care of yourself.

Time to Master

Some people master assertiveness skills sufficiently for symptom relief with just a few weeks of practice. For others, several months of step-by-step work are necessary to experience significant change.

Instructions

1. *Three Basic Interpersonal Styles*

Assertiveness is a skill that can be learned, not a personality trait that some are born with and others are not. The first step in assertiveness training is to identify the three basic styles of interpersonal behavior.

Aggressive style. In this style, opinions, feelings, and wants are honestly stated, but at the expense of someone else's feelings. The underlying message is, "I'm superior and right, and you're inferior and wrong." The advantage of aggressive behavior is that people often give aggressive individuals what they want in order to get rid of them. The disadvantage is that aggressive individuals make enemies, and people who can't avoid them entirely may end up behaving dishonestly toward them in order to avoid confrontations.

Passive style. In this style, opinions, feelings, and wants are withheld altogether or expressed indirectly and only in part. The underlying message is, "I'm weak and inferior, and you're powerful and right." The advantage of passive communication is that it minimizes responsibility for making decisions and the risk of taking a personal stand on an issue. The disadvantages are a sense of impotence, lowered self-esteem, and having to live with the decisions of others.

Assertive style. In this style, you clearly state your opinions, feelings, and wants without violating the rights of others. The underlying assumption is, "You and I may have our differences, but we are equally entitled to express ourselves to one another." The major advantages include active participation in making important decisions, getting what you want without alienating others, the emotional and intellectual satisfaction of respectfully exchanging feelings and ideas, and high self-esteem.

To test your ability to distinguish interpersonal styles, label person A's behavior in the following scenes as aggressive, passive, or assertive:

Scene 1

A: Is that a new dent I see in the car?

B: Look, I just got home, it was a wretched day, and I don't want to talk about it now.

A: This is important to me, and we're going to talk about it now.

B: Have a heart.

A: Let's decide now who is going to pay to have it fixed, when, and where.

B: I'll take care of it. Now leave me alone, for heaven's sake!

A's behavior is ☐ Aggressive   ☐ Passive   ☐ Assertive

Scene 2

A: You left me so by myself at that party ... I really felt abandoned.

B: You were being a party pooper.

A: I didn't know anybody—the least you could have done is introduce me to some of your friends.

B: Listen, you're grown up. You can take care of yourself. I'm tired of your nagging to be taken care of all the time.

A: And I'm tired of your inconsiderateness.

B: Okay, I'll stick to you like glue next time.

A's behavior is ☐ Aggressive   ☐ Passive   ☐ Assertive

Scene 3

A: Would you mind helping me for a minute with this file?

B: I'm busy with this report. Catch me later.

A: Well, I really hate to bother you, but it's important.

B: Look, I have a four o'clock deadline.

A: Okay, I understand. I know it's hard to be interrupted.

A's behavior is ☐ Aggressive   ☐ Passive   ☐ Assertive

Scene 4

A: I got a letter from Mom this morning. She wants to come and spend two weeks with us. I'd really like to see her.

B: Oh no, not your mother! And right on the heels of your sister. When do we get a little time to ourselves?

A: Well, I do want her to come, but I know you need to spend some time without my relatives underfoot. I'd like to invite her to come in a month, and instead of two weeks, I think one week would be enough. What do you say to that?

B: That's a big relief to me.

A's behavior is ☐ Aggressive   ☐ Passive   ☐ Assertive

Scene 5

A: Boy, you're looking great today!

B: Who do you think you're kidding? My hair is a fright and my clothes aren't fit for the Goodwill box.

A: Have it your way.

B: And I feel just as bad as I look today.

A: Right. I've got to run now.

A's behavior is ☐ Aggressive   ☐ Passive   ☐ Assertive

Scene 6

(While at a party, A is telling her friends how much she appreciates her boyfriend taking her out to good restaurants and to the theater. Her friends criticize her for being unliberated.)

A: Not so. I don't make nearly as much as a secretary as he does as a lawyer. I couldn't afford to take us both out or pay my own way to all the nice places we go. Some traditions make sense, given the economic realities.

A's behavior is ☐ Aggressive   ☐ Passive   ☐ Assertive

Now that you have labeled person A's responses in these scenes as aggressive, passive, or assertive, compare your assessment with ours:

Scene 1. A is aggressive. A's seemingly innocent question is actually an accusation in disguise. A's insistence on immediate action with total disregard for B's state of mind sets up a polarized conflict in which B is likely to feel wrong, withdrawn, and defensive.

Scene 2. A is aggressive. The tone is accusing and blaming. B is immediately placed on the defensive and no one wins.

Scene 3. A is passive. A's timid opening line is followed by complete collapse. The file problem must now be dealt with alone.

Scene 4. A is assertive. The request is specific, nonhostile, and open to negotiation.

Scene 5. A is passive. A allows the compliment to be rebuffed and surrenders to B's rush of negativity.

Scene 6. A is assertive. She stands up to the prevailing opinion of the group and achieves a clear, nonthreatening statement of her position.

2. *The Assertiveness Questionnaire*

(Adapted from Sharon and Gordon Bower's *Asserting Your Self*.)

The second step in assertiveness training is to identify those situations in which you want to be more effective. Having clarified the three interpersonal styles, now reexamine your responses to the six problem situations you responded to at the beginning of this chapter. Label your responses as falling primarily in the aggressive, passive, or assertive style. This is a start in objectively analyzing your behavior and finding out where assertiveness training can most help you.

To further refine your assessment of the situations in which you need to be more assertive, complete the following questionnaire. Put a check mark in column A by the items that are applicable to you and then rate those items from 1–5 in column B:

1. comfortable

2. mildly uncomfortable

3. moderately uncomfortable

4. very uncomfortable

5. unbearably threatening

(Note that the varying degrees of discomfort can be expressed whether your inappropriate reactions are hostile or passive.)

	A *Check here* *if the item* *applies to me*	*B* *Rate* *from 1–5* *for discomfort*
WHEN do I behave nonassertively?		
Asking for help	_____	_____
Stating a difference of opinion	_____	_____
Receiving and expressing negative feelings	_____	_____
Receiving and expressing positive feelings	_____	_____
Dealing with someone who refuses to cooperate	_____	_____
Speaking up about something that annoys me	_____	_____
Talking when all eyes are on me	_____	_____
Protesting a rip-off	_____	_____
Saying "no"	_____	_____
Responding to undeserved criticism	_____	_____
Making requests of authority figures	_____	_____
Negotiating for something I want	_____	_____
Having to take charge	_____	_____
Asking for cooperation	_____	_____
Proposing an idea	_____	_____
Asking questions	_____	_____
Dealing with attempts to make me feel guilty	_____	_____
Asking for service	_____	_____

	A *Check here if the item applies to me*	B *Rate from 1–5 for discomfort*
Asking for a date or appointment	_____	_____
Other _____	_____	_____

WHO are the people with whom I am nonassertive?

Parents	_____	_____
Fellow workers, classmates	_____	_____
Strangers	_____	_____
Old friends	_____	_____
Spouse or mate	_____	_____
Employer	_____	_____
Relatives	_____	_____
Children	_____	_____
Acquaintances	_____	_____
Sales people, clerks, hired help	_____	_____
More than two or three people in a group	_____	_____
Other _____	_____	_____

WHAT do I want that I have been unable to achieve with nonassertive styles?

Approval for things I have done well	_____	_____
To get help with certain tasks	_____	_____
More attention, or time with my mate	_____	_____
To be listened to and understood	_____	_____
To make boring or frustrating situations more satisfying	_____	_____
To not have to be nice all the time	_____	_____
Confidence in speaking up when something is important to me	_____	_____
Greater comfort with strangers, store clerks, mechanics, and so on	_____	_____
Confidence in asking for contact with people I find attractive	_____	_____
To get a new job, ask for interviews, raises, and so on	_____	_____
Comfort with people who supervise me or work under me	_____	_____

	A Check here if the item applies to me	B Rate from 1–5 for discomfort
To not feel angry and bitter a lot of the time	_____	_____
To overcome a feeling of helplessness and the sense that nothing ever really changes	_____	_____
To initiate satisfying sexual experiences	_____	_____
To do something totally different and novel	_____	_____
To have time by myself	_____	_____
To do things that are fun or relaxing for me	_____	_____
Other _____	_____	_____

Evaluating your responses. Examine your answers, and analyze them for an overall picture of what situations and people threaten you. How does nonassertive behavior contribute to the specific items you checked on the *What* list? In constructing your assertiveness program, focusing initially on items you rated as falling in the 2–3 range will be useful. These are the situations that you will find easiest to change. Items that are very uncomfortable or threatening can be tackled later.

3. *Describing Your Problem Scenes*

The third step in assertiveness training, according to Sharon and Gordon Bower, is to describe your problem scenes. Select a mildly to moderately uncomfortable situation that suggests itself from items on the Assertiveness Questionnaire. Write out a description of the scene, being certain to include *who* the person involved is, *when* it takes place (time and setting), *what* bothers you, *how* you deal with it, your *fear* of what will take place if you are assertive, and your *goal*. Always be specific! Generalizations will make it difficult later on to write a script that will make assertive behavior possible in this situation. The following is an example of a poor scene description.

> I have a lot of trouble persuading some of my friends to listen to me for a change. They never stop talking, and I never get a word in edgewise. It would be nice for me if I could participate more in the conversation. I feel that I'm just letting them run over me.

Notice that the description doesn't specify *who* the particular friend is, *when* this problem is most likely to occur, *how* the nonassertive person acts, what *fears* are involved in being assertive, and a specific *goal* for increased involvement in the conversation. The scene might be rewritten as follows:

> My friend Joan *(who)*, when we meet for a drink after work *(when)*, often goes on nonstop about her marriage problems *(what)*. I just sit there and try to be interested *(how)*. If I interrupt her, I'm afraid she'll think I just don't care *(fear)*. I'd like to be able to change the subject and talk sometimes about my own life *(goal)*.

Here is a second poor scene description:

A lot of times I want to strike up a conversation with people, but I worry that maybe they don't want to be disturbed. Often I notice someone who seems interesting, but I can't imagine how to get their attention.

Once again there is a lack of detail. No clear statement is made as to *who* these people are, *when* the experience takes place, *how* the nonassertive person behaves, or the specific *goal*. The described scene will become much more useful by including these elements:

There is an attractive girl *(who)* who always brings a bag lunch and often sits at my table in the cafeteria *(what, where)* at lunch *(when)*. I just eat in silence and read my book *(how)*. I would like to start a conversation by asking about her boss, who has a very hard-to-get-along-with reputation *(goal)*, but she looks so intent on her book I'm afraid she would be put out if I interrupted *(fear)*.

Write three or four problem scenes, and for each scene try to relive the thoughts and feelings you actually experienced. You might notice, for example, that in each problem scene you gun yourself down with negative thoughts ("I can't do it . . . I'm blowing it again . . . boy, do I look stupid"), or you usually feel tense in the stomach and seem to be breathing way up in your chest. Some of the strategies in other chapters of this workbook that will help you cope with distressing habitual thoughts and physical reactions when you act assertively are: refuting irrational ideas, coping skills training, deep muscle relaxation, and breathing exercises. This chapter, however, primarily focuses on changing your habitual way of behaving in these problematic interpersonal situations.

4. *Your Script for Change*

The fourth step in assertiveness training is writing your script for change. A script is a working plan for dealing with the problem scene assertively. There are six elements in a script:

1. **Look at your rights, what you want, what you need, and what your feelings are about the situation**. Let go of blame, the desire to hurt, and self-pity. Define your goal and keep it in mind when you negotiate for change.

2. **Arrange a time and place to discuss your problem that is convenient for you and for the other person.** This step may be excluded when dealing with spontaneous situations in which you choose to be assertive, such as when a person cuts ahead of you in line.

3. **Define the problem situation as specifically as possible.** This is essential for focusing the discussion. Here is your opportunity to state the facts as you see them and share your opinion and beliefs. For example: "It's time to make a decision about where we're going to eat tonight. I know you love Mexican food, but we've eaten at Tijuana Joe's the last three times we've gone out for dinner. We're in a rut!"

4. **Describe your feelings so that the other person has a better understanding of how important the issue is to you.** Once they are expressed, your feelings can often play a major role in helping you get what you want, especially when your opinion differs markedly from that of your listener. If nothing else, the listener may be able to relate to and understand your feelings about an issue even when

he totally disagrees with your perspective. When you share your feelings, you become less of an adversary.

There are three important rules to remember when assertively expressing your feelings:

1. Do not substitute an opinion for a feeling ("I feel that Mexican food should be abolished!"). A more accurate feeling statement is, "I hate Mexican food!"

2. Use "I messages" that express your feelings without evaluating or blaming others. Rather than saying, "You are inconsiderate" or "You hurt me," the *I* message would be, "I feel hurt."

3. *I* messages connect the feeling statement with specific behaviors of the other person. For example, "I feel hurt when you ignore my wishes about where we eat." Contrast the clarity of this message with the vague blame statement, "I feel hurt because you are inconsiderate."

5. **Express your request in one or two easy-to-understand sentences.** Be specific and firm! Instead of expecting others to read your mind and magically meet your needs, as in the case of the passive individual, clearly state your wishes and needs. Rather than assuming that you are always right and entitled to getting your way, as an aggressive person might, state your wants as preferences, not commands. For example, "I would really like to go to a French restaurant tonight."

6. **Reinforce the other person to give you what you want.** The best reinforcement is to describe positive consequences. "We'll save money. . . . We'll have more time together. . . . I'll give you a backrub. . . . My mother will only stay a week. . . . I'll be less tired and more fun to be with. . . . I'll be able to get my work in on time. . . . Little Julia will do better in school," and so on.

In some cases, positive reinforcement may be ineffective. If the person you're dealing with seems resistant or you feel that you're having trouble motivating him or her to cooperate with you, consider describing some negative consequences for failure to cooperate. The most effective negative consequences are descriptions of the alternative way you will take care of yourself if your wishes aren't accommodated.

- If we can't leave on time, I'll have to leave without you. Then you'll have to drive over later on your own.

- If you can't clean the bathroom, I'll hire someone to do it once a week and add it to your rent.

- If you won't fold and put away your clothes, I'll just leave them in this box. I guess you can sort through it whenever you need something.

- If you keep talking in this loud, attacking way, I'll leave. We can talk again tomorrow.

- If you drink heavily again at these office functions, I won't go with you.

- If your check bounces again, we'll have to work on a cash basis only.

- If you keep talking during the movie, I'm going to ask the manager to come in here.

- If you can't give me an accurate idea of when you'll be home, I'm not going to cook and keep things warm for you.

Notice that these examples are different from threats. The consequence of noncooperation is that the speaker takes care of his or her interests. The consequences are not designed to hurt, merely to protect the speaker. Threats usually don't work because they make people so angry. If you do make a threat ("You won't go to my sister's wedding? I won't go to your family reunion!"), make sure you are willing and able to back it up. Even then it will often do more harm than good.

The first letters of each script element (Look, Arrange, Define, Describe, Express, and Reinforce) combine to spell LADDER. You may find this a useful mnemonic device to recall the steps toward assertive behavior. The LADDER script can be used to rewrite your problem scenes so that you can assert what you want. Initially, LADDER scripts should be written out and practiced well in advance of the problem situation they are created for. Writing the script forces you to clarify your needs and increases your confidence in success.

As an example of a LADDER script, let's say that Jean wants to assert her right to half an hour each day of uninterrupted peace and quiet while she does her relaxation exercises. Frank often interrupts with questions and attention-getting maneuvers. Jean's script goes like this:

Look at your rights and goal in this situation.
It's my responsibility to make sure Frank respects my needs, and I am certainly entitled to some time to myself.

Arrange a time and place to discuss the situation.
I'll ask him if he's willing to discuss this problem when he gets home tonight. If he isn't, we'll set a time and place to talk about it in the next day or two.

Define the problem specifically.
At least once, and sometimes more often, I'm interrupted during my relaxation exercises— even though I've shut the door and asked for the time to myself. My concentration is broken and I find that relaxing deeply is harder.

Describe your feelings using *I* messages.
I feel angry when my time alone is broken into and I feel frustrated that the exercises are then made more difficult.

Express your request simply and firmly.
I would like not to be interrupted when my door is closed, except in a dire emergency. As long as it is closed, assume that I am still doing the exercises and want to be alone.

Reinforce the other person to give you what you want.
If I'm not interrupted, I'll come in afterward and chat with you. If I am interrupted, I will take more time to do the exercises.

In another example, Harold has felt very reluctant to approach his boss to find out why he was turned down for a promotion. He's received no feedback about the reasons for the decision, and Harold is now feeling somewhat negative toward the company and toward his boss in particular. Harold's script is as follows:

Look at rights and goal:
Resentment won't solve this. I need to assert my right to reasonable feedback from my employer.

Arrange meeting:
I'll send him a memo tomorrow morning asking for time to discuss this problem.

Define problem:
I haven't gotten any feedback about the promotion. The position I applied for has been filled by someone else, and that's all I know.

Describe feelings:
I feel uncomfortable not knowing at all why I didn't get it and how the decision was made.

Express request:
I'd like to get some feedback from you about how my performance is seen, and what went into the decision.

Reinforce:
I think your feedback will help me do a better job.

These scripts, like the problem scenes described earlier, are specific and detailed. The statement of the problem is clear and to the point, without blaming, accusing, or being passive. The feelings are expressed with *I* messages and are linked to specific events or behaviors, not to an evaluation of Jean's husband or Harold's boss. *I* messages provide a tremendous amount of safety for the assertive individual because they usually keep the other person from getting defensive and angry. You are not accusing anyone of being a bad person, you are merely stating what you want or feel entitled to.

Successful LADDER scripts do the following:

1. When appropriate, establish a mutually agreeable time and place to assert your needs.

2. Describe behavior objectively, without judging or devaluing.

3. Describe clearly, using specific references to time, place, and frequency.

4. Express feelings calmly and directly.

5. Confine your feeling response to the specific problem behavior, not the whole person.

6. Avoid delivering put-downs disguised as "honest feelings."

7. Ask for changes that are reasonably possible, and small enough not to incur a lot of resistance.

8. Ask for no more than one or two very specific changes at a time.

9. Make the reinforcements explicit, offering something that is really desirable to the other person.

10. Avoid threats or negative consequences that you're not willing or able to do.

11. Keep your mind on your rights and goals when being assertive.

Using these rules, we can now distinguish between good and bad scripts. For example, for two semesters running, Julie has wanted to take a night class in ceramics. Each time, her husband has an excuse for why he can't watch the children on the class night. Here's Julie's script:

L   *I'm sick of being pushed around,*

A   *so I'm going to tell him tonight.*

D   *A year is long enough to wait.*

D   *He's too selfish to help,*

E   *so he's just going to have to suffer every Wednesday night.*

R   *If he doesn't like it, he can just kiss this marriage good-bye.*

Julie has violated these rules for a good script:

1. She didn't get an agreement on the time and place for the discussion.

2. She used nonspecific and accusing phrases such as "pushed around."

3. She failed to specify exactly what the problem is.

5. She described her husband as selfish, rather than expressing her feelings about specific behaviors.

8. She did not specify times, or duration of the semester.

9. She threatened negative consequences that she isn't willing or able to carry out.

Julie's script could be successfully rewritten as follows:

L   *I have a right to have time to myself during which I can pursue interests of my own. I want to attend this ceramics class.*

A   *I'll ask him to discuss it after breakfast Saturday morning, or as soon afterward as possible.*

D   *I've missed two previous ceramics classes because you weren't available for baby-sitting on class night. I've waited a year and I would like to enroll this time.*

D   *I feel frustrated that I haven't been able to explore something that really excites me. I also feel hurt when you do other things rather than help me take the class.*

E   *I'd like you to look after the children on Wednesday nights between 6:30 and 9:00. The semester ends June 2.*

R   *If you're willing, I'll cook my special meatloaf for you on Wednesdays, but if you're not, we'll have the expense of a baby-sitter.*

The described problem behavior has become specific and the expressed feelings are now nonthreatening. Julie's reinforcements are realistic and explicit. Note that negative reinforcement is often not necessary, and that positive reinforcement may require no more than the assurance that you will feel good if a certain behavior change is made. Elaborate promises can usually be avoided.

Now you can write your own LADDER scripts, using copies of the blank from on the next page. Then you can rehearse your written scripts in front of a mirror. If possible, tape-record your rehearsals to further refine your assertive style. Rehearsing scripts with a friend to get immediate feedback is helpful. Let yourself imagine or, better yet, act out, the worst possible response that could be made to your assertive request. Get desensitized to the "nightmare" response by facing it, and then prepare your countermeasures.

Assertive Ladder Script

Look at your rights and goal in this situation.

_____

_____

_____

Arrange a time and a place to discuss the situation.

_____

Define the problem specifically.

_____

_____

_____

Describe your feelings using "I messages."

_____

_____

_____

Express your request simply and firmly.

_____

_____

_____

Reinforce the other person to give you what you want.

_____

_____

_____

Short Form Assertiveness Technique

The short form assertiveness technique is designed for situations where you lack the time or energy to prepare an entire LADDER script. Assertiveness can be condensed to three basic statements:

1. **Your thoughts** about the problematic situation. This is a nonblaming, nonpejorative description of the problem as you see it. You stick as closely as possible to objective facts, making no inferences about the motives or feelings of others.

2. **Your feelings.** These are *I* statements about your emotional reaction to the problem. Try to avoid the implication that you're holding the other person responsible for your feelings. You're angry, sad, hurt, or disappointed. But your main message should be that you are trying to solve a problem, not blame or prove the other person wrong.

3. **Your wants.** As in the LADDER script, make your request specific and behavioral. Don't ask your tardy spouse to be "more considerate." Request specifically that he call if he'll be more than fifteen minutes late.

Whenever you're in a situation that requires an assertive response, quickly run through the three short form components in your mind:

I think . . . we've been working every night for two weeks on our bathroom remodel.

I feel . . . tired, grumpy, and pressured by your desire that it be done in one month's time.

I want . . . not to work more than three nights without one night off.

Make sure you've developed some idea of what you think, feel, and want before you start to speak. Try to express each component of your assertive statement in order. Finish one part before going on to the next.

Make a great effort to follow the rules about being nonblaming and making *I* statements. If you stick to these two simple rules, you'll find the other person far less defensive and far more cooperative. Stay away from attempts to prove that your needs are more important or more legitimate than the other person's. Just keep on track with a statement of facts, feelings, and a specific request for change.

Annie usually eats lunch with her co-worker, Marge. Once or twice a week Marge asks Annie to drop her by a bank or store on the way to eat. Annie finally reaches the boiling point when Marge has her drive forty minutes to get something notarized. Annie quickly reviews the three statements in short-form assertiveness:

I *think* . . . Once a week or more I help you with errands and we miss fifteen to thirty minutes of our lunch.

I *feel* . . . tired from rushing and disappointed that I don't get to relax at lunch.

I *want* . . . to stop being a taxi service for you during my lunch hour.

The "I want" seemed a bit harsh and attacking, so Annie changed it to, "Let's eat on our own if either of us has errands."

Recall a problematic situation in your life. As an exercise in thinking on your feet, try mentally composing an assertive message:

I *think* . . . (just the facts)

I *feel* . . . (expressed as an *I* statement)

I *want* . . . (specific behavior change)

Now keep practicing. Think of at least three situations where you'd like to be more assertive. As you recall each one, pretend you are really there and have to make some response. Quickly go over the three parts of your assertive statement, then say them out loud. Listen to how they sound. Are they blaming? Is your request specific enough? Are you saying clearly what you want? Are you criticizing the other person's motives or feelings? Correct what doesn't sound right and try saying it again.

5. *Assertive Body Language*

The fifth step in assertiveness training is to develop assertive body language. Practicing with the mirror will help you follow these five basic rules:

1. Maintain direct eye contact.

2. Maintain an erect body posture.

3. Speak clearly, audibly, and firmly.

4. Don't whine or use an apologetic tone of voice.

5. Make use of gestures and facial expression for emphasis.

6. *Learning How to Listen*

The sixth step of assertiveness training involves learning how to listen. As you practice being assertive in real-life situations, you will find that sometimes you need to deal with an issue that is important to the other person before he or she will be able to focus on what you have to say. This is especially true when what you want directly conflicts with long unspoken and unmet needs of the listener. For example, "You say you want an hour of silence when you first get home from work? Well, I haven't said this before because you're working so hard, but I'm ready to tear out my hair after spending the day with the kids. I have needs too, you know." At this point, it might be wise to practice assertive listening.

In listening assertively, you focus your attention on the other person so that you can accurately hear the speaker's opinions, feelings, and wishes. Assertive listening involves three steps:

1. **Prepare.** Become aware of your feelings and needs. Are you ready to listen? Are you sure that the other person is really ready to speak?

2. **Listen and clarify.** Give your full attention to the other person; listen to the speaker's perspective, feelings, and wants. If you are uncertain about one of these three elements, ask the speaker to clarify with more information: "I'm not quite sure how you view the situation . . . could you say more about it?" "How do you feel about this?" "I don't understand what you want . . . could you be more specific?"

3. **Acknowledge.** Communicate to the other person that you heard his or her position. For example, "I hear you don't want to take on this new project because

you're feeling overwhelmed with your current responsibilities and want to catch up." Another way to acknowledge the other person's feelings is to share your feelings about what has been said: "I'm feeling overwhelmed too, and I feel terrible about having to ask you to do more work."

Assertive listening and assertive expressing go together. Here is a sequence in which both people use assertive listening and expressing skills to solve a problem. John is unhappy about the way Carmen communicates her needs to him.

John: Is this a good time to talk about something that's bugging me a little? (*Arrange.*)

Carmen: Okay.

John: Yesterday you told me you were feeling cut off and kind of abandoned by me. (*Define.*) I felt like I was doing something horrible to you. I felt very wrong, but totally confused about exactly what I was doing. (*Describe feeling.*) Rather than making general complaints like that, could you say what I'm not doing that you need, or what I could change? (*Express request.*) I think I could be a lot more responsive that way. (*Reinforce.*)

Carmen: What was it you needed more information about? (*Clarify.*)

John: What you needed me to do, at that moment, to feel closer.

Carmen: Okay, so what you're saying is that my talking about my feelings without making any specific requests for change leaves you feeling confused and responsible. (*Acknowledge.*)

John: Right.

Carmen: Well, sometimes I'm just telling you how I feel. I don't know why I feel that way or what to do about it. Telling you is an attempt to open the discussion. (*Redefining problem.*)

John: I see. So you really aren't sure what I could do at that point. (*Acknowledge.*) How about just saying you aren't sure and asking what we could do about it together? Making it *we* instead of *me* would help a lot on my end. (*New request.*)

Carmen: That sounds right. I like it.

Notice that Carmen clarifies and acknowledges before attempting any further explanation of the problem from her point of view. Then, in a nonblaming way, she explains why she can't go along with John's request. John, in turn, acknowledges what Carmen has said. He then uses this new information to make a second proposal that works better for Carmen.

Here's the rub: You can't always expect the other person to play by the rules. There are times when you'll have to express and listen assertively in the face of defensive or hostile reactions. Consider the case of Hal and Sara.

Sara: I have a problem with the cash projections, can we talk? (*Arrange.*)

Hal: Whatever.

Sara: Currently you're only running them out to the next three months, and I can't see how sales, inventory, and costs are going to interact six to eight months down the line. (*Define.*) I'm getting pretty nervous about the big printing bills because we don't know if the money will be there. (*Describe feeling.*) Could you run out the cash projection at least six months? (*Express request.*) I think we'd all breathe easier. (*Reinforce.*)

Hal: Forget it, Sara. There's no time. I haven't got the bodies in my department to do stuff like that. Take a Valium and cool off.

Sara: How much extra work would it take? (*Clarify.*)

Hal: (loudly) Forget it, Sara. Forget it, okay?

Sara: I hear you. You're overworked and haven't the staff to take on anything extra. (*Acknowledge.*) But I'm wondering, how many extra hours of work are involved? (*Clarify.*)

Hal: At least twenty. Keep pushing, Sara. I'm up to here with everybody's demands.

Sara: I hear how stressed you are. (*Acknowledge.*) If once a month I got a twenty-hour bookkeeper from the pool for you, could you handle it? (*New request.*)

Hal: Probably, Sara. Let me see the body first.

In the face of sarcasm and anger, Sara continues to clarify and acknowledge until she understands Hal's problem. She doesn't get sidetracked by hostile resistance. She keeps working to understand Hal's stresses and needs so she can make a new, more acceptable proposal.

7. Arriving at a Workable Compromise

The seventh step of assertiveness training is learning to arrive at a workable compromise. When two people's interests are in dire conflict, a fair compromise that totally satisfies both parties is difficult, if not impossible, to achieve. Instead, look for a workable compromise you both can live with, at least for a while. Although a compromise may naturally emerge in your discussion, sometimes you might need to make a list of all the alternative solutions you can think of. Cross off the ones that are not mutually acceptable. Finally, decide on a compromise you can both live with. This brainstorming process is most effective if you let your imaginations run wild while generating ideas. It's best to agree to review a workable compromise in a specified length of time, such as a month. At that time, you can examine the results of your changed behavior. If you aren't both sufficiently satisfied, you can renegotiate.

Typical compromise solutions include:

- My way this time, your way next time.

- Part of what I want with part of what you want.

- Meeting halfway.

- If you'll do ———— for me, I'll do ———— for you.

- We'll do this one my way, but we'll do ———— your way.

- We'll try my way this time, and if you don't like it you can veto it next time.

- My way when I'm doing it, your way when you're doing it.

If you feel resistant to brainstorming and making lists of alternatives, try this simpler approach. When a person doesn't want to give you what you want, ask for a counterproposal. If the counterproposal isn't acceptable to you, make a new one of your own. But first do a little assertive listening to uncover the other person's feelings and needs in the situation. Keep going back and forth with counterproposals until something works for both of you.

A second route to compromise is to ask this question: "What would you need from me to feel okay doing this my way?" The answer may surprise you and offer solutions you never thought of.

8. *Avoiding Manipulation*

The eighth and final step to becoming an assertive person is learning how to avoid manipulation. Inevitably, you will encounter blocking gambits from those who seek to ignore your assertive requests. The following techniques are proven ways of overcoming the standard blocking gambits.

Broken record. When you find that you are dealing with someone who won't take no for an answer or refuses to grant you a reasonable request, you can carefully choose a concise sentence to use as your broken-record statement that you'll say over and over again. You could say to your insistent four-year-old, "Jeff, I am not going to give you any more candy." You might say to the aggressive used-car salesman, "I am not going to buy a car today; I'm just looking." You might say to the uncooperative store clerk, "I want you to give me back my money for this defective radio." Briefly acknowledge that you have heard the other person's point, and then calmly repeat your broken-record statement without getting sidetracked by irrelevant issues. "Yes, but. . . . Yes, I know, and my point is . . . I agree, and . . . Yes, and as I was saying . . . Right, but I'm still not interested."

Content-to-process shift. Shift the focus of the discussion from the topic to an analysis of what is going on between the two of you. "We're getting off the point now." "We've been derailed into talking about old issues." "You appear to be angry with me."

Defusing. Ignore the content of someone's anger, and put off further discussion until he has calmed down. "I can see that you are very upset and angry right now. Let's discuss it later this afternoon."

Assertive delay. Put off a response to a challenging statement until you are calm, have more information, or know exactly how you want to respond. "Yes . . . very interesting point . . . I'll have to reserve judgment on that . . . I don't want to talk about it at this time."

Assertive agreement. Acknowledge criticism you agree with. You don't need to give an explanation unless you wish to. "You're right. I did botch the Sudswell account." "Thanks for pointing out that I was smiling when I was trying to say no to that salesman. No wonder I couldn't get rid of him." "You're right, boss, I am half an hour late . . . my car broke down."

Clouding. When someone is putting you down as a person, acknowledge something in the criticism you can agree with, and ignore the rest. *Agree in part:* "You're right. I am late with the report." *Agree in the probability:* "You may be right that I am often late." *Agree in the principle (agreeing with the logic without agreeing with the premise):* "If I were late as often as you say, it certainly would be a problem." When clouding, rephrase the critic's words so that you can honestly concur. By giving the appearance of agreeing without promising to change, you soon deplete the critic of any reason to criticize you.

Assertive inquiry. Invite criticism in order to find out what is really bothering the other person. "I understand you don't like the way I chaired the meeting last night. What is it about my behavior that bothered you? What is it about me that you feel is pushy? What is it about my speaking out that bothers you?"

Prepare yourself against a number of typical blocking gambits that will be used to attack and derail your assertive requests. Some of the most troublesome blocking gambits include:

Laughing it off. Your assertion is responded to with a joke. "Only three weeks late? I've got to work on being less punctual!" Use the content-to-process shift ("Humor is getting us off the point") and the broken record ("Yes, but . . . ").

Accusing gambit. You are blamed for the problem. "You're always so late cooking dinner, I'm too tired to do the dishes afterward." Use clouding ("That may be so, but you are still breaking your commitment") or simply disagree ("Eight o'clock is not too late for the dishes").

The beat-up. Your assertion is responded to with a personal attack. "Who are you to worry about being interrupted, you're the biggest loudmouth around here." The best strategies to use are assertive irony ("Thank you") in conjunction with the broken record or defusing ("I can see you're angry right now, let's talk about it after the meeting").

Delaying gambit. Your assertion is met with, "Not now, I'm too tired," or "Another time, maybe." Use the broken record, or insist on setting a specific time when the problem can be discussed.

Why gambit. Every assertive statement is blocked with a series of "why" questions, such as, "Why do you feel that way. . . . I still don't know why you don't want to go . . . why did you change your mind?" The best response is to use the content-to-process shift (*"Why* isn't the point. The issue is that I'm not willing to go tonight") or the broken record.

Self-pity gambit. Your assertion is met with tears and the covert message that you are being sadistic. Try to keep going through your script using assertive agreement ("I know this is causing you pain, but I need to get this resolved").

Quibbling. The other person wants to debate with you about the legitimacy of what you feel, or the magnitude of the problem, and so on. Use the content-to-process shift ("We're quibbling now, and have gotten off the main concern") with the assertion of your right to feel the way you do.

Threats. You are threatened with statements such as, "If you keep harping at me like this, you're going to need another boyfriend." Use assertive inquiry ("What is it about my requests that bothers you?") as well as content-to-process shift ("This seems to be a threat") or defusing.

Denial. You are told, "I didn't do that," or "You've really misinterpreted me." Assert what you have observed and experienced, and use clouding ("It may seem that way to you, but I've observed . . . ").

Further Reading

Alberti, R. E., and Michael Emmons. 1995. *Your perfect right*. Twenty-fifth Edition. San Luis Obispo, Calif: Impact Press.

Bower, S. A., and G. H. Bower. 1991. *Asserting Yourself*. Reading, Mass.: Addison-Wesley.

Butler, P. E. 1992. *Self-Assertion for Women*. San Francisco: HarperCollins.

Fensterheim, H., and J. L. Baer. 1975. *Don't Say Yes When You Want to Say No*. New York: Dell.

Gabor, D. 1994. *Speaking Your Mind in 101 Different Situations*. New York: Simon & Schuster.

Jakubowski-Spector, P. 1973. Facilitating the growth of women through assertiveness training. *The Counseling Psychologist*. 4:75–86.

Lazarus A. 1966. Behavioral rehearsal vs. nondirective therapy vs. advice in effecting behavior change. *Behavioral Research and Therapy*. 4:20–12.

Phelps, S., and N. Austin. 1997. *The Assertive Woman*. San Luis Obispo, Calif.: Impact Press.

Smith, M. J. *When I Say No, I Feel Guilty*. 1985. New York: Bantam.

Wolpe J. 1958. *Psychotherapy by Reciprocal Inhibition*. Stanford, Calif.: Stanford University Press.

18

Job Stress Management

In this chapter you will learn to:

- ☐ Identify your symptoms and sources of job stress

- ☐ Motivate yourself to take control of your job stress

- ☐ Pace and balance yourself

Background

The classic symptoms of job burnout include pessimism, increased dissatisfaction, absenteeism, and inefficiency at work. While you may not be on the verge of job burnout, you may be one of the growing majority of Americans who report that their job causes them stress. Job stress accounts for a tremendous amount of personal misery and billions of dollars lost annually in productivity, wages, and medical bills. Americans are waking up to the fact that job stress management makes personal and financial sense.

What Causes Job Burnout?

Every job includes some built-in difficulties that the worker is paid to adjust to. Job difficulties alone do not cause burnout. Rather, it is the worker's lack of control over her job situation that leads to uncertainty, frustration, reduced motivation, and eventually burnout. For example, you can become demoralized because you are unable to meet the impossible expectations of your boss, because you can't get the support of your coworkers, because you are inadequately trained, or because no matter how well you do your efforts are not recognized.

Even minor factors beyond your control can have a stressful impact. Consider the many unexpected interruptions in the course of your day: special meetings, phone calls, people dropping in, and equipment breakdown. Think about having to go through channels and deal with bureaucratic red tape. Think about the faulty air conditioning system or the constant din of machines, elevator music, and voices. Your daily commute probably adds to your accumulated stress for the day as well.

It is a common error to associate only excessive stress with lowered productivity. As early as 1908, Robert Yerkes and John Dodson pointed out that the symptoms of stress underload are quite similar to those of stress overload: reduced efficiency, irritability, a sense of time pressure, diminished motivation, poor judgment, and accidents. We all have a unique "performance zone" within which we experience manageable stress that stimulates our energy, motivation, decision making, and productivity.

Burnout is not simply caused by too much stress in your job. If your job made no demands on you, you would be bored. Job stress management, like stress management in general, involves finding the right types and amounts of challenge to stimulate your interest and performance without overloading you. It also requires managing those distressing areas of your job that are inevitable. Finally, it includes balancing leisure and work-related activities so that they complement one another. Job stress management is a dynamic process you can exercise personal control over.

Symptom Effectiveness

Job-stress management is effective in increasing your sense of control in the work setting. Increased feelings of control can improve job-related symptoms of guilt, irritability, depression, anxiety, and low self-esteem. Jobstress management can also reduce job-related psychosomatic symptoms such as insomnia, ulcers, headaches, eating disorders, and lowered immunity to infection.

Time to Master

The initial assessment of your job stressors and your response to them can be completed in one day. Learning how to respond more effectively to job stress will take at least a month. The habit of effective job stress management may take between two months and a year to integrate into your daily life.

Eight Steps Toward Managing Your Job Stress

Step 1. Identify Your Symptoms of Job Stress

Instructions: Rate each of the following items in terms of how often the symptom was true for you during the last three months:

0 = never
1 = occasionally
2 = somewhat often
3 = frequently
4 = almost always

_____ 1. I feel little enthusiasm for doing my job.

_____ 2. I feel tired even with adequate sleep.

_____ 3. I feel frustrated in carrying out my responsibilities at work.

_____ 4. I am moody, irritable, or impatient over small inconveniences.

_____ 5. I want to withdraw from the constant demands on my time and energy.

_____ 6. I feel negative, futile, or depressed about my job.

_____ 7. My decision-making ability seems less than usual.

_____ 8. I think I am not as efficient as I should be.

_____ 9. The quality of my work is less than it should be.

_____ 10. I feel physically, emotionally, or spiritually depleted.

_____ 11. My resistance to illness is lowered.

_____ 12. My interest in sex is lowered.

_____ 13. I am eating more or less; drinking more coffee, tea, or sodas; smoking more cigarettes; or using more alcohol or drugs than usual in order to cope with my job.

_____ 14. I am feeling emotionally callous about the problems and needs of others.

_____ 15. My communication with my boss, co-workers, friends, or family seems strained.

_____ 16. I am forgetful.

_____ 17. I am having difficulty concentrating.

_____ 18. I am easily bored.

_____ 19. I feel a sense of dissatisfaction, of something wrong or missing.

_____ 20. When I ask myself why I get up and go to work, the only answer that occurs is "my paycheck."

If you scored 0 to 25, you are probably coping adequately with the stress of your job. If you scored 26 to 40, you are suffering from job stress and would be wise to take preventative action. If you scored 41 to 55, you need to take preventative action to avoid job burnout. If you scored 56 to 80, you are burning out and must develop a comprehensive job stress management plan.

Step 2. Identify the Sources of Your Job Stress

Instructions: Rate your experience in your job during the past year, using the following 5-point scale:

0 = never
1 = occasionally
2 = somewhat often
3 = frequently
4 = almost always

Lack of Control

___ 1. I lack the authority to carry out certain responsibilities.

___ 2. I feel trapped in a situation without any real options.

___ 3. I am unable to influence decisions that affect me.

___ 4. There are a lot of requirements that get in the way of my doing certain tasks.

___ 5. I can't solve the problems assigned to me.

___ Subtotal

Information Gap

___ 6. I am unsure about the responsibilities of my job.

___ 7. I don't have enough information to carry out certain tasks.

___ 8. I am underqualified for certain tasks I'm expected to do.

___ 9. Others I work with are not clear about what I do.

___ 10. I don't understand the criteria used to evaluate my performance.

___ Subtotal

Cause and Effect

___ 11. There is no relationship between how I perform and how I am rated.

___ 12. I sense that popularity and politics are more important than performance.

___ 13. I don't know what my supervisor thinks of my performance.

___ 14. I don't know what I am doing right and what I am doing wrong.

___ 15. There is no relationship between how I perform and how I am treated.

___ Subtotal

Conflict

___ 16. I am expected to satisfy conflicting needs.

___ 17. I disagree with co-workers.

___ 18. I disagree with my supervisor.

___ 19. I am caught in the middle.

___ 20. I can't get what I need to get the job done.

___ Subtotal

Blocked Career

_____ 21. I feel pessimistic about opportunities for advancement or growth in my job.

_____ 22. My supervisor or boss is critical.

_____ 23. I feel unaccepted by the people I work with.

_____ 24. My good work is not noticed or appreciated.

_____ 25. My progress on the job seems less than it could be.

_____ Subtotal

Alienation

_____ 26. I experience little meaning in my work.

_____ 27. I feel unsupported by my co-workers or boss.

_____ 28. My values seem at odds with those of the management.

_____ 29. The organization seems insensitive to my individuality.

_____ 30. I find I cannot be myself at work because I feel different from my co-workers.

_____ Subtotal

Overload

_____ 31. I have too much to do and too little time in which to do it.

_____ 32. I take on new responsibilities without letting go of any of the old ones.

_____ 33. My job seems to interfere with my personal life.

_____ 34. I must work on my own time (during breaks, lunch, at home, and so on).

_____ 35. The size of my workload interferes with how well I do it.

_____ Subtotal

Underload

_____ 36. I have too little to do.

_____ 37. I feel overqualified for the work I actually do.

_____ 38. My work is not challenging.

_____ 39. Most of my work is very routine.

_____ 40. I miss contact with people in my job.

_____ Subtotal

Environment

_____ 41. I find my work environment unpleasant.

_____ 42. I lack the privacy I need to concentrate on my work.

_____ 43. Some aspects of my environment seem hazardous.

_____ 44. I have too much or too little contact with people.

_____ 45. I have to deal with many little hassles.

_____ Subtotal

Value Conflict

_____ 46. I must do things that are against my better judgment.

_____ 47. I must make compromises in my values.

_____ 48. My family and friends do not respect what I do.

_____ 49. I observe my co-workers doing things that I don't approve of.

_____ 50. The organization that I work for pressures employees to do things that are unethical or unsafe.

_____ Subtotal

_____ Grand total

If your score is over 100, you have more than an average number of job stressors. If your score is 130 or higher, the number of job stressors is unusually high. Identify the categories in which you scored 12 or more. In addition to dealing with your specific major stressors, you will want to give consideration to these general areas.

Step 3. Identify How You Respond to Your Specific Job Stressors

What are your specific job stressors and how do you tend to respond to them? In addition to looking over your responses on the job stress inventory, reflect back over your recent experiences at work. In the far left-hand column of the following form, list your specific stressors. For each stressful item, write down your feelings when it occurs, what you say to yourself about it, and what you do in response to it.

For example, Patty, a computer programmer, wrote down the specific stressors in her job and her response to them in the following shorthand manner:

Your Job Stressor	Your Feelings	Your Thoughts	Your Behavior
Programming	Bored, numb	"Non-stop programming makes Patty a dull girl."	Plodding, inefficient; eat sweets, drink coffee
Deadlines	Anxious	"I'll never make it!"	Work faster and longer; mistakes
Meetings	Annoyed, impatient	"What a waste, I've got work to do."	Critical, resistant to suggestions
Vague supervisor	Insecure, confused, annoyed	"What does it take to please this jerk?"	Guess what he wants; complain
Chatty co-worker	Angry	"Why does he keep interrupting me? He's so inconsiderate!"	Respond politely and return to my own work
Uncooperative secretary	Angry, frustrated, dissatisfied	"She's lazy, slow, and utterly useless."	Refuse to talk to her
No privacy	Annoyed	"Hard to focus."	Tense my muscles; neck and backache
Terminal	Strained, tired	"I wish I didn't have to do this."	Eye strain, headache
Down time	Frustrated, refreshed	"Damn, I lost it!"	Eat, drink coffee, socialize
No raise	Angry, frustrated	"I deserve better than this!"	Complain bitterly

Exercise: List your specific stressors and how you respond to them. Use as little or as much detail as you need.

Your Job Stressor	Your Feelings	Your Thoughts	Your Behavior
_____	_____	_____	_____
_____	_____	_____	_____
_____	_____	_____	_____
_____	_____	_____	_____
_____	_____	_____	_____
_____	_____	_____	_____

_____   _____   _____   _____

_____   _____   _____   _____

_____   _____   _____   _____

_____   _____   _____   _____

_____   _____   _____   _____

_____   _____   _____   _____

_____   _____   _____   _____

_____   _____   _____   _____

_____   _____   _____   _____

_____   _____   _____   _____

_____   _____   _____   _____

Now that you have written out your specific job stressors and how you typically respond to them, review your list and see if any patterns emerge. When Patty did this, she noticed the following patterns:

1. I respond to boredom and frustration by eating and drinking coffee.

2. Working at a computer terminal for long periods of time and having to concentrate in spite of a lack of privacy causes me to have a variety of physical and emotional symptoms of stress.

3. I waste time because I'm not assertive enough to ask questions of my supervisor, say no to my office mate, or firmly request secretarial support.

4. I tend to be highly critical of myself, others, and my environment, but rarely do anything constructive to improve my situation. I can see why I feel chronically irritated and tense at work.

In looking over your list of specific job stressors and your responses to them, what patterns can you find?

_____

_____

_____

_____

_____

_____

_____

_____

_____

_____

Step 4. Set Goals to Respond More Effectively to Your Job Stressors

Now that you have identified your patterns of stress, you can begin to formulate a more effective plan for responding to those stressors you can anticipate. Maybe you can avoid some of them altogether. Perhaps you can be better prepared for them when they happen. The name of the game is taking more control . . . and this is where you begin to do it.

You will probably want to make changes in one or more of these general areas:

1. Change the external stressor (quit the job, assertively tell the boss not to overload you, take regular breaks, reorganize your time).

2. Change your thoughts (turn off the job when you go home, alter your perfectionist attitude, stop assuming that you are responsible for others' problems).

3. Change physically (relax, exercise, eat properly, get sufficient sleep).

When you are designing goals for yourself, remember the following guidelines. Useful goals are generally:

- specific,

- observable,

- achievable within a certain time frame,

- broken down into small intermediate steps,

- compatible with long-term goals,

- written down in simple self-contract form,

- reevaluated at specified intervals, and

- rewarded when achieved.

For example, Patty decided to set a new, more effective response to each of her four stress patterns as a goal for herself. She wrote out the following self-contract:

I, Patty Bowers, agree to change the following four old patterns of responding to stress as follows:

Patterns 1 and 2. Rather than eating or drinking coffee when I am bored or frustrated, I will take regular breaks once an hour in which I either do a brief relaxation exercise or get up and walk around and talk to people. I'll take advantage of flex time and go to an aerobics class three days a week and run personal errands two days a week in the middle of the day. I will eat three nutritious meals, rather than snack on junk.

Pattern 3. I will take a one-day workshop on Assertiveness Training and ask my supervisor more questions until I am sure I know what he wants. I also will tell my co-worker not to interrupt me with small talk, other than when I get up and walk around. I will assertively ask the secretary for help.

Pattern 4. I will take each one of my critical thoughts and turn it into a constructive action thought. For instance, rather than saying about meetings, "What a waste, I have work to do," I could say, "Whew, a break from programming! What constructive contribution can I make here?"

I will revaluate my progress for each goal on a weekly basis. I plan to spend a weekend at a local hot springs as a reward for changing these four patterns for one month.

Patty Bowers

If making such a contract would increase your motivation, do so with a friend or co-worker. Then report back to each other weekly on your progress toward each goal.

Exercise: Using the form on the next page, write out goals to modify a few of your responses to specific stressors in your life in the form of a self-contract.

Step 5. Motivate Yourself

Create specific rewards for every goal you establish:

- Give yourself one point for each relaxation break you take. Twenty-five points means new clothes or CDs.

- You'll buy that book you've been wanting to read after clarifying with your boss some of his or her expectations.

- You'll rent that spicy new murder mystery after you tell John not to interrupt you when you're writing.

- You'll call Rebekah for a little chat after you write that memo requesting flex time.

- After you've requested a limit on the number of cases you're expected to take, you'll call Art and invite him to dinner at Walker's.

- You'll assign one dollar toward a shopping spree for each stress-producing thought you catch and change (see step 6).

Here's a way of motivating yourself to perform stress-reducing activities that you normally feel too rushed to do. Sometimes a work-related task that you enjoy has no

I, _____ agree to:

1. _____

_____

_____

2. _____

_____

_____

3. _____

_____

_____

I will monitor my progress every _____ (*length of time*).

I will reward myself with _____ .

immediate payoff, so you postpone it and focus your attention on tasks that have immediate deadlines. Such was the case with Marty, who kept putting off writing a professional article he had outlined two years earlier. Administrative responsibilities swallowed up his time, so he decided to deal with the problem by setting aside half an hour each morning to work on his article before letting himself tackle the demands of the day. He used the motivating power of immediate deadlines to prompt him to accomplish something fun and rewarding.

Step 6. Change Your Thinking

Job stress occurs because your thoughts trigger a painful emotional reaction. There are three generic thoughts that do you in:

1. I've got to do _____ (*a certain task*) _____ (*perfectly*) (*on time*) (*so my boss will be pleased*) or _____ (*something painful*) will happen.

2. They're doing this to me and it's not fair.

3. I'm trapped here.

Thought 1 makes you anxious, thought 2 triggers anger, and thought 3 generates depression. You can do something about these thoughts and the job stress they create. Right now, list the things you tell yourself about your job that fit into each of the above three categories.

Category 1

_____

_____

_____

Category 2

_____

_____

_____

Category 3

_____

_____

_____

Here's how you can cope with these stress-producing thoughts.

1. Make a *realistic appraisal* of what exactly will happen if the task isn't on time, flaw-less, or totally pleasing to your boss. A realistic appraisal means looking at what has happened to yourself and others in the past when tasks such as this were late, had errors, and so on. Realistic also means being specific. It's time to get rid of that vague sense of doom. Exactly what is your boss likely to say to you? What, if anything, is likely to happen to you?

Now complete this sentence: "If _____ isn't (*perfect, on time, totally acceptable*), the boss's response will likely be _____ . I can handle it."

Mentally repeat this coping statement each time you catch yourself catastrophizing about vague and dire consequences. Note: If you have no idea how your boss would respond, ask him. "If I'm a day late with the Crocker report, will that be a problem?"

2. There's absolutely no good that can come from blaming anybody for your job stress. Blaming maintains your sense of being stuck and helpless. You see yourself as a victim who has no alternatives and has lost the power of choice. Blaming trig-gers anger and stress hormones such as adrenaline that deplete your energy and over the long run damage your health.

As stated in the chapter on refuting irrational ideas, "The conditions for things or people to be otherwise than they are don't exist. . . . Things are what they are because of a long series of causal events." Saying to yourself that your boss or the company president should act differently is like saying Nixon should never have tried to cover up Watergate. The conditions necessary for Nixon to be fearful and obsessed with secrecy existed, and the means and opportunity existed. His values, needs, ambitions, advisors, and personal history all pushed him to deny it.

No one is *supposed* to take care of or protect you on this job. They are all busy taking care of and protecting themselves. This is natural; this is the inescapable fact of working life. So what can you say to yourself to avoid chronic blaming and anger?

The first thing you can do is ask yourself this question: "What steps can I take to change the conditions I don't like?" If you can't think of any way to change the job, you have two rational choices. You must either adapt to and accept the conditions or look for another job.

If you decide to accept the current situation, the second coping statement you can make is: "_____ is acting exactly as he should. The conditions necessary for him to act this way (*his needs and coping strategies to meet those needs, past successes and failures, fears, attitudes toward our relationship*) all exist, and this is why he did _____ (*to*) (*with*) me."

3. You are not trapped. You may have difficult choices, but you aren't trapped. Right now the pain of this job seems less than the pain associated with other available choices. Is this really true? Here's a chance to list your options for change.

What specific steps could you take to change a major stress producer on your job?

_____

_____

What would you risk in attempting that change?

_____

_____

What steps could you take to change jobs altogether?

_____

_____

What would you risk in attempting that change?

_____

_____

What steps could you take to change your perception of a risk so that you would be willing to attempt a change?

_____

_____

Typically this involves getting additional information so that you feel more confident you can cope with the challenge involved in making a change. For example, if you think that the risk in changing jobs is that you are too old, you could set as a goal for yourself to ask someone your age in the type of position you want if age really makes a difference. If you believe that you will risk blowing an interview for a new position in your present company, you could set as a goal to take an interview class.

If you are not ready to do what is necessary to change, rather than saying, "I'm trapped," the more accurate thing to say to yourself is, "I choose to stay with the current conditions on this job because right now it seems less painful than _____ _____ (*the steps to change*). I may choose differently in the future."

Step 7. When in Conflict, Negotiate

Whether you disagree with your boss regarding your salary or with your co-workers about who is going to make the coffee, you need to present your position and negotiate a compromise you can all live with.

Read chapter 17, Assertiveness Training, to learn how to express your opinions, feelings, and wants as you negotiate for change. At the very least, read the section Arriving at a Workable Compromise. Here is a four-step model to follow when you want to discuss a specific problem with your supervisor or co-workers with the aim of arriving at a mutually acceptable outcome.

State:

1. the problem (what you perceive to be the cause of your stress),

2. how you feel about the problem,

3. how it affects your productivity and motivation, and

4. a win-win solution (both sides of the conflict get something positive from your solution).

For example, Randy, a creative high school teacher, was refused compensation for the time he spent developing new courses. Randy told his boss, "Ever since I realized I wouldn't receive money for my course-development work, my enthusiasm for teaching has deteriorated. I think my students have gained tremendously from my special classes. They're now suffering as a result of my loss of motivation. It's important to me and to the school to continue creating new classes and to be compensated in some way. Since the money isn't available, I would be satisfied if I could take one class period each day for a semester to develop my new class."

The principal's response was, "I can't spare you a period every day, but I would agree to three hours a week." Randy accepted this workable compromise.

Step 8. Pace and Balance Yourself

Do you pace yourself at work? If you are a sprinter, you can afford to throw everything you've got into the race. This is because at the end of a fast short run you know you have plenty of time to recover from your intense effort. Most jobs, however, require you to be more like a marathon runner who must pace himself in order to get across the finish line in a timely manner without collapsing. Like the marathon runner, you need to maintain a certain detachment from the immediate demands of your job so that you will remember to reserve enough energy to deal with what you anticipate down the road as well as any surprises.

Here are eight tips for pacing and balancing yourself:

1. Pay attention to your natural rhythms to determine when you tend to perform optimally, and schedule your most difficult tasks at that time.

2. Try to set up your day so you shift back and forth between pleasant and more difficult tasks. After something tough, make an effort to schedule something you enjoy.

3. Schedule inviolate periods of time into your day for work-related tasks that are pleasurable though not terribly productive. Try to do this even when you feel rushed.

4. Take advantage of your coffee breaks and lunches to do things that will reverse the stress response. For example, go to a quiet place and do a relaxation exercise. A ten-minute brisk walk will give you as much energy as a cup of coffee. A light conversation with your co-workers will release tension and may be just what you need to get a fresh perspective on a problem that was weighing you down.

5. If you are fortunate enough to have a flexible schedule, consider taking a long break in the middle of the day to do aerobic exercise, a relaxation exercise, or personal errands.

6. Take minibreaks throughout your day to reduce or prevent symptoms of tension and stress. These breaks need not take more than a few minutes, and the payoff can be seen in increased mental alertness and productivity. See chapter 10, Brief Combination Techniques, for exercises appropriate for short breaks.

7. Choose leisure activities that balance the unique stresses of your job.

If your job requires:	*Consider a complementary leisure activity such as:*
Much sitting or mental concentration	Aerobic exercise
Mindless repetition	Intellectually challenging hobbies and interests
A controlled environment	Hiking in nature; adventure
Boring tasks or no recognition	Competitive or achievement-oriented activities
Responding to people demands	Solitary activities

Dealing with conflicts   Peaceful activities

Working alone   Social activities

8. Carefully plan the timing and type of vacations that you take to maximize their recuperative effects.

Exercise

List five ways that you can better pace yourself at work and create more balance in your life:

_____

_____

_____

_____

_____

Further Reading

Davis, M. 1984. *Job Stress Management*. In *Relax: The Stress Reduction System*. Richmond, Calif.: Synapse Software Corporation.

Kemper, D., J. Giuffre, and G. Drabinski. 1985. *Pathways: A Success Guide for a Healthy Life*. Boise, Idaho: Healthwise, Inc.

Potter, B. A. 1987. *Preventing Job Burnout: Transforming Work Pressures into Productivity*. Los Altos, Calif.: Crisp Publications.

Nutrition

In this chapter you will learn to:

☐   Assess your current eating habits

☐   Eat a balanced diet to optimize health and manage stress

☐   Eat to prevent or minimize specific physical conditions

Background

Eating is one of the natural joys in life. Preparing and anticipating a meal and enjoying its colors, aromas, and tastes are delightful ways of giving yourself pleasure as well as taking good care of yourself. Since meals are often a time to relax and socialize, they can help reduce stress. Most cultures celebrate holidays and the passages of life with feasting; these times bring people together and give life meaning. However, eating right is a learned skill and not something that just comes naturally.

Unfortunately, the foods that people eat for pleasure are not always nutritionally sound. America's love affair with snack foods has led some to joke that the four food groups are candy, cookies, coke, and chips. The average American diet, with its emphasis on convenience foods, often does contain too much fat, sugar, and sodium. Obesity is only one of the risks run by physically inactive people who eat a high-fat, high-calorie diet. These habits also increase the danger of degenerative joint diseases and high blood pressure, and research indicates that diets high in fat may contribute to cardiovascular disease and some cancers.

Symptom Effectiveness

A healthy body responds better to the inevitable stresses of life, and good nutrition is a building block of good health. Eating well can help prevent or control high blood pressure, heart disease, indigestion, constipation, hypoglycemia, diabetes, and obesity. Good eating habits may also reduce irritability, PMS, headaches, and fatigue.

Time to Master

Plan to keep track of your food intake for three days. After reading the guidelines for a healthy diet, you will compare them with your own eating habits and decide what changes you want to make. You can begin to apply the recommendations in this chapter in a matter of hours. To make lasting changes in your diet, plan on *gradually* introducing a few changes at a time that you can stick with for a minimum of one month.

Ten Steps to Positive Eating

The first five of these ten steps to positive eating follow the format of the food pyramid illustrated below, starting at the top of the pyramid and working toward the base. The top represents the fat, sugar, and salt that we tend to overindulge in because of the flavor and fun that they add to our diets. The middle level of the pyramid represents milk, meat, eggs, legumes, and nuts, which provide protein. The bottom level contains fruit and vegetables, and the base represents grains such as bread, rice, cereal, and pasta. The last five of the ten steps cover weight control, caffeine, alcohol, vitamins, and tips for making food preparation and eating less stressful.

Recommended Pyramid   Common Pyramid

1. *Cut Back on Fats*

Despite all the bad press that fat receives, the average American still ingests 37 to 42 percent of their calories from fat, instead of the recommended 20 to 30 percent. We talk about cutting fat, but when we get hungry we reach for our high-fat favorites, despite the presence of so many alternatives. The food industry has come up with dozens of new lower-fat snack and cookie products to help you make the change (and fruit is still one of the best low-fat snacks). Any bookstore has shelves full of low-fat cookbooks that offer a menu of tasty and creative dishes. Fat-free salad dressings and flavored vinegars provide still another attractive way to reduce the fat in your diet. Even those with no time to cook can fall back on lean frozen entrée products. Be sure to check the label and select items with three grams or less of fat per serving.

There are three kinds of fat. Saturated fat is solid at room temperature and usually of animal origin. Examples are meat fat, butter, and Crisco. Unsaturated or monosaturated fat is liquid at room temperature but solidifies when chilled, similar to olive oil and margarine. Polyunsaturated fats such as corn oil and safflower oil remain liquid even when refrigerated. Although the exact relation of fats to hypertension and heart disease is still controversial, the most widely accepted theory is that saturated fats contribute to heart disease and strokes by elevating the body's cholesterol level.

Fat "replacers," such as Olestra, are now on the market, usually as components of high-fat snack foods. They reduce the fat content while contributing taste and texture to the foods and are considered safe by the FDA.

How do you score on fat intake? Answer the following questions by circling the number in the column that best describes how often you select or limit the foods listed on the scorecard. Add up the numbers you circled for your total score.

Your fat score: Do you . . . ?	*Rarely*	*Often*	*Almost always*
Choose lean meat, chicken, or fish?	1	5	10
Eat high-fat meats like bacon, lunch meats, or sausage?	10	5	1
Limit eggs to four yolks per week?	1	5	10
Read labels and select foods with less than three grams of fat per serving?	1	5	10
Choose low-fat or nonfat dairy products?	1	5	10
Limit fried foods?	1	5	10
Choose doughnuts, croissants, or sweet rolls for breakfast?	10	5	1
Choose reduced-fat or fat-free products when they are available?	1	5	10
Limit margarine, butter, salad dressings, and sauces on foods?	1	5	10
Balance a high-fat dinner with a low-fat breakfast and lunch?	1	5	10

Scoring. If you scored 10 to 59 points, you can do better. At 60 to 79 points, you're on your way. If you scored over 80 points, keep up the good work!

2. *Avoid Too Much Sugar*

Americans have a sweet tooth. If you've been abroad, you've probably noticed that American desserts tend to be much sweeter than Asian, Mexican, or European desserts. Including table sugar, sugar in soft drinks, canned foods, baked goods, and other sweets, the average American eats 130 pounds of sugar and sweeteners annually . . . and many of these items provide few nutrients.

As children, we were given sweets to comfort us. So now, when we are stressed, we still reach for cookies, candy, or sweets. Studies indicate that women are more likely to seek solace in sweets than men. Other evidence suggests that sweets trigger the release of endorphins, natural opiates that create euphoric feelings. Though sugar may provide a temporary high, it also stimulates the pancreas to secrete insulin to process the sugar. In some people, the pancreas overreacts and secretes excess insulin. The result is hypoglycemia, a condition characterized by dizziness, irritability, nausea, and hunger pangs that may in turn prompt another sweet treat.

Cravings for sweets are better satisfied with a piece of fruit. Fruit provides the complex sugars, fiber, and vitamins that sugar will not.

Tips for cutting sugar:

- Use less sugar, raw sugar, honey, and syrup.

- Eat fewer foods that contain sugar such as candy, cookies, and soft drinks.

- Select fresh fruit or fruits canned in juice or light syrup.

- Read labels and avoid foods that list sucrose, glucose, maltose, dextrose, lactose, or fructose as one of their first four ingredients.

3. *Limit Sodium Intake*

Sodium is an essential mineral, but adults in the United States ingest about ten to twenty times more sodium than the body needs. Sodium is used to regulate body fluids, maintain pH balance, and control nerve and muscle activities. Although our major sodium sources are table salt (composed of 40 percent sodium and 60 percent chloride) and processed foods, sodium is also a natural component of milk, cheese, meats, and bread. A single slice of bread actually provides the minimum daily requirement for salt (230 milligrams). Recommended sodium intake is three thousand milligrams daily. A low-sodium diet of two thousand milligrams is often prescribed for people with high blood pressure.

Though research is inconclusive, a high intake of sodium correlates with high blood pressure and increased risk of stroke. Since stress also aggravates these conditions, you will be wise to reduce your salt intake. Salt also increases edema, an excess accumulation of fluid that adds to the stress and discomfort of premenstrual syndrome.

Tips for shaking the salt habit:

- Avoid salty snacks such as chips, crackers, pretzels, and nuts.

- Limit your intake of salty condiments such as soy sauce, pickles, and cheese.

- Restrict use of cured meats, sausages, and bacon.

- Learn to savor less salt and to substitute new herb-based condiments at the table.

- Use herbs and spices while you cook, and reduce the salt in recipes.

- Avoid foods with salt or sodium as one of the first three or four ingredients.

4. *Eat a Variety of Foods*

You need over forty nutrients for optimum health. These are classified as macronutrients (proteins, carbohydrates, and fats) and micronutrients (vitamins and minerals). You need the former in larger quantities and the latter in smaller amounts. While an excess of macronutrients will lead to weight gain, an excess of micronutrients may actually be toxic for you, or at least a waste of the money you spend on unnecessary vitamin, mineral, or herbal supplements.

There is no perfect food. Even milk, which provides the backbone of a baby's diet, does not supply vitamin C or iron, which is why we include juice and cereal among baby's first foods. Although natural foods are favored by many health-conscious individuals, these can sometimes have toxic components. Varying your diet helps maximize your nutrients and minimize your exposure to any one toxic substance or contaminant. A wide variety of foods provides a wide variety of nutrients.

The tip of the food guide pyramid represents the extras that add pleasure to our diet, but use of these items needs to be carefully controlled. Level two of the pyramid adds protein to the diet, but may provide too much fat. Select low-fat or nonfat meat and dairy products whenever possible. Using beans and legumes liberally in your diet will help keep protein up and fat down. Despite the widespread perception that fish is a better source of protein than red meat, some fish actually has more fat than lean red meat, and red meat also contains the iron that most women need. Informed food preparation can also help. Take the skin off chicken, because the skin alone on a chicken breast has five grams of fat. Bake, broil, or barbecue to reduce fat.

Level three of the pyramid reminds us to eat at least five fruits and vegetables daily for the valuable fiber and vitamins they provide. A serving is usually half a cup. Add up juice at breakfast, an apple for lunch, and a potato, a salad, and a vegetable for dinner, for a total of five servings. Spaghetti sauce is equal to one or two servings of tomato. Make "five a day" your rule and stick to it.

The pyramid base is composed of bread, rice, and cereal and pasta products, all variants of the proverbial "staff of life." Six to eleven servings are suggested daily. That may seem like a lot, but it really isn't. Many people eat two servings of cereal at breakfast. A sandwich provides two more servings of bread, and a plate of spaghetti easily provides three to four more servings of pasta of a half a cup each. A few pretzels for a snack is another serving. Total: nine servings.

5. *Eat More Complex Carbohydrates*

Eating foods with adequate starch and fiber will add to your sense of well-being. You'll notice that complex carbohydrates and fiber make meals filling and satisfying.

Eating lots of fresh fruits and vegetables is also good for your peace of mind, since these "power foods" contain the fiber, vitamins, minerals, and nutrients that can protect you against chronic illnesses, including diabetes, cancer, and heart disease.

Choose whole-grain breads or pastas more often. Enriched grain products restore the known nutrients that may be removed by milling. Yet although some enriched foods actually provide more nutrients than natural foods, unrefined foods may well contain nutrients that we have not yet discovered. When you do buy refined foods, be sure they are enriched to restore the B vitamins and iron lost in milling.

Evidence continues to build that dietary fiber (including cellulose, gums, pectin, and lignin) is an essential component of a healthy diet. Fiber helps reduce constipation by increasing stool bulk and water absorption, controls blood sugar and blood lipids by binding nutrients, and decreases stool transit time, thus reducing the risk of colon cancer and diverticulitis. Unfortunately, although the recommended intake of dietary fiber is twenty-five to forty grams daily, the average American consumes only five to ten grams. For most of us, fresh vegetables and fruits and whole grains and legumes are the chief sources of fiber in our diets. You can supplement your fiber intake by increasing your use of legumes and bran products or by adding bran to homemade foods. Plan to increase fiber gradually, as rapid increases may lead to bloating and flatulence.

Dietary Fiber in Common Foods

Food group	*Dietary fiber content*
Legumes and bran cereals	5 to 8 grams per serving
Fruits and vegetables	2.5 grams per serving
Grains and starches	2.5 grams per serving
Nuts	2.5 grams per ounce

Source: *Journal of the American Dietetic Association.*

Carbohydrates also seem to function as edible tranquilizers. They contain tryptophan, an amino acid that stimulates the production of serotonin in the brain. Serotonin has a calming effect that eases tension and may cause drowsiness. Is this the explanation for that happy full feeling that a big spaghetti dinner usually seems to create?

6. *Attain or Maintain Your Ideal Weight*

There are currently three methods used to estimate healthy body weight. The first is the old standby height and weight chart originated by the insurance companies. Note that healthy weights do not increase with age; health risks appear to be more weight related than age related. Newer methods of assessing healthy weights are the waist-to-hip ratio and the body-mass index (BMI).

To determine the waist-to-hip ratio, measure your waist comfortably and then your hips at the widest part. Divide your waist measurement by your hip measurement. If the number exceeds 1, you're at greater risk for heart disease. A healthy ratio is below 0.8 for women and below 0.95 for men.

Healthy Weights for Men and Women

Height	*Men*	*Women*
4'10"		91-199 lbs.
4'11"		94-122 lbs.
5'0"		96- 125 lbs.
5'1"		99-128 lbs.
5'2"	112-141 lbs.	102-131 lbs.
5'3"	115-144 lbs.	105-134 lbs.
5'4"	118-148 lbs.	108-138 lbs.
5'5"	121-152 lbs.	111-142 lbs.
5'6"	124-156 lbs.	114-146 lbs.
5'7"	128-161 lbs.	118-150 lbs.
5'8"	132-166 lbs.	122-154 lbs.
5'9"	136-170 lbs.	126-158 lbs.
5'10"	140-174 lbs.	130-163 lbs.
5'11"	144-179 lbs.	134-168 lbs.
6'0"	148-184 lbs.	138-173 lbs.
6'1"	152-189 lbs	
6'2"	156-194 lbs.	
6'3"	160-199 lbs.	
6'4"	164-204 lbs.	

Source: U. S. Department of Health, Eduction, and Welfare.

The body-mass index is another method of assessing body composition. BMI factors in body-fat ratios, since body fat, not body weight, correlates with health risk. Use the chart below to figure out your BMI. A BMI of 22 is considered low risk for weight-related health problems. A BMI over 27 is considered overweight and a BMI over 32 is defined as obese. Your ideal body weight is probably the weight you were between the ages of 20 and 25, if you were lean at that time.

Although there are thousands of weight-reduction diets, the best weight-control strategy is a lifelong sensible eating plan. Diets just don't work. Research indicates that "yo-yo dieting" damages health and makes each successive weight-loss effort even harder.

Body Mass Index

Weight in Pounds

Height in inches

	58	59	60	61	62	63	64	65	66	67	68	69	70	71	72	73	74
110	23.0	22.2	21.5	20.8	20.1	19.5	18.9	18.3	17.8	17.2	16.7	16.2	15.8	15.3	14.9	14.5	14.1
115	24.0	23.2	22.5	21.7	21.0	20.4	19.7	19.1	18.6	18.0	17.5	17.0	16.5	16.0	15.6	15.2	14.8
120	25.1	24.2	23.4	22.7	21.9	21.3	20.6	20.0	19.4	18.8	18.2	17.7	17.2	16.7	16.3	15.8	15.4
125	26.1	25.2	23.4	23.6	22.9	22.1	21.5	20.8	20.2	19.6	19.0	18.5	17.9	17.4	17.0	16.5	16.0
130	27.2	26.3	25.4	24.6	23.8	23.0	22.3	21.6	21.0	20.4	19.8	19.2	18.7	18.1	17.6	17.2	16.7
135	28.2	27.3	26.4	25.5	24.7	23.9	23.2	22.5	21.8	21.1	20.5	19.9	19.4	18.8	18.3	17.8	17.3
140	29.3	28.3	27.3	26.5	25.6	24.8	24.0	23.3	22.6	21.9	21.3	20.7	20.1	19.5	19.0	18.5	18.0
145	30.3	29.3	28.3	27.4	26.5	25.7	24.9	24.1	23.4	22.7	22.0	21.4	20.8	20.2	19.7	19.1	18.6
150	31.4	30.3	29.3	28.3	27.4	26.6	25.7	25.0	24.2	23.5	22.8	22.2	21.5	20.9	20.3	19.8	19.3
155	32.4	31.3	30.3	29.3	28.4	27.5	26.6	25.8	25.0	24.3	23.6	22.9	22.2	21.6	21.1	20.4	19.9
160	33.4	32.3	31.2	30.2	29.3	28.3	27.5	26.6	25.8	25.1	24.3	23.6	23.0	22.3	21.7	21.1	20.5
165	34.5	33.3	32.2	31.2	30.2	29.2	28.3	27.5	26.6	25.8	25.1	24.4	23.7	23.0	22.4	21.8	21.2
170	35.5	34.3	33.2	32.1	31.1	30.1	29.2	28.3	27.4	26.6	25.8	25.1	24.4	23.7	23.1	22.4	21.8
175	36.6	35.3	34.2	33.1	32.0	31.0	30.0	29.1	28.2	27.4	26.6	25.8	25.1	24.4	23.7	23.1	22.5
180	37.6	36.4	25.2	34.0	32.9	31.9	30.9	30.0	29.1	28.2	27.4	26.6	25.8	25.1	24.4	23.7	23.1
185	38.7	37.4	36.1	35.0	33.8	32.8	31.8	30.8	29.9	29.0	28.1	27.3	26.5	25.8	25.1	24.4	23.8
190	39.7	38.4	37.1	35.9	34.8	33.7	32.6	31.6	30.7	29.8	28.9	28.1	27.3	26.5	25.8	25.1	24.4
195	40.8	39.4	38.1	36.8	35.7	34.5	33.5	32.4	31.5	30.5	29.6	28.8	28.0	27.2	26.4	25.7	25.0
200	41.8	40.4	39.1	37.8	36.6	35.4	34.3	33.3	32.3	31.3	30.4	29.5	28.7	27.9	27.1	26.4	25.7
205	42.8	41.4	40.0	38.7	37.5	36.3	35.2	34.1	33.1	32.1	31.2	30.3	29.4	28.6	27.8	27.0	26.3
210	43.9	42.4	41.0	39.7	38.4	37.2	36.0	34.9	33.9	32.9	31.9	31.0	30.1	29.3	28.5	27.7	27.0
215	44.9	43.4	42.0	40.6	39.3	38.1	36.9	35.8	34.7	33.7	32.7	31.8	30.8	30.0	29.2	28.4	27.6
220	46.0	44.4	43.0	41.6	40.2	39.0	37.8	36.6	35.5	34.5	33.5	32.5	31.6	30.7	29.8	29.0	28.2
225	47.0	45.4	43.9	42.5	41.2	39.9	38.6	37.4	36.3	35.2	34.2	33.2	32.3	31.4	30.5	29.7	28.9
230	48.1	46.5	44.9	43.5	42.1	40.7	39.5	38.3	37.1	36.0	35.0	34.0	33.0	32.1	31.2	30.3	29.5
235	49.1	47.5	45.9	44.4	43.0	41.6	40.3	39.1	37.9	36.8	35.7	34.7	33.7	32.8	31.9	31.0	30.2
240	50.2	48.5	46.9	45.3	43.9	42.5	41.2	39.9	38.7	37.6	36.5	35.4	34.4	33.5	32.6	31.7	30.8
245	51.2	49.5	47.8	46.3	44.8	43.4	42.1	40.8	39.5	38.4	37.3	36.2	35.2	34.2	33.2	32.3	31.5
250	52.3	50.5	48.8	47.2	45.7	44.3	42.9	41.6	40.4	39.2	38.0	36.9	35.9	34.9	33.9	33.0	32.1

Interpretation:
Underweight: less than 19.8
Normal Weight: 19.8–26.0
Overweight: 26.0–29.0
Obese: greater than 29.0

Source: National Academy of Science 1992.

First of all, diets don't work because most dieters don't reach their diet objectives. After all, diets represent food deprivation, which is emotionally difficult for most of us. In addition, your body interprets the diet as a famine, which means that it goes into a reduced metabolic state to decrease the severity of the impact on your overall well-being. The harder you diet, the more your body resists losing weight. For those who do manage to lose weight, over 95 percent do not keep the weight off for even a year, and most end up dieting again. This sets the yo-yo spinning, because with each new diet the body lowers the energy required for maintenance a little bit more, making weight control even harder.

Research suggests that it is better for you to maintain a moderate weight gain than to continually diet to lose the same ten pounds over and over again. The simple math is that you must expend more calories than you eat in order to avoid gaining weight. The ideal combination is to eat a little less and exercise a little more. If you cut the fat content of your food, you can eat the same quantity of food, or even more. The best approach to weight control is to reduce your daily intake by 100 calories and increase your exercise by 100 calories. This means that you cut out one cookie and walk one mile a day more than you walk now. Continue this regimen for a year, and you will be twenty pounds lighter!

Diets are just a temporary quick fix, while weight control is a lifestyle issue throughout our lives. This means a lifelong commitment to learning to cook using low-fat methods; consistently choosing low-calorie, low-fat foods; and being satisfied with smaller portions.

Commercial weight-loss programs that provide good nutrition education and realistic exercise goals may be a help in making that commitment. Weight Watchers, one of the most reputable programs, advocates eating lots of vegetables and cutting down on fat, while increasing exercise. It also offers behavior modification and support. There are chapters in most cities; look in your local phone book to find a convenient location. Other organizations that provide educational and support programs include Overeaters Anonymous, the YMCA and YWCA, and many health insurance programs, local colleges, and community centers.

Good weight-control programs emphasize behavior changes that enhance weight control:

Eat slowly. Take small bites and truly enjoy the color, taste, and texture of the food. Remember that it takes twenty minutes for the hypothalamus (your "appestat") to provide feedback on satiety, or sense of fullness.

Concentrate on eating. Don't read or watch TV while eating. Enjoy eating as a primary activity so you can be aware of flavors, colors, and portion size.

Eat regularly. Studies show that people who eat three to five meals daily control their weight successfully. This may be because they do not get excessively hungry and overeat. Studies also indicate that people who eat breakfast consume fewer total calories daily.

Control portion size. Portions are generally a half a cup. You can eat anything you want as long the portion fits in a four-ounce cup!

When you're bored: Substitute a pleasurable activity such as a walk, a phone call, or engaging in a hobby.

When you're angry: Write a letter to the person you're angry with (but don't send it) or go jogging or do some gardening. If you must chew something, choose a carrot or gum.

When you're tired: Go to bed or take a hot bath. You may be surprised to find that a walk or a bike ride may reenergize you.

When you're anxious: Engage in physical activity, go to a movie, or find a way to deal with the issues causing the anxiety.

7. Avoid or Limit Caffeine

Coffee, tea, chocolate, colas, and some medications are all high in this stimulant, which can make some people feel irritable or nervous, interfere with sleep, and contribute to gastrointestinal distress. If you drink regular coffee, a daily limit of 200 milligrams of caffeine is recommended by the American Medical Association.

Beverage	Serving	Caffeine
Regular brewed coffee	10 oz	170–200 mg
Decaffeinated brewed coffee	10 oz	10 mg
Instant coffee	10 oz	90–140 mg
Brewed tea	10 oz	60–100 mg
Canned ice tea	12 oz	25–35 mg
Cola drinks	12 oz	40–60 mg
Dark chocolate	1 oz	20 mg
Milk chocolate	1 oz	6 mg

Source: *Journal of the American Dietetic Association*, August 1987.

8. If You Drink, Drink in Moderation

As a tool for reducing stress, alcohol has the bothersome side effect of reducing reality as well. Although some research indicates that a drink a day will increase longevity, reliance on alcohol to deal with daily life is a dangerous practice. Alcoholic beverages are high in calories and low in nutrients. In excess, alcohol depletes B vitamins, alters blood sugar, elevates blood pressure, and disrupts relationships. If you drink, limit yourself to one to two drinks.

9. Take a Multivitamin Tablet Daily

Vitamins and minerals are necessary in small amounts, and without them metabolism is impaired. The recommended dietary allowances listed here reflect considerable research by the academic community and are approved by the National Research Council. The quantities given include allowances for individual variation.

Recommended Dietary Allowance

	Men		Women	
Age	25–50	51+	25–50	51+
Weight (lbs)	174	170	138	143
Height (inches)	70	68	64	63
Protein (grams)	63	63	50	50
Fat-soluble vitamins				
Vitamin A (µg RE)	1,000	1,000	800	800
Vitamin D (µg)	5	5	5	5
Vitamin E (µg TE)	10	10	8	8
Vitamin K (µg)	80	80	65	65
Water-soluble vitamins				
Vitamin C (mg)	60	60	60	60
Thiamine (mg)	1.5	1.2	1.1	1.0
Riboflavin (mg)	1.7	1.4	1.3	1.2
Niacin (mg)	19	15	15	13
Pyridoxine (mg)	2.0	2.0	1.6	1.6
Folate (µg)	200	200	180	180
Vitamin B12 (µg)	2.0	2.0	2.0	2.0
Minerals				
Calcium (mg)	800	800	800	800
Phosphorous (mg)	800	800	800	800
Magnesium (mg)	350	350	280	280
Iron (mg)	10	10	15	10
Zinc (mg)	15	15	12	12
Iodine (µg)	150	150	150	150
Selenium (µg)	70	55	55	55

Source: National Research Council, Food and Nutrition Board, National Academy of Sciences. Revised 1989.

Since we do not all eat according to the food pyramid every day, a multivitamin tablet is recommended as an "insurance policy." However, taking vitamins is not a substitute for not eating well. There are compounds in foods we have not yet identified that are nutritionally important adjuncts to the metabolic functioning of vitamins and minerals.

Multivitamins can provide you with extra amounts of the B vitamins (linked to stress) and vitamins A, E, and C (which have anticancer properties). Multivitamins can also supplement any minerals that may be inactivated by fiber in the diet. Vitamins marketed as "stress tabs" or as "stress formulations" are meant for physical stress rather than psychological stress. More is not better when supplementing vitamins and minerals; fat-soluble vitamins can become toxic because they accumulate in the liver, and new evidence indicates that water-soluble vitamins may also be toxic. We do know that consistent doses of over three grams of vitamin C a day increase the risk of kidney stones. Vitamin and mineral function is interrelated: vitamin C enhances iron absorption; vitamin D, calcium, and phosphorus work together in bone metabolism; and B vitamins are necessary for burning glucose as a fuel for the body. Trace minerals are interrelated, so increasing intake of one mineral may cause an imbalance in another. Supplements should supply no more than 1 RDA of each mineral. Additional vitamin C (250–1000mg), vitamin E (200–400IU), and calcium (1000–1500mg) are often recommended.

10. *Eat Frequent, Calm Meals*

Positive eating includes taking the time to prepare and eat frequent meals or snacks and relaxing as we eat them. Our fast-paced society, along with our many available fast-food options, encourages eating on the run and denies us the time to relax as we eat. Our bodies run better if we refuel them frequently. Blood sugar is like gasoline to a car, and we all know a car does not run if the fuel lines are empty. Eating three to five small meals a day will help maintain an even blood-sugar level.

To reduce the daily stress of meal preparation, plan and shop weekly. When you cook, cook with the idea of leftovers or snacks in mind. It's cheaper, quicker, easier, and healthier to reheat something in the microwave than to run out for fast food. Reheated leftovers can make tasty lunches the next day.

At work, take time away from your workstation to sit and relax with your meal or snack. Likewise, take some time alone to relax and reflect during your breaks. Learn to savor the flavors, textures, and colors of your food.

Self-Assessment

Daily Food Diary

If you are interested in making significant changes in your eating habits, it will be worth your while to keep a record of everything you eat and drink for the next three days. You will discover exactly how much you neglect certain food groups and overindulge in others, and you will be amazed to see how sugars and fats sneak into your diet. You will see important connections between the circumstances in which you eat and drink, your feelings, and your diet. With this factual account of your eating habits, you will also be motivated to use the guidelines in this chapter to create a more nutritionally balanced diet. You may want to repeat this exercise periodically to measure your progress.

Before you start, look at the first day of Sharon's diary as an example of how to do this. In addition to writing down everything that she ate, she also noted the setting in which she ate and how she felt while she was eating.

Refer to Sharon's diary and to the food pyramid to fill in the Food Guide Points column of your diary. Sharon's example shows you how to use the pyramid to count servings. Here are some specific guidelines to keep in mind:

- Note that low-fat milk counts as one milk serving and one fat serving; nonfat milk is a basic milk serving.

- Similarly, count all cookies, donuts, or Danish as one serving each of bread, fat, and sugar. (These treats actually may have more fat and sugar than bread, but counting them this way will help you begin to realize how these items sneak into your total diet.)

- Four ounces of ice cream count as one-half serving of milk and one serving each of fat and sugar.

- If you put butter or margarine on vegetables or a potato, don't forget to count it: one teaspoon of either equals one fat serving.

- French fries contain at least three teaspoons of oil (equal to three servings of fat).

- Salad dressing is one serving of fat for every two tablespoons of dressing.

Make some extra copies of the blank Daily Food Diary and use them to record your intake for at least the next three days. Be sure to write down where and when you eat, the setting and the people with you at the time, and your feelings. What a person eats is often tied to internal and external cues, and keeping track of this information may give you clues about why you eat the way you do.

Summarizing Your Food Diary

For each of the three days that you kept your Daily Food Diary, add up the total number of points in each food group, divide by three, and write this number in the Daily Average column for each food group. You will then be able to compare your daily averages for each food group with the ideal servings listed in the sixth column of the summary form. Refer to Sharon's Food Diary Summary as an example and then fill out the blank Food Diary Summary from the data in your Daily Food Diary.

Taking Charge of Your Nutritional Well-Being

The food pyramid provides a goal for daily food choices. Review your Food Diary Summary and compare your average servings per food group against the ideal servings. Put a check mark in the margin of the groups in which you were below the recommendation. Put a star in the margin by the groups in which you were over the recommendation.

Having digested the facts presented in this chapter, you shouldn't be too surprised to find that your usual food intake looks a lot more like the typical American diet than like the recommended pyramid. Chances are good that it is top-heavy with fats and sugars and skimpy on fruits, vegetables, grains, bread, and cereals.

Sharon's Food Diary

Meal	Food	Amount	Food guide points	Setting	Feelings
Breakfast	Cereal Low-fat milk	1/2 cup 1 cup	1 bread 1 milk 1 fat	Kitchen, alone	Hungry, hurried
Snack	Crumb donut Coffee w/sugar	One 2 cups	1 bread 1 fat 2 sugar 2 caffeine	Coffee room	Happy, social
Lunch	Tuna sandwich with mayo Diet Coke Apple	3 oz 2 tsp One One (lg)	1 fish 2 fat 2 bread 1 caffeine 1 fruit	Alone at my desk, working	Busy, pressured
Snack	Cookie	One (lg)	1 bread 1 fat 1 sugar	Coffee room	Tense, headache
Dinner	Hamburger with lettuce, tomato, mayo, catsup, bun French fries	6 oz 2 tsp 4 oz	2 meat 1 veg 2 fat 2 bread 1 veg 3 fat	Home, with family	Tired, grumpy
Snack	Rocky Road ice cream	8 oz	1 milk 1 fat 1 sugar	TV, alone	Tired, bored

Daily Food Diary

Meal	Food	Amount	Food guide points	Setting	Feelings

Sharon's Food Diary Summary

	Day 1	Day 2	Day 3	Daily average	Ideal servings
Breads and grains A serving equals 1 slice of bread; ½ cup rice, cereal, or pasta	7	4	7	6	6–11
Vegetables and fruits A serving equals ½ cup or 1 small apple, orange, or potato	3	3	1	2	5–9
Milk, cheese, yogurt A serving equals 1 cup low-fat milk; 1 oz cheese	2	2	2	2	2–3
Meat, poultry, fish A serving equals 2½–3 oz meat or fish; 1½ cup legumes; 1 cup nuts	3	2	4	3	2–3
Fats and sweets A serving equals 2 tbs salad dressing; 1 tsp butter or margarine; 1 oz candy	15	9	6	8+	2–5
Alcohol A serving equals 12 oz beer, 3 oz wine, 1 bar drink	0	1	0	⅓	0–1
Caffeine A serving equals 1 cup regular coffee or tea	3	5	3	4	0–1

Food Diary Summary

	Day 1	Day 2	Day 3	Daily average	Ideal servings
Breads and grains A serving equals 1 slice of bread; ½ cup rice, cereal, or pasta					6–11
Vegetables and fruits A serving equals ½ cup or 1 small apple, orange, or potato					5–9
Milk, cheese, yogurt A serving equals 1 cup low-fat milk; 1 oz cheese					2–3
Meat, poultry, fish A serving equals 2½–3 oz meat or fish; 1½ cup legumes; 1 cup nuts					2–3
Fats and sweets A serving equals 2 tbs salad dressing; 1 tsp butter or margarine; 1 oz candy					2–5
Alcohol A serving equals 12 oz beer, 3 oz wine, 1 bar drink					0–1
Caffeine A serving equals 1 cup regular coffee or tea					0–1

After Sharon reviewed her summary, she sat down and filled out her Goal-Setting Chart. The solutions she developed may suggest some positive steps that you can take.

Sharon's Goal-Setting Chart

Food group	Problem	Solution
Sugar	Too much sugar	Replace sweets with fresh fruit
Fat	Too much fat: Salad dressing Mayonnaise Fried foods Ice cream	Fat-free dressing Omit Bake, broil Use low-fat frozen Yogurt instead
Vegetables	I hate vegetables	Add one new vegetable per month
Portions	My portions are huge	Use a measuring cup
Caffeine	I'm drinking too much	Switch to herbal teas, take walks

Now it's time to fill in your own positive eating goals.

Now go back to your Daily Food Diary again and review the settings in which you ate. Note anything about the setting that might contribute to unhealthy eating behavior. For example, it's clear from Sharon's sample diary that eating alone at her desk provided no break from work and may have actually made her less efficient as her tension level grew in the afternoon. Lunch with friends or at least in a different locale could have provided a change of scene. She takes her breaks in the coffee room, where high-fat, high-sugar snacks are a constant temptation. If she plans to take a piece of fruit to the coffee room, she can still have the benefits of socializing but markedly improve the nutritional value of her break.

Your Personal Positive Eating Goals

Food group	Problem	Solution

What changes or improvements would you make regarding the setting in which you eat?

_____

_____

_____

Now review the feelings that you recorded in your Daily Food Diary. Note any feelings that contributed to unhealthy eating behavior. For instance, you can probably see that Sharon uses comfort food to try to feel better when she has negative feelings and sensations (tension, a headache, boredom, fatigue). Aerobic exercise, socializing, or a relaxation exercise might be more effective in alleviating these symptoms. She can also plan ahead to have a favorite low-calorie substitute available for those times when she knows she is likely to feel down. Going to bed earlier might also help prevent snacking when she feels bored or tired at night. If an earlier bedtime led to getting up earlier in the morning, she would also have time for a less hurried breakfast.

How do your feelings contribute to your dietary intake? What changes can you make?

_____

_____

_____

Changing your eating habits will take some time. Concentrate on no more than a few goals at a time for a minimum of one month. When you have integrated these new eating habits into your daily life, move on to a few more goals. Depending on how many habits you wish to change, you should be enjoying a healthier diet in one to six months. Making too many changes at a time can be stressful, so insure your success by going slowly. The changes you make also need to be tasty ones, otherwise you will feel deprived and have difficulty sticking with your plan.

Final Thoughts

You have the power to take charge of your eating habits, and taking charge will make a positive difference. Just keep the ten steps of positive eating in mind and gradually make changes in your food selections. Put a copy of the food pyramid on the refrigerator as a reminder and keep it in mind when you shop. Go to your local bookstore and check the cookbook section for a new low-fat cookbook or magazine to inspire you. If you need a personalized nutrition plan, consult a registered dietitian at your medical clinic or check the Yellow Pages. If you have a nutrition question, call the Center of Nutrition and Dietetics hotline listed at the end of this chapter. Food is a necessity and a pleasure in life, so make positive, healthy choices!

Pharma-Foods

"Pharma-foods" offer enhanced nutrient intake, through supplementation of certain nuritients, but care is still required in food selection. A good example is calcium-supplemented orange juice. Many women do not achieve optimum calcium intake, and this is a good way to start the day with healthy vitamin C, folate, vitamin A, and calcium. Another example is mega-fortified cereals for children, who may have limited nutrient intake due to dietary restrictions, personal preference, or economic status. Look for more and more of these foods in the marketplace.

Coming Soon—Genetically Personalized Nutrition

Thanks to modern science, you will soon be able to give a small sample of blood, or perhaps saliva, and have your nutritional needs determined. A nutrition professional will be able to take the results of this genetic testing and translate the information into a diet- and food plan with nutrients tailored to your specific metabolism. Finally, researchers will soon begin to be able to recognize the individual differences in metabolism and required nutrients. This will be a fantastic advance in preventative health.

Further Reading

Christie, C., and S. Mitchell. 1999. *Smart Cookies Don't Go Stale: Eat to Stay Young and Stress Free*. New York: Kensington Publishing Corp.

Connor, K. 1999. *Kava: Nature's Stress Relief*. New York: Avon Books.

Duyff, R. 1996. *The American Dietetic Association's Complete Food and Nutrition Guide*. Minneapolis: Chronimed Publishing.

Firshein, R. 1998. *The Neutraceutical Revolution*. New York: Riverhead Books.

Somer, E. 1995. *Mood & Food*. New York: Henry Holt.

Tyler, V. E. 1993. *The Honest Herbal*. New York: Pharmaceutical Products Press.

Other Resources

Center for Nutrition and Dietetics Nutrition hotline: 800-366-1655.

Weight Watchers Program locations: 800-726-6108.

Web Sites

http://www.eatright.org
   The American Dietetic Association
   Web site of professional dietitians providing comprehensive nutrition resources: daily nutrition tips, reading lists, healthy lifestyle hints, and special sections on nutrition for children, women, and the elderly.

http://navigator.tufts.com
   Tufts University Nutrition Navigator
   Sections on general nutrition, nutrition commentator on news, and section on dietary needs rates other nutrition Web sites for content and accuracy.

http://www.weightwatchers.com
   Weight Watchers International
   Worldwide weight management program Web site with meeting locations, program description, recipes, fitness, and support.

http://www.cyberdiet.com
   Cyberdiet.com
   Nutrition Web site rated among the best by the Tufts Web site. Covers self-assessment including Body Mass Index calculation, diet and nutrition, fitness, as well as support and motivation.

http://webMD.com
   WebMD/Healtheon
   Click on Living Better and choose Diet and Nutrition. Information on diet and nutrition, online consultation with a dietitian, diet and nutrition chat room, as well as live Webcasts.

http://drkoop.com
   Dr. Koop, former U.S. Surgeon General, "Best Prescription Is Knowledge"
   Dieting basics, diet programs and products, exercise, and healthy shopping and dining.

http://dietary-supplements.info.nih.gov
   National Institutes of Health, Office of Dietary Supplements
   Information, research, and scientific papers on dietary supplements.

http://vm.cfsan.fda.gov/~dms/dietsupp.html
   Food and Drug Administration, Center for Food Safety and Applied Nutrition
   Covers the Dietary Supplement Health and Education Act of 1994, food safety, food and cosmetics fact sheets, and offers a section on bioengineered foods.

Exercise

In this chapter you will learn to:

☐ Use exercise to decrease the stress response

☐ Apply three categories of exercise to create a balanced program

☐ Monitor your response to exercise

☐ Motivate yourself to get started and stay committed to your exercise program

Background

Exercise is one of the simplest and most effective means of stress reduction. Vigorous physical exertion is the natural outlet for the body when it is in the "fight or flight" state of arousal. Exercise returns your body to its normal equilibrium by releasing natural chemicals that build up during the stress response.

Types of Exercise

There are three broad categories of exercise: aerobic exercises, stretching exercises, and toning exercises. All three types should play a role in any balanced exercise program.

Aerobic Exercises

Aerobic exercises are repetitive, rhythmic, and varied. They involve sustained use of the large muscles in your body, especially the legs and arms. The goal of aerobic exercise is to strengthen your cardiovascular system and increase your stamina. To produce this effect, you need to exercise at least three days a week. Each time you do aerobic exercise, your heart rate should reach the target heart rate appropriate for your age and remain at that rate for twenty minutes. Instructions for determining your target heart rate are given on page 278.

Popular aerobic exercises include running, jogging, brisk walking, swimming, bicycling, dancing, martial arts, and a number of other activities. Fortunately, this wide variety of choices offers alternatives to suit every lifestyle and range of physical conditions.

You probably get a certain amount of exercise each day in activities such as walking, climbing stairs, housecleaning, shopping, and gardening. To find out how much activity you get in a day, use a pedometer. This device, adjusted to your walking stride, clips to your clothing and measures the number of miles that you walk or run. Wear it for one week, removing it when you do aerobic exercises, and record how far you have walked at the end of each day. If you walk less than 2 miles per day, you should consider yourself an inactive person and begin your exercise program slowly. In addition to these everyday activities, both stretching and toning exercises should be incorporated into your exercise program.

Prescription for Aerobic Exercise

Frequency: Three to five days per week

Duration: A minimum of twenty minutes of uninterrupted, continuous exercise

Intensity: 60 to 75 percent of your maximum heart rate

Stretching and Toning Exercises

Stretching and toning exercises are not vigorous or prolonged enough to produce the cardiovascular strengthening that results from aerobic exercise. They can be used to increase muscle strength, flexibility, and joint mobility. If you are very sedentary or in poor physical condition, stretching and toning exercises will help prepare you for aerobic exercise with a minimal risk of cardiovascular strain.

Stretching exercises are slow, sustained, and relaxing. Specific stretches are available to decrease muscle tension, improve the flexibility of specific muscle groups, and help maintain joint mobility. Stretching improves circulation and helps to prevent injury when used during the warm-up and cooldown periods before and after aerobic exercise. It also helps you feel good, by soothing your mind and body and helping to focus and center your thoughts. You can also stretch before going to bed in preparation for a good night's sleep.

Both yoga and tai chi offer well-balanced stretching programs. Stretching exercises are convenient. You do not need special clothing or equipment. Weather is irrelevant, because you can do them indoors as well as outdoors.

Prescription for Stretching Exercises

Frequency: Stretch both before and after aerobic exercises, i.e. during your warm-up and cooldown periods. You can also stretch whenever you're feeling stressed, tense, stiff, or tired.

Duration: Begin by holding the stretch position for thirty seconds. Do not bounce in and out of the stretch. Gradually increase the stretch to two minutes over a period of a few weeks. Breathe rhythmically and notice how your body relaxes.

Toning exercises focus on specific muscles that need to be firmed or tightened. Some good examples are crunches for stomach muscles, squats for thigh muscles, toe raises for calf muscles, and push-ups for arm and chest muscles.

Most toning exercises can be placed in one of these two categories:

1. *Isotonics* involve the shortening of muscles against resistance through a range of movement. Weight lifting or the use of resistive weight machines is the most popular form of isotonic exercise. Isotonics can be used to increase the size of the muscle or simply for toning. Bigger muscles can mean more power, endurance, and speed. Toned muscles yield a firmer looking body and are important in protecting joints.

2. *Isometrics* require the contraction of muscles against resistance, without any change in the length of the muscle fibers. For example, you can push your two hands together at chest level and feel your chest muscles tighten. Isometrics do not make muscles larger, but they do increase muscle strength.

Prescription for Toning Exercises

To tone muscles, rather than increase muscle size, use less resistance and do more repetitions. Doing three sets of ten repetitions with moderate weight is a good rule of thumb.

To increase muscle size, use more resistance and do fewer repetitions. One set of eight to twelve repetitions with heavy weight is a good rule of thumb.

Stretching Exercises

A. Side body stretch. (1) Stand erect, arms at sides, feet shoulder width apart, and legs relaxed with knees slightly bent. (2) Raise one arm over your head to the side. Keeping stomach tucked in and chest high, continue to bend your arm and trunk to the side until you feel a stretch in your waist. Hold this position for thirty seconds. (3) Return to starting position. (4) Repeat on the other side.

figure A-1   figure A-2

figure A-3   figure A-4

B. Leg and back stretch. (1) Stand with feet together, arms at sides, and eyes looking straight ahead. (2) Squat down, keeping heels on floor and reaching your arms straight ahead. Hold thirty seconds. (3) Reach hands forward to floor, come down onto knees, and slide body back onto heels. Hold for thirty seconds. (4) Slide forward until front of body touches floor. (5) With hands on floor in front of shoulders, press chest away from floor by straightening elbows. Keep front of hips in contact with floor. Keep head and neck relaxed, eyes looking at the floor. Hold thirty seconds. (6) Push back into the squatting position. (7) Return to starting position.

C. Full body stretch. (1) Lie on the floor with legs straight and arms overhead. (2) Stretch right arm and leg in opposite directions. Hold thirty seconds. (3) Stretch left arm and left leg in opposite directions. Hold thirty seconds. (4) Stretch left arm and right leg in opposite directions. Hold thirty seconds. (5) Stretch right arm and left leg in opposite directions. Hold thirty seconds. (6) Stretch both arms and legs in opposite directions. Hold thirty seconds.

figure B-1

figure B-2   figure B-3

figure C-1   figure C-2   figure C-3

figure B-4

figure B-5

figure B-6   figure B-7

figure C-4   figure C-5   figure C-6

Toning Exercises

D. Arm and upper back toner (modified push-ups). (1) Place hands about shoulder width apart on the wall. Move your feet back until your legs and back are in a straight line, your body supported by your feet and hands. Always keep head up. (2) Bend arms at elbow, lowering your upper body as close to wall as possible. (3) Push up, straightening arms, and return to starting position. *Begin with ten repetitions.*

figure D-1

figure D-2

figure D-3

E. Leg toner (squats). (1) Stand with feet comfortably apart, hands on hips. (2) Bend knees to half-squat position as you bring arms forward with palms down. Be sure to keep your heels on the floor and hips slightly higher than knees. (3) Return to starting position. *Begin with ten repetitions.*

F. Tummy toner (abdominal crunches). (1) Lie on back with knees bent and feet flat on the floor. Interlace fingers behind head. (2) Tucking chin into chest, curl forward, lifting only head, neck, and shoulders without pulling on neck. Hold for five seconds. (3) Slowly return to starting position. *Begin with ten repetitions.*

figure F-1

figure E-1

figure E-2

figure E-3

figure F-2

figure F-3

Symptom Effectiveness

Regular and adequate exercise is the best choice for increasing muscular strength, endurance, and flexibility. It is also an excellent way to relieve chronic muscle tension caused by stress. The greater flexibility and better posture gained through exercise can relieve lower back pain caused by stress. Improved metabolism can relieve indigestion and chronic constipation caused by stress. Exercise will fight both chronic fatigue and insomnia caused by stress. Exercise also provides relief from emotions such as depression and anxiety.

Time to Master

Set up a schedule of at least three exercise sessions per week over a six- to eight-week period. Make the commitment to stick with this schedule in order to incorporate exercise as a regular part of your life. Keeping a diary, similar to the diary described later in this chapter on page 280, will help give you a picture of the progress you are making during this initial period.

Precautions

It is always wise to check with your doctor or health care provider before beginning an exercise program. Abruptly starting a strenuous program of aerobic exercise could overstrain your heart if you are not used to the exertion. If you lead a sedentary lifestyle, are overweight, eat fatty or salty foods, or smoke, you may encounter difficulty with certain exercises. Likewise, if you are resuming an exercise program after a serious illness or an operation, start gradually and follow any special precautions suggested by your doctor or health care provider.

If you are obese (more than 20 percent over your ideal weight) or have any medical problems that require regular medications and regular checkups, do not start any regular exercise program without seeing a doctor or your primary health care provider for a complete physical examination. Once you have begun your exercise program, contact your doctor or primary health care provider if you develop any of the following symptoms:

- Your heart rate becomes irregular and begins to skip beats
- Your heart rate takes longer than fifteen minutes to slow down
- You feel a tightness, pressure, or pain in your chest, shoulders, arms, or neck
- You feel dizzy or nauseous
- You feel extreme breathlessness after only mild exertion
- You feel exhausted long after your exercise session is over

Developing Your Own Exercise Program

Daily Diary of Opportunities to Exercise

The benefits of exercise are easy to understand and commonly appreciated. Unfortunately, the many barriers to beginning an exercise program are also widely shared. Do any of these excuses sound familiar?

- I'm too tired.

- I don't have enough time.

- I get enough exercise in my job.

- I'm too out of shape.

- The weather is bad.

- I'm too embarrassed in front of others.

- I don't want to look like a bodybuilder.

- It will increase my appetite and I'll just gain more weight.

- I'm too old.

- Exercise is boring.

- I have more important things to do.

- I'm afraid I'll hurt myself.

The reasons you give yourself for not exercising are powerful; they have succeeded in depriving you of one of your basic needs. Facing up to these excuses is an essential step in overcoming an inactive lifestyle.

You can begin by keeping a daily Diary of Opportunities to Exercise, which will help you discover times in your schedule when you can increase your exercise. Make a note in your diary each time you have at least ten minutes free to take a walk or do some other kind of exercise. Also write down the things you say to yourself that hold you back or give you an excuse for not exercising.

Here is a sample Diary of Opportunities to Exercise:

Angela's Diary of Opportunities to Exercise

Time	Opportunity to exercise	Reasons for and against exercising
7:45	Let dog out to run in the yard.	I'm running late, so I can't walk the dog this morning.
8:15	Drive to work.	It's too far to walk, and my bike has a flat.
10:00	Drive with coworker to a special conference three blocks away.	I would have walked, but I couldn't very well say no to a friend offering a ride.
12:00	Drive to lunch.	I want to save time. Besides, it looks like rain.
1:00	Make calls to people who work on different floors of my building.	It's more efficient to phone.
3:00	Walk to post office.	I need to stretch my legs.
5:00	Collapse on sofa at home.	I could go jogging, but I'm exhausted and too out of shape since gaining those five pounds at Christmas.
7:30	Back on the sofa.	I could walk the dog, but it's dark and this isn't a safe neighborhood. Also, I have a headache. Maybe tomorrow ...

Make a minimum of three copies of this form to fill out over the next few days:

Diary of Opportunities to Exercise

Time	*Opportunity to exercise*	*Reasons for and against exercising*

Look over your diary and examine the statements that you made to yourself. Are they really valid reasons for not doing something that is essential to your health and well-being? Consider the implications of the following common excuses.

❑ "I don't have enough time."

❑ "I'm feeling rushed."

❑ "I have more important things to do."

❑ "My other obligations don't leave me enough time."

If these excuses sound familiar, it may mean that exercise is at the bottom of your list of priorities. Instead of saying, "I can't exercise," try saying "I choose not to exercise." What does that statement say about you?

If exercise really is important to you, you will create a space for it in your life. Remember that for a busy person, exercise is an especially important outlet for daily pressures. Without exercise, you will become increasingly tense, out of shape, and low on physical energy. Your ability to cope with the stresses of your busy life will be jeopardized.

For help in sorting out your priorities and finding ways to schedule in the activities that really do matter to you, see chapter 16, Goal Setting and Time Management. Now consider the implications of these excuses.

❑ "I'm too old to exercise."

❑ "I'm too fat to exercise."

❑ "I'm too out of shape to exercise."

Even though you recognize the advantages of exercise, you may persist in a sedentary lifestyle because you see yourself in a negative light. Such beliefs can make it hard for you to initiate an exercise program on your own. You should take a class, join a group, or get together with a friend who already exercises regularly and would happily encourage you to do so. Others will soon show you that exercise is for all ages and shapes. What are the implications of these excuses?

❑ "I'm afraid I'll hurt myself."

❑ "I'm afraid that I'll look silly."

❑ "I'm afraid of embarrassing myself."

Of the many fears associated with exercise, fear of a heart attack is one of the most common. If this is your fear or if you have a family history of heart conditions, get a physical exam and clearance from your doctor before you begin an exercise program, and start slowly. You may be afraid of injuring yourself. In this case, books, classes, and experienced people can provide you with information about how to exercise safely, what to expect as you progress, and how to cope with any difficulties you encounter.

When Angela reviewed her exercise diary, she took a close look at the reasons she was choosing not to exercise. Since she knew these reasons were a barrier to doing something that she needed and wanted to do, she took the time to write out ways of overcoming these obstacles.

Angela's Responses to Reasons for Not Exercising

Reason for not exercising	*Response or solution*
Running late . . . can't walk the dog.	I rarely have time to walk the dog in the morning because I don't get up early enough to do it. I'll set the alarm fifteen minutes earlier and get up as soon as it goes off.
Can't bike to work . . . flat tire.	It's not a matter of "can't": I just don't want to bike to work. But I can fix the flat so that I can bike on weekends, when I do enjoy biking in the country.
Can't decline a ride from a friend.	I'm full of "can'ts." Obviously I can say no, but sometimes I choose not to. I'll ask my friend to walk with me to meetings in the future.
Save time by driving to lunch.	An hour is plenty of time to walk to lunch, eat, and walk back.
Drive to lunch because it looks like rain.	This is the dumbest excuse yet! So what if it's cloudy? If I'm so concerned about the weather, I'll carry an umbrella or eat in the cafeteria downstairs.
It's more efficient to phone.	True, but face-to-face contact is valuable. And I do have the time to make the rounds in person.
I'm too exhausted, out of shape, and overweight to jog.	These are all signs of exercise deprivation and the very reasons why I should jog.
The neighborhood is unsafe after dark.	I could ask my husband to walk with me, or do some indoor exercises, or join a health club, or plan my exercises for earlier in the day.
I have a headache.	Another possible sign of exercise deprivation and stress accumulation.
Maybe tomorrow . . .	My favorite strategy for avoiding exercise! I'll go walk the dog right now!

Use this form to record your responses to reasons for not exercising. If your own excuses for not exercising seem particularly hard to dispute, try reading chapter 12, Refuting Irrational Ideas.

Your Responses to Reasons for Not Exercising

Reason for not exercising	Response or solution

Choosing the Best Type of Exercise for You

If you aren't sure which forms of exercise you'd like to try, then there are a few key questions that can help you decide. Think carefully about your answers and write them down in the space provided. Be honest with yourself, because the answers to these questions may determine how successful your exercise program will be.

1. How physically fit are you now? Circle a number and add any comments:

 1   2   3   4   5   6   7   8   9   10

_____

_____

2. What do you want to achieve with your exercise program?

_____

_____

3. Do you prefer to exercise alone or with others?

_____

_____

4. Do you prefer to exercise indoors or outdoors?

_____

_____

5. How much time are you willing to spend exercising each day or each week?

_____

_____

6. What time of day do you prefer to exercise? Will this fit into your current schedule? What changes do you need to make to incorporate exercise into your regular routine?

_____

_____

7. How far are you willing to travel to exercise?

_____

_____

8. How much money are you willing to spend on exercise equipment, classes, or club membership?

_____

_____

Your answers to these questions should give you a sense of which kinds of activities are appropriate for you. Walking may be the best way to start if you are middle-aged or somewhat overweight or have been inactive. Swimming is good for people who are substantially overweight or have bone or joint problems. The list of common aerobic exercises at the end of this chapter highlights some of the typical advantages and disadvantages of each.

Establishing Goals

Your Diary of Opportunities to Exercise can give you a sense of the time already available to you for exercise. (If you feel that you need more time than you have now, read chapter 16, Goal Setting and Time Management.) You are now ready to use this information to set goals and develop a plan for increasing the amount of exercise that you get during the day. Make sure that the goals you set are realistic and achievable, taking into account your current exercise level, the resources available to you, your time limitations, and your personal interests.

In establishing your goals, you'll want to pick the times that are most convenient for you. Once you have determined the optimal times for you, use them consistently. Set a short-term goal for each week. Keep the following considerations in mind:

- Morning offers the advantage of cooler weather and fewer people. On cold days, be sure to wear several layers of clothing and a hat that will prevent heat loss.

- Midday offers warmer weather and more people. On hot and humid days, drink lots of water and be aware of signs of heat stroke: feelings of dizziness, weakness, light-headedness, or excessive tiredness. If sweating stops, your body temperature can become dangerously high.

- Evening again offers cooler weather, but probably more people.

- If your schedule requires you to exercise at night on city streets, be sure to wear reflective clothing, travel on well-lighted streets, and carry identification, a loud whistle, and enough change for a phone call. (This is a good time to exercise with a friend.)

- Plan to exercise before meals or at least two hours after your last meal.

- Exercise any day during the week, at least three to five days per week. It is not necessary to exercise seven days per week.

Here are a few more suggestions to help you stay on track:

- Make a promise to yourself to stick with your program at least three times a week for two months.

- Tell your friends, family, and coworkers who you know will offer support and encouragement about your plans and goals.

- Choose a time in the day that is convenient for you.

- Write down your goals and post them where you'll see them each day.

- Continue to write down your excuses for not exercising—and how you'll deal with them when they arise—in your diary.

Types of Aerobic Exercises

Exercise	Advantages	Disadvantages
Basketball	Challenging An excellent whole-body exercise	Cannot be done alone Requires a court to play on
Bicycling (outdoors)	Changing scenery makes it interesting Not stressful on bones or joints Good exercise for the legs and heart	Requires a bicycle and a helmet You need to know how to fix a flat Traffic can be dangerous You need an alternative when the weather is bad Your arms don't get exercised
Bicycling (stationary)	Weather or traffic make no difference No flat tires	Requires access to a stationary bicycle Can be monotonous
Dancing	It's fun, especially if you enjoy music Can be an excellent whole-body exercise	If done on a hard, non-wooden floor, can cause harm to bones and joints
Hiking	Takes you outdoors into the fresh air and lets you experience nature	Requires hiking boots May require other equipment or precautions if hiking in remote or unfamiliar territory
Martial Arts	Challenging An excellent whole-body exercise	Requires skill Usually requires a partner or a class Requires space
Racquetball	An excellent whole-body exercise	Requires access to a court Requires some skill Requires a partner May be too strenuous for beginners
Rope jumping	Cheap and convenient Equipment is small and portable Can be done alone Can be done almost anywhere	Requires some skill
Rowing a boat	Can be very relaxing A scull with a sliding seat provides an excellent full-body workout	Requires a boat and access to water

Rowing (stationary)	Can be done indoors	Requires access to equipment Can be monotonous
Running or jogging	You can enjoy changing scenery You only need a pair of running shoes You can do this alone or with others Good exercise for the legs and heart	Can increase wear and tear on joints Can lead to injuries if not properly done May be too difficult for beginners or overweight individuals Takes a longer time to learn to enjoy than other forms of exercise
Skating (roller skates or on ice)	Can be done alone or with others	Can give you skinned knees and elbows Requires some skill Requires equipment and access to facilities
Skiing (cross-country or alpine)	An excellent way to enjoy nature	Requires some skill Requires equipment and access to snow
Skiing (cross-country on a ski machine)	Can be done indoors	Requires some skill and coordination Requires access to equipment
Stair climbing	Requires no skill	Can be very monotonous
Swimming	A good way to stay cool Good for joint pain or muscle weakness Good for large muscles in arms, legs, and chest	Requires an ability to swim and access to a pool Not a good choice if you are sensitive to chlorine
Tennis (singles)	A good whole-body workout Can be done with others	Requires some skill Requires equipment and access to a court Cannot be done alone
Walking briskly	Can be done anytime, anywhere Requires only a pair of shoes	It takes longer to reach your target heart rate than other forms of exercise

Sample Exercise Program

This program will take you from thirty to eighty minutes to complete and will stretch and tone the major muscle groups in your body. For best results, do a full set of exercises three to five days each week. If you don't have time for such an ambitious program, try to get some form of exercise for at least twenty minutes per day. Always start with gentle warm-up stretches first to avoid putting too much sudden stress on your body.

Begin by Warming Up

- Length: Ten minutes before aerobic exercise.

Warm-up exercises increase your metabolism and your body temperature and prepare your muscles, heart, and lungs for vigorous exercise. They also decrease your chance of injury. The stretching and toning exercises described earlier in this chapter can be used as warm-ups.

Follow with Aerobics

- Easy length: Ten to twenty minutes.

- Intermediate length: Twenty to forty minutes.

- Advanced length: Forty to sixty minutes.

The simplest, most readily available form of aerobic exercise is brisk walking or jogging. Accordingly, a walking and jogging program is used in this section to illustrate the principles of aerobic exercise. You can use a similar graduated approach for running, bicycling, swimming, cross-country skiing, jumping rope, or any other aerobic exercise that you choose to do.

As you exercise, your large skeletal muscles rhythmically tense and relax, stimulating the blood flow through your vascular system, heart, and lungs. Your heart rate is particularly important. Much like the speedometer in your car that tells you how fast you are going, your heart rate tells you how hard you are working. If you are traveling too fast in your car, you slow down; likewise, if you are going too slowly, you speed up.

Just as the speed of your car is measured in miles per hour, the work of your heart is measured in beats per minute. You can find out how fast your heart is going by taking your pulse. Practice taking your pulse while sitting quietly. Wear a watch with a sweep second hand on your left arm. Turn the palm of your right hand toward you. Firmly place the fingertips of your left hand on your right wrist near the bone that joins your thumb to your wrist. You will feel your pulse. To determine your heart rate for one minute, simply take your pulse for ten seconds and then multiply this number by six. You can also find this number by referring to the following chart.

Heart Rate in Beats Per Ten Seconds and Per Minute

If you got this number in ten seconds	10	11	12	13	14	15	16	17	18	19	20	21	22	23	24	25
This is your heart rate in beats per minute	60	66	72	78	84	90	96	102	108	114	120	126	132	138	144	150

A normal resting pulse may range from forty to one hundred beats per minute, depending on your level of physical fitness. In order to benefit from aerobic exercise, your heart must reach and stay within a range known as your target heart rate for at least twenty minutes. You reach this range when your heart is beating at a rate of between 60 and 75 percent of its maximum rate. It is the safest exercise range for you, and exercising at this pace stimulates the relaxation response. Exercising below your target heart rate will not strengthen your cardiovascular system. Exercising consistently above your target rate could put too much strain on your heart. The following table shows the estimated heart rates for different age groups.

Estimated Heart Rates for Selected Ages Table

Age (years)	Average maximum heart rate (beats per minute)	Target heart rate (60 to 75 percent of maximum rate)
20–24	200	120–150
25–29	195	117–146
30–34	190	114–142
35–39	185	111–138
40–44	180	108–135
45–49	175	105–131
50–54	170	102–127
55–59	165	99–123
60–64	160	96–120
65–69	155	93–116
70+	150	90–113

Exercise at your target level places a moderate stress on your heart that will gradually improve its efficiency. By monitoring your heart rate during exercise and comparing it to your target rate, you have immediate feedback about whether you are doing too much exercise or not enough exercise. If your heart rate is greater than your target rate, you slow down; if your heart rate is less than your target rate, you speed up.

If you are out of shape, brisk walking may push your pulse over 60 percent of the maximum heart rate for your age group. As your heart and lungs become conditioned, you will have to exert more effort (by walking faster or jogging) to attain your target rate. Here are three simple tests that you can do to determine how fast you should walk or jog in order to reach your target rate.

Test #1   Walk five minutes at a comfortable pace. Take your pulse immediately, because the rate falls off rapidly. If it is less than the target rate for your age group, go on to the second test. If you have already reached your target rate, continue to walk at this pace every other day until your heart rate falls below 60 percent of your maximum rate, and then go on to the second test.

Test #2   Walk five minutes at a vigorous pace. Again, take your pulse immediately. If you have not reached 60 percent of your maximum heart rate, go on to the third test. If your pulse is within your target range, continue at this pace with aerobic walks every other day until your pulse falls below your target rate, and then go on to the third test.

Test #3   Alternate one minute of slow jogging with one minute of brisk walking for five minutes, and then take your pulse. If you still haven't reached your target rate, you are ready to continue with slow jogging every other day. If you have reached 60 percent of your maximum heart rate, continue to alternate one minute of jogging with one minute of brisk walking every other day until your pulse falls below the target level. Then increase the amount of time you spend jogging as you decrease your time walking.

You will need to check your pulse frequently until you find a pace that will keep your heart rate within your target range for at least twenty minutes. After that, monitor your pulse once per week to make sure that you are maintaining your target rate.

As you become more conditioned, you will find that you need to gradually spend more time jogging or even running in order to stay within your target heart rate zone. A good rule of thumb is to continue to jog until you feel winded, and then slow to a brisk walk for about a minute. If you can sing while exercising, you're not exercising hard enough. Note, though, that you should be able to carry on a conversation while you're jogging without becoming excessively short of breath. If you can't, you're going too fast.

End by Cooling Down

- Length: Ten minutes after your aerobic exercise.

A period of cooling down helps decrease your metabolism and body temperature and prevents your muscles from becoming sore. When jogging or running, always end your session with five minutes of slow walking. Take long, exaggerated steps, stretching your legs. Let your arms dangle loosely, and shake your hands. The stretching and toning exercises that you used to warm up can be used.

Special Considerations

Avoiding Injury

Here are a few things to consider in order to avoid injury:

- Have a physical checkup. Get cleared by your primary health care provider before beginning a regular exercise program. This is especially important if you are older, out of shape, or recovering from a serious illness or operation.

- Start slowly and build up gradually. Progress at a steady pace. Set realistic goals.

- Spread your exercise over the week, rather than exercising only on weekends.

- Exercise within your target heart rate zone. Remember that you should be able to talk comfortably while you are exercising. If you are too breathless, you need to slow down.

- Always warm up and cool down.

- Drink plenty of fluids to replace those lost during vigorous exercise.

- Don't exercise if you are feeling sick. Your body needs rest at this time.

- Don't exercise after a large meal, because blood flow to the large muscles is limited.

- Don't use ankle or arm weights, which can place added stress on your back and joints.

- Wear comfortable shoes that offer good support to your feet and ankles.

- Wear comfortable, lightweight, loose-fitting layers of clothing. Be prepared to remove clothing as your body temperature increases during the warm-up and aerobic phases and to add clothing as your body temperature decreases when you are cooling down.

- Use any equipment that is recommended for your protection.

Keeping at It

There are two major obstacles to overcome in undertaking an exercise program. The first is just to get started. The second is to keep at it. If you have followed the instructions in the preceding sections, you have jumped the first hurdle. The second may be more difficult. The following suggestions will help you keep at your exercise program until it becomes as automatic as eating or sleeping.

- Choose exercise activities that you enjoy.

- Start slowly and never overdo.

- Monitor your progress.

- Make copies of the exercise diary on the following page and keep it up to date.

- Give yourself small rewards.

- Focus on the benefits of exercise.

- Visualize success.

- Get support from your family and friends.

- Join an exercise class, running club, or fitness center.

Exercise Diary

Week of _____

Target heart rate: _____

Remember to WARM UP and COOL DOWN.

Day	*Activity*	*Location*	*Distance or Duration*	*Comments, Thoughts, Feelings*
Monday				
Tuesday				
Wednesday				
Thursday				
Friday				
Saturday				
Sunday				

Further Reading

Anderson, B. 1980. *Stretching.* Bolinas, Calif.: Shelter Publishers.

Bailey, C. 2000. *The Ultimate Fit or Fat.* Boston: Houghton Mifflin.

Cooper, K. 1982. *The Aerobics Program for Total Well Being.* New York: Bantam Books.

Dworkis, S., P. Moline, and M. Fox. 1994. *Extension: The 20-Minute-a-Day Yoga-Based Program to Relax, Release, and Rejuvenate the Average Stressed-Out Over-35-Year-Old Body.* New York: Poseidon Press.

Finger, A., and A. Bingham. 2000. *Yoga Zone Introduction to Yoga: A Beginner's Guide to Health, Fitness & Relaxation.* New York: Three Rivers Press.

Fixx, J. F. 1980. *Jim Fixx's Second Book of Running.* New York: Random House.

Francina, S. 1997. *The New Yoga for People over 50.* Deerfield Beach, Fla.: Health Communications.

Gerrish, M. 1997. *When Working Out Isn't Working Out: A Mind/Body Guide to Conquering Unidentified Fitness Obstacles.* Glendale, Calif.: Griffin Trade.

Katz, J. 1993. *Swimming for Total Fitness.* New York: Doubleday.

Meyers, C. 1992. *Walking.* New York: Random House.

Parry, R., and L. Wickenden. 1997. *Tai Chi Made Easy: A Step By Step Guide to Health and Relaxation.* Allentown, Pa.: People's Medical Society

Fitness and Aerobic Exercise Brochures

For a catalog, write or call:
Krames Communications
312 90th Street
Daly City, CA 94015-8800
1-800-333-3032

When It Doesn't Come Easy—Getting Unstuck

This book has covered many techniques to reduce stress and tension. Essentially they provide alternatives to your old stressful habits. You may have found that just practicing the new skills and observing the positive effects has caused you to give up the old habits. For instance, you may have found that practicing slow, deep breaths rather than short, constricted breaths results in a relaxed sense of well-being. This positive feedback from your body may have provided ample motivation for you to give up your old anxiety-provoking shallow breathing habit. However, if you are like most people, at some point you probably encountered some difficulty in exchanging old familiar habits for new ones. This chapter takes a look at why old habits are hard to part with, even when they are obviously contributing to your stress. It also offers some suggestions for how to deal with your own resistance to change.

If you find yourself skipping an exercise session you have contracted with yourself to do, or are aware that you are just going through the motions of the exercises, ask yourself some of the following questions:

1. Why am I doing these exercises?

2. Are these reasons really important to me?

3. What am I doing or would I like to be doing instead of these exercises?

4. Is this alternative activity more important to me than my doing the exercises?

5. Can I schedule my life so that I can do the exercises *and* this alternative activity?

6. If I do not want to do the exercises now, exactly when and where will I do them next?

7. What would I have to give up if I succeeded with my exercises?

8. What would I have to confront if I succeeded with my exercises?

Chapter 16, Goal Setting and Time Management, covers many topics that could help you get back on track by: 1.) clarifying what is most important to you; 2.) setting goals; 3.) developing an action plan; 4.) evaluating how you spend your time; 5.) combating procrastination; and 6.) organizing your time.

Taking Responsibility for Your Decisions

It is difficult to learn new habits on your own when at first the rewards for your efforts may be minimal. When distractions occur, decide whether you want to be detoured or to continue on your chosen route. If you decide to take the detour, do so with full awareness, after weighing the pros and cons. Before going off on the detour, make an appointment with yourself for when and where you are next going to do your exercises. In this way you are taking responsibility for your decision. In addition, you are less likely to feel bad about yourself for not following through on your original plan, if that is your conscious choice.

What are the reasons you give yourself for skipping your exercises? Typical reasons are: "I'm too busy today," "I'm too tired," "Missing once won't hurt," "David needs my help," "This isn't working," "This is boring," "I feel relaxed and unstressed today, so I don't need to exercise," or "I feel too bad today to do exercises." These excuses are seductive because they are partially true. That is, you may really feel very busy or tired, somebody may want your help, and missing one session probably won't hurt. The part that isn't true is the implication that because you are busy or tired or someone needs your help, you cannot do the exercise sessions. A more truthful statement would be, "I am tired. I could do the exercises, but I choose not to," or "I could do my exercises, but I choose to help David rather than do them." The important point here is that you take responsibility for your decision to choose one activity over another, rather than pretend that you are the passive victim of circumstances such as your fatigue, David's demands, or other priorities that keep you busy.

Confront Your Excuses

The excuses you give yourself for not doing your exercises are likely to be the same ones that you have used for years to keep yourself locked into a stressful situation. These excuses are based on faulty premises. For example, a middle-aged housewife believed that she had no right to relax until all her work was done. She predicted that if she took time for herself, the pile of chores would grow rapidly into an unassailable mountain. Over the years, she became anxious and depressed and developed a number of physical complaints. Her perfectionist belief that she had to do all of her work before she had a right to relax had caused a gradual depletion of her energy. Realistically, the work of a housewife and mother is never done; therefore she could never relax. But she had overlooked her innate right (and some would call it an obligation) to relax and replenish her vital store of energy. This woman had defined her priorities as being "housewife first" and "me second," without taking into account the importance of relaxation and getting away from stressful activities for maintaining good mental health and physical health. If you, as this woman, say to yourself, "I'm indispensable. Things won't get done without me and may even fall apart . . . ," consider putting your mental and physical health at the top of your list of priorities.

If you are an energetic person who likes to succeed or who likes to get things done yesterday, slow down your pace when learning these exercises. Having to prove yourself or rushing creates stress. Enthusiasm may push you to take on many exercises at once or do the sessions for too long. You run a high risk of burning out and losing interest if you do too much too fast. Furthermore, you are likely to feel guilty for not keeping up the rigorous program you have set for yourself. Soon you will find yourself coming up with excuses to avoid exercising at all ("I'm overextended already in many areas of my life. Why add to the burden?"). You may feel confused when you begin to experience more energy as a result of doing the relaxation and stress reduction exercises. Resist the temptation to pour this extra energy back into your work. Rather, use it for further rest and enjoyment.

If you find yourself saying, "I just don't feel like it . . . may tomorrow I will . . . " day after day, give yourself a mental kick in the butt. It is simply not true that you have to be motivated to do something before you do it. Motivation is often sparked by action. For example, if you take a brisk ten-minute walk, you are likely to feel good from the results and want to continue. Tell yourself that you only have to do an activity for five or ten minutes. Often once you are into an activity, the momentum of doing it will carry you through to its completion. At the very least, you can work on a project five or ten minutes a day until it is done without an ounce of motivation. Lack of motivation is sometimes a symptom of depression. Depression often improves when you become more active. Tell yourself, "Of course you don't feel like doing it. So what. Do it anyway!"

Confronting Roadblocks in the Road to Stress Management and Relaxation

If you read this workbook without doing any of the exercises, it's likely that you are only dabbling. Intellectually, you see the value of the exercises, but you somehow never get much past the stage of thinking about them; or you may actually do some of the exercises, but never apply them to everyday situations. For the dabbler, this is just another book with some interesting ideas, rather than a workbook promoting experiential learning of new ways to deal with stress.

There are some individuals who are frightened by novel experiences, and this fear becomes a roadblock to success. You might become overwhelmed by some side effect of a relaxation technique such as tingling in your arms and legs. Unfortunately, you may then stop the exercise instead of going on to find that the tingling is not harmful and goes away with time. You can get turned off by a single element of an exercise and, rather than changing the exercise to fit your needs, drop the exercise. Perhaps you don't understand a step in the instructions and rather than ad lib, you chuck the whole thing. It can be a valuable growth experience to work through these difficulties on your own.

When Symptoms Persist

Sometimes symptoms of stress persist in spite of regular relaxation and stress reduction. If you are a conscientious person, and have been practicing regularly, this is disheartening. The following are just a few of the most common reasons why this might be happening to you.

Some people are highly suggestible and begin to experience every symptom that they hear about. For example, one very tense policeman joined a relaxation group to overcome his tendency to hyperventilate when under stress. He began to experience all of the physical symptoms described by the other group members: migraines, lower back pain, rapid heartbeat, and so forth. Doing deep breathing, thought stopping, or coping skills training helped him combat these tendencies.

A surprising number of people are attached to their symptoms, which serve a very definite purpose. For example, your headaches may get you out of interpersonal situations you want to avoid, without having to take responsibility for disappointing others. You can soon find out whether your symptoms rescue you from more unpleasant experiences by keeping a log of when you get your symptoms and the activities (or would-be activities) that surround them. If you suspect that your symptoms provide you "secondary gain" in this manner, refer to the chapter on assertiveness training. It should provide you with the incentive and the tools to be more direct in saying "no."

Your symptoms of tension may be a signal that you are not dealing effectively with something in your life and that you are covering up your feelings. For example, you may be angry with your family but not sharing this fact with them. You might be putting off talking about a particular conflict because you don't see any way of improving matters. A nurse was visited every other weekend by a very spoiled stepdaughter. She had agreed to the arrangement when she married and now felt trapped by it. Within three years, the visits invariably produced a migraine headache. To counteract this symptom, she finally negotiated a new contract with her husband to spend Sundays on her own while he baby-sat.

The people around you are apt to be aware that you are withholding stressful feelings and that something is wrong. Nevertheless they cannot read your mind, and are unlikely to come to your rescue. You know best what you need. Letting others know your feelings and what you want opens the way to engaging them in helping you make a change.

Your symptom may be a way of getting taken care of when you feel that you cannot directly ask for help or consideration. If you feel tired and have a backache, someone else may have to do the cooking and cleaning and keeping the house quiet. Ask yourself when your symptoms first began. What was going on in your life that might have contributed to them? One elderly woman who had suffered from periodic colitis since childhood recalled that her abdominal cramps began when her younger twin brothers were born. She remembered that the only time her busy mother ever held her and rocked her was when she had the symptoms. She noted that she tended to get symptoms of colitis only when her husband left her alone in the evenings.

It is possible that you have developed a symptom of an important person in your life as part of your identification with them. For example, you may not only have learned to be hardworking and successful from your father, but also to deal with stress in a similar manner. Carrying your tension in your jaw, you may come to the point of grinding your teeth just like your father. Since characteristic ways of responding to stress are generally learned, ask yourself who in your family shares your same symptoms. It's often easier to learn how they are not dealing effectively with the stress in their lives than to see it in yourself. The next step is to observe and see if the same is true for you.

If you continue to have difficulty reducing the stress in your life, consider consulting a professional. You may be interested in one-on-one psychotherapy sessions, or in joining a relaxation and stress reduction group. Your medical doctor, company health plan, community health organization, adult education program, and community colleges are good places to start looking for professional help.

Persistence Pays

Finally, don't give up. Your ability to relax, learn to handle stress, and heal yourself is a tremendous power. Change might not always come easy—you may feel stuck in your old stressful habits—but you can do it. All it takes is patience, persistence . . . and time.

Index

Some Other
New Harbinger Titles

Surviving Your Borderline Parent, Item 3287 $14.95

When Anger Hurts, second edition, Item 3449 $16.95

Calming Your Anxious Mind, Item 3384 $12.95

Ending the Depression Cycle, Item 3333 $17.95

Your Surviving Spirit, Item 3570 $18.95

Coping with Anxiety, Item 3201 $10.95

The Agoraphobia Workbook, Item 3236 $19.95

Loving the Self-Absorbed, Item 3546 $14.95

Transforming Anger, Item 352X $10.95

Don't Let Your Emotions Run Your Life, Item 3090 $17.95

Why Can't I Ever Be Good Enough, Item 3147 $13.95

Your Depression Map, Item 3007 $19.95

Successful Problem Solving, Item 3023 $17.95

Working with the Self-Absorbed, Item 2922 $14.95

The Procrastination Workbook, Item 2957 $17.95

Coping with Uncertainty, Item 2965 $11.95

The BDD Workbook, Item 2930 $18.95

You, Your Relationship, and Your ADD, Item 299X $17.95

The Stop Walking on Eggshells Workbook, Item 2760 $18.95

Conquer Your Critical Inner Voice, Item 2876 $15.95

The PTSD Workbook, Item 2825 $17.95

Hypnotize Yourself Out of Pain Now!, Item 2809 $14.95

The Depression Workbook, 2nd edition, Item 268X $19.95

Beating the Senior Blues, Item 2728 $17.95

Shared Confinement, Item 2663 $15.95

Handbook of Clinical Psychopharmacology for Therpists, 3rd edition, Item 2698 $55.95

Getting Your Life Back Together When You Have Schizophrenia, Item 2736 $14.95

Do-It-Yourself Eye Movement Technique for Emotional Healing, Item 2566 $13.95

Call **toll free, 1-800-748-6273,** or log on to our online bookstore at **www.newharbinger.com** to order. Have your Visa or Mastercard number ready. Or send a check for the titles you want to New Harbinger Publications, Inc., 5674 Shattuck Ave., Oakland, CA 94609. Include $4.50 for the first book and 75¢ for each additional book, to cover shipping and handling. (California residents please include appropriate sales tax.) Allow two to five weeks for delivery.

Prices subject to change without notice.